THE PASTOR OF FISH STREET

The Journals of the Rev George Lambert, Congregational Minister

Edited by

JOHN MARKHAM

East Yorkshire Local History Society
2008

E Y LOCAL HISTORY SERIES No.57
Series editor Arthur G. Credland

No part of this book may be reproduced, stored in a retrieval system, or transmitted in any form, or by any means electronic, mechanical, photocopying, recording or otherwise without the prior permission of the publishers and the Copyright holders.

ISBN-0-900349-57-3 / ISBN-978-0-900349-57-7

EAN 9780900349577

Copyright EYLHS © 2008

Printed by Highgate Print Limited, Beverley, England

Cover illustration: Pastel portrait of the Rev George Lambert (*Ferens Art Gallery*)

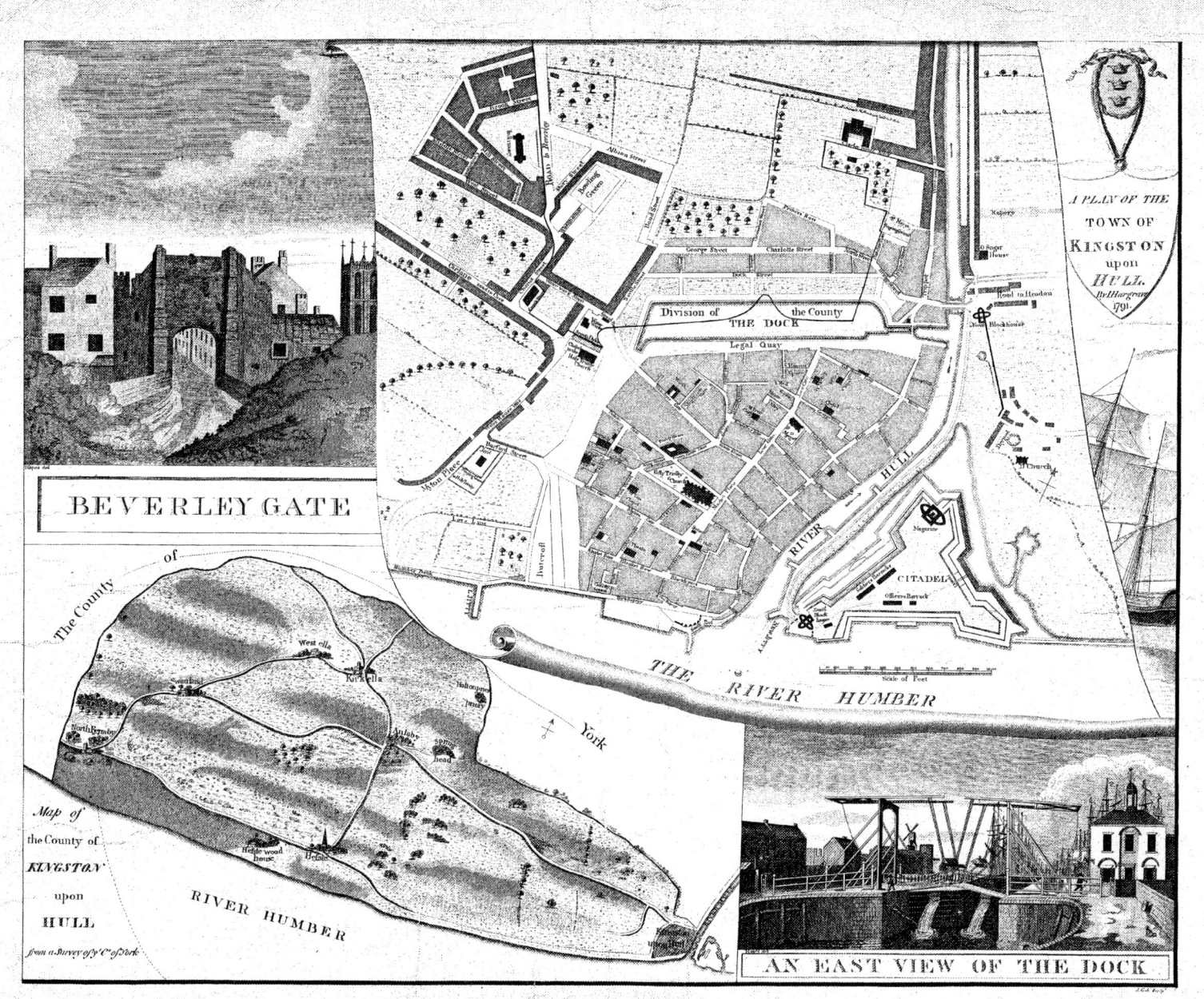

1 Hull in 1791 by J. Hargrave; engraved by J. Gale. (Hull Local Studies Library)

2 Hull in 1817 by C.Mountain; engraved by Consitt and Goodwill. Published by J.Cragg. (Hull Local Studies Library)

Contents

Editor's Introduction 7
Acknowledgements 10
Bibliography 11
George Lambert (1742-1816): The Pastor of Fish Street 13
George Lambert: The Man and his Family 17
The golden verses of Pythagoras 21
Soul Memorials Vol 1 1769-1781 22
Vol 2 1782-1783 45
Vol 3 1784-1785 64
Vol 4 1786-1788 79
Vol 5 1789-1790 102
Vol 6 1791-1794 117
Vol 7 1795-1798 131
Vol 8 1799-1802 146
Vol 9 1803-1807 157
Vol 10 1808-1810 169
Vol 11 1811-1813 194
Vol 12 1814-1816 211
Appendix A Some remarks on the experience of me Geo Lambert 217
Appendix B The Last Public Execution in Hull 222
Appendix C Place Name Spellings 225
Appendix D George Lambert's Publications 226
Index 227

Editor's Introduction

George Lambert's journals consist of 12 octavo volumes of good quality unlined paper bound in marbled boards, some of which have become detached.

3 **Some volumes of the Lambert diary**

He started keeping a regular diary in 1780, the date of an autobiographical summary of his spiritual development (reproduced in Appendix A), though he begins with items scattered over earlier years recording exceptional blessings to his family. The fact that these have specific dates and that a journal, the *Criterion*, published a long account of his prison visits in 1778 to John Rogerson, the last man to be publicly executed in Hull, 'drawn from an unpublished journal' (see Appendix B) indicates that he had kept previous records, some of which he apparently copied into the journal now maintained systematically and clearly labelled Vol 1.

The 12 volumes, extending until 10 March 1816, one week before his death, have previously been used by C E Darwent in his *Story of Fish Street Church* (1899), a book of considerable interest and value, though a word of caution is needed. Some of the 'quotations' printed within inverted commas are, in fact, paraphrases, and it is not always possible to reconcile his references to the dated entries in the journals.

This edition of George Lambert's writings differs significantly from Darwent's use of the materials. His prime purpose was to illustrate the life of the church in its crucial first years and to show George Lambert's contribution as its pastor. George Lambert described his journals as Soul Memorials, a narrative of his spiritual life. The progress he made, the difficulties he encountered and the outlines of his sermons (with his texts methodically listed) were his major concern. Yet he did include what he would have regarded as the far less important *obiter dicta*, among them family incidents, events in Hull, references to the national and international affairs which were causing him so much unease, medical matters, extreme weather conditions and the vagaries of travel. Though he would probably have used his favourite word, 'trifling', to dismiss these subjects, trivial in comparison to his inner life, these are a substantial portion of the extracts selected for this edition, which provide another strand of local and social history. Entries were made more frequently in the early years than in the later years; though some of the latter are lengthy, they tend to omit the personal and domestic details which provide so much interest.

Religion remains prominent. It permeated the whole of his existence and, as the journals show, he saw divine intervention in everything he did. Not a slip of his foot on a step or a stumble from which he emerged unharmed was allowed to pass without a prayer of praise to a protective Providence. To avoid repetitions which would now be regarded as tediously sanctimonious, many of these sincere expressions of gratitude have been omitted.

Yet it is through the repetitive recording of the orderly routine of a Dissenting minister in the reign of George III that these journals convey the impressive picture of a man and the people of his particular sector of society in a significant period of history. The thoughtful choosing of his texts, the meticulous, prayerful planning of his sermons, his never neglected calls on the sick and the dying and his visits to preach at other chapels were the essence of his life. While a selected edition by its very nature has to omit much, the ordinary in this context is as important as the unusual, and I have aimed at including sufficient of the daily and weekly tenor of George Lambert's ways to avoid distorting the picture of his life and his role in the community. Others would have selected different extracts, though there are some 'purple patches' which everyone would include, like his dramatic account of a hazardous crossing of a Humber blocked by ice and his poetic musings on the transformation of a pastoral scene by the opening of the Humber Dock.

Hull was a staunchly Protestant town in which Nonconformity was a powerful force and where religion and doctrinal niceties could be matters of intense interest and often heated controversy. The serious atmosphere of the milieu in which George Lambert moved is, I hope, conveyed by the entries I have included. The Protestant work ethic was a fundamental, if unstated, tenet of faith, and leading members of the business community were active in the chapels and in the Anglican churches of an Evangelical persuasion. Whether rich or poor, members of these large congregations formed an important section of Hull society and the historical value of George

Introduction

Lambert's journals lies largely in the insight it gives into the thoughts and activities of people who contributed to the distinctive character of the town at that time and to its future development.

Some of George Lambert's associates were well-known figures who have left their mark on local history and others can be identified through modest research. But some make only a fleeting appearance in his journals and otherwise remain unknown. They were part of the fabric of his life and were probably more important to him that these odd references suggest.

For myself, working on these journals has provided an entrée into a world of which I have no personal knowledge. The importance of Hull's Nonconformist heritage is appreciated by all historians but perusing the details of George Lambert's life over nearly half a century has given me a privileged, close-up view of the intimacies of this powerful cultural and religious element in Hull's society.

George Lambert's handwriting is generally clear and regular, with a few idiosyncrasies which, with practice, one learns to decipher. Understandably there was some deterioration with age. Errors are more noticeable at times of great stress. A small number of names, where there is no contextual reference to aid interpretation, pose problems. The aim throughout the editing of his journals has been accessibility and intelligibility. He wrote an excellent classical prose style but many of the entries are in non-sentence structure, often separated by colons. When considered necessary, punctuation has been added according to modern conventions.

Most abbreviated words have been given in full and, on the principle that the value of his writing is as a historical record not a literary text, minor errors and occasional odd spellings and usages (whether mistakes or his own preferred version) have been corrected. He seems uncertain about the difference between 'were' and 'where', 'affect' and 'effect', and 'of' and 'off', 'slipped' is spelt with one 'p', he tends to split such words as 'anybody' and 'today' into their separate elements and he is not consistent in the use of upper case letters and apostrophes. All these have been standardised. Most place names have, when they differ, been given their modern spellings, though a list is included (see Appendix C) of his version of names which have some historical interest. Omissions from the text have been indicated by three stops and editorial additions by square brackets.

John Markham
October 2008

Acknowledgements

First in the list of the many people who have assisted me in the preparation of this edition is unquestionably Miss Sheila Lambert, great-great-great-granddaughter of the Reverend George Lambert. Sheila generously loaned me the six volumes of the journals in her possession and arranged for me to borrow the further six volumes in the possession of a relation so that photostat copies could be made for my detailed study. In addition Sheila has provided valuable information on aspects of the Lambert family not covered in the journals of her distinguished ancestor.

I also owe a debt of gratitude to Barry Sage, who wordprocessed my original manuscript version of the edited text and Sue Hyde, who completed the process with a revised version including the footnotes and appendices and who also compiled the index.

The staffs of the Beverley Reference Library (some now in the Treasure House) and of Hull Reference Library and Local Studies Library have been a most reliable source of help and information on many occasions. Mr Alan Humphries, Librarian of the Thackeray Museum, Leeds, quickly answered my queries on George Lambert's many health problems, and Jonathan Morgan, Archivist of Dr Williams's Library, London, was equally generous with information on many points of Congregational history which I could never have explained without the aid of his expertise in this field of scholarship. The Ferens Art Gallery generously granted permission to reproduce the portrait of George Lambert. I also thank Wilberforce House for finding and allowing reproduction of the print of Fish Street Chapel.

During the long period I have been engaged on this project I have asked questions of many people and received answers which saved me hours of searching in libraries. I have not kept a record of their names, and I regret that I will have omitted to give specific mention of some who deserve my gratitude, but I do recall with thanks the generous help give by Judith Preston Anderson, Geoff Bell, Stephen L Deas, Mary Fowler, Sheila Gardner, Christopher Ketchell, Alan Marshall, Berna Moody and Barbara Robinson. To others who are not named I give my sincere apologies and record my indebtedness.

Not least, I thank the East Yorkshire Local History Society for undertaking to publish this work, and Arthur Credland, the Society's editor, who has guided me so wisely on many aspects of the text and its final presentation.

Bibliography

Abbreviated titles shown as [ ].

K J Allison, *Hull Gent Seeks Country House*, (East Yorkshire Local History Society, 36, 1981) [Allison]

Archives of Fish Street church currently located in Hull Local Studies Library, under the classification DCFS. Of particular relevance are the Church Book (DCFS/1/1/1) and The transcriptions of the Baptism Registers (DCFS/1/3/5/1)

J Bellamy, 'Some aspects of the economy of Hull in the nineteenth century with special reference to business history' (unpublished University of Hull PhD thesis, 1965)

Beverley, Yorkshire (1791), a copy of the entry from a national directory of 1791, including both Beverley and Hull [D1791]

J A R Bickford and M E Bickford, *The Medical Profession of Hull 1400-1900* [Hull n.d.] [Bickford]

S Cooper Scott, ed F Brooks, *Things That Were* (1923)

Rev George Thomas Coster, *Pastors and People* (Hull 1869)

A G Cox and D Stather, *A History of the Parish of Market Weighton* (Market Weighton 1971)

J N Crosse, *Account of Hull Subscription Library* (Hull 1810)

C E Darwent, *The Story of Fish Street Church, Hull* (1899) [Darwent]

E M Forster, ed E Hanquart-Turner, *Marianne Thornton* (2000 edn, first published 1956)

M Fowler, *Holderness Road* (Beverley 1990)

I & E Hall, *Georgian Hull* (York 1978/9)

R Heathcote, *Anlaby* (Beagle Publications 1999)

H McLachlan, *English Education Under The Test Acts* (Manchester 1931)

Victoria History of the County of York, East Riding, ed K J Allison, Vol I, The City of Kingston upon Hull (Oxford 1969) [VCH]

R Lovett, *The History of the London Missionary Society 1795-1895*, Vol 1, (1899)

J G Miall, *Congregationalism in Yorkshire* (1868)

D Neave, *Lost Churches and Chapel of Hull* (Hull 1991)

Oxford Dictionary of National Biography (Oxford 2004) [ODNB]

W G B Page, *History of Fish Street Congregational Church* (Hull 1889)

J G Patton, *A Country Independent Chapel* (Hull 1943)

J J Sheahan, *General and Concise History and Description of the Town and Port of Kingston upon Hull* (Beverley 1864)

E B Smith, *Zion, A History of the United Reform Church, Cottingham, 1692-1992*, 3rd edition (Cottingham 1992)

P Stubley, *A House Divided: Evangelicals and the Establishment in Hull 1770-1914* (Hull 1995) [Stubley]

George Lambert (1742-1816): The Pastor of Fish Street

George Lambert made his first visit to Hull in 1769, the occasion the opening of a new Congregational chapel in Blanket Row, formed by 11 former members of Dagger Lane Chapel who had become dissatisfied with the preaching of the minister there, the Rev John Burnett. Dissenting sects were prone to disputes over Scriptural interpretation and religious practices, the intensity of the debate sometimes leading to the secession of the dissatisfied and the formation of a new church where the preaching and procedures would be more to their taste.

George Lambert attended the ceremony on 9 April as a representative of the Dissenting Academy at Heckmondwike[1] where he had been a student. His words and his impressive bearing made such a profound impact on all who were present that he was invited to return as their pastor. He took his time replying. The invitation was made on 30 July 1769. His acceptance was dated 12 October. Although it is reported that he had once dutifully declared that he would be willing to go to any place Providence might direct, he revealed his human frailty by interposing a hope that he should not be sent to Hull. God moves in a mysterious way and it was in Hull that he was to spend the 47 years of a ministry which ended only with his death in 1816.

4 Heckmondwike Academy (Miall)

When he arrived in 1769 he was described as a 'broad, full-set man, clad in leather breeches, with ruddy cheeks and shrewd bright grey eyes'. Many years after his death, a woman, probably a member of the church, retained a clear memory of him in old age: 'I see him now, with his white wig and three-corner hat, his dark blue cloak, his silver buckles, black silk stockings, and black smallclothes.'

George Lambert was to establish a reputation as a preacher which spread way beyond Hull, but Blanket Row was small and in 1781 he was strongly tempted to accept an invitation to take up an offered post in Kidderminster. the deacons were anxious for him to stay and, after some rather tricky negotiations and an abortive attempt to take over the New Chapel in Dagger Lane (with some suspicion that he was exerting moral blackmail to have his ambitions fulfilled), it was resolved to build a new, much larger, chapel in Fish Street. The site acquired from Samuel Wright (with whom there was later an acrimonious legal/financial dispute) cost £450, Lambert himself subscribing 100 guineas (£105).

5   **Print of the Congregational Chapel, Fish Street. Restored 1869. Sam Musgrave, Architect. The date 1782 should be in the pediment (KINCM:2006.6474, Wilberforce House, Hull)**

Opened on 31 July 1782, Fish Street was far more spacious than its predecessor: Hadley described it as 'a large, elegant and commodious chapel'. Yet it proved to be too small for the growing congregation attracted by his preaching and in 1802 it was extended. During these alterations the Methodist meeting house in George Yard was borrowed. When Fish Street reopened on 31 October that year, George Lambert could note with some satisfaction that from an uncertain 20 or so hearers when he began in Hull he now had at least 1,000.

He was a most conscientious pastor, regularly visiting the sick (a demanding and dangerous duty in times of serious epidemics like smallpox which spread rapidly through the town), and to those nearing the end of their lives he brought consolation, in his own quaint phrase 'improving' these harrowing moments. In addition to the Sunday services there were week-day commitments at Fish Street, a routine which drew derision from Anglicans who sarcastically pitied 'that poor devil Lambert, who had to preach twice a week to the same people'. There were many journeys out of Hull to preach in local villages or sometimes further afield, engagements not undertaken lightly in view of the vagaries of travel and his obvious lack of natural ability as a horseman. He became a founding member of the London Missionary Society and two-day journeys to and from the capital were uncomfortable and sometimes hazardous experiences, which he was always grateful to have completed in safety. He was the complete antithesis of the contemporary Jane Austen clergymen who spent the week enjoying the agreeable social life of large country houses, interrupting it only on Sundays when they rode over to their parish to read a published sermon at matins.

Though he may have preached with passion, his religion had a firmly intellectual base. He spent long hours in his upstairs study and had to conceal his frustration when callers at the house interrupted the reading and meditation which he regarded as an essential part of his daily round. He was elected a committee member of the Hull Subscription Library and read widely, including poetry. According to Darwent, he kept a commonplace book, in which he would have recorded quotations for future reference. This passed to a descendant, Colonel William Lambert White of Hedon, but its present location, if it still exists, is unknown.

George Lambert's journals reveal how thoroughly he prepared his sermons, often recording a summary of their structure and the development of his theme. He claimed to be poor at impromptu preaching and there could be mounting tension if he had not fixed on his text as the next Lord's Day drew nearer. Only on rare occasions did he have to admit preaching an old sermon. A few were published – admirers would have liked more – and he also wrote hymns.

His impact on his hearers must have been profound, not infrequently life-changing. There were times when privately and unnecessarily he confessed his awareness of his lack of ability, particularly when he heard other, brilliant preachers. Strain and stress as well as emotional crises affected his voice, in old age his eyesight deteriorated and embarrassing problems with his false teeth affected his diction. But there were many days when he could record with gratitude the 'liberty' he had experienced as he stood in the pulpit, a modest acknowledgement of the inspired eloquence which made him one of the most influential figures in Hull's religious history.

George Lambert did not know how fortunate he was to live in an age when Christianity was still to be confronted by German theologians questioning its texts and by the challenge to its account of creation posed by Darwin. For him the Bible was the Word of God. His duty was to interpret its true meaning through study, meditation and prayer and to present this truth for the edification of those to whom he was privileged to be pastor.

Though he had friendly relationships with other Dissenting ministers and with Evangelical clergy of the Church of England, he could never blur any fundamental differences separating them. Just as Fish Street owed its origin to members who had seceded from elsewhere on doctrinal grounds, so did George Lambert have to contend with dissidents who objected to perceived errors in his interpretation of the Scriptures, told him of their dissatisfaction and in some cases went elsewhere. As a Congregational chapel, Fish Street was a democratic organisation, its members were well aware that they were all entitled to their own opinion, even on matters more secular than religious, and disputes over the preferential allocating of pews or the opening or closing of windows in hot weather exercised the full extent of George Lambert's diplomatic skills and Christian forbearance. Matters theological aroused intense interest in Hull. Sectarian preachers arriving in the town attracted – in his view – gullible adherents and threatened to undermine the faith of his congregation.

There was in Hull at this period an informal Evangelical alliance, wrote Mrs Gilbert, the wife of a later minister at Fish Street. As a connoisseur of sermons George Lambert would attend other churches and chapels and he was a friend of a number of Anglican clergy, including Thomas Clarke and Joseph Milner of Holy Trinity and Mr King of St Mary's, Lowgate. A subsequent vicar of Holy Trinity, the Rev J H Bromby, however, regarded by those more scrupulous in matters of doctrine as a man of a suspiciously liberal and broad-minded tendency, he dismissed as one who knows not the Gospel. Though a firm adherent to courteous behaviour, he could never bring himself to speak dishonestly and there were difficult situations when he struggled to combine truth with charity. In the privacy of his journal he could be brutally frank about the inadequacies of other preachers at Fish Street or the other places of worship in Hull and about the incursions of those who arrived in the town and seduced the pliable from the paths of truth. He was a Protestant of his time. To Roman Catholics ('Papists') he was as fervently hostile as he was to Jews, though in the latter case one might have expected a shared reverence for the Old Testament to have created more understanding.

[1] Heckmondwike: 'a famous centre of evangelical Christian life and almost alone in the north of England' (Darwent), founded by the Rev Mr Hitchins and 'Fuller the banker', as an Academy or College in the North England which would supply orthodox Dissenting ministers (ie not Arian or Unitarian). GL joined the Academy in 1763. See Darwent 20-1. Heckmondwike contributed £14 13 6 to the building of Fish Street chapel.

George Lambert: The Man and his Family

Fortunately for a man who found so much to worry about, his marriage in 1770 to Hannah Ansley of Leeds was made in heaven. He was well aware that he had been favoured by Providence and paid tribute to her: 'What reason I have to be thankful that God gave me so good a woman and so good a wife. She has been a helper indeed.' [15 June 1793]. Marital bliss was sometimes darkened by concern about her ill health, to which her many pregnancies must have contributed. Darwent's total of 11 must include the John born in 1772, who evidently died very young, his Christian name being re-used for the John born in 1782 who features in the journals. George Lambert mourned with great anguish the early death of another child, Maria: 'Sweet babe, I loved her much.' [4 December 1791].

He was a loving father who cared deeply for his children's well-being, both secular and spiritual and he suffered with them in their not infrequent illnesses and in the aftermath of their many accidents. He records inflicting corporal punishment, but this was an accepted practice at that period. A highly strung man who struggled to control his nervous equilibrium, he soon regretted giving way to his temper and being more severe than he had intended. A home so permeated with religion and stern morality created problems as they grew older and their ideas and desires (notably those of his eldest son) came into conflict with his own immutable standards. But the bond remained strong.

He lived modestly but his income would exceed that of the majority of Hull people of the time and he repeatedly expressed his gratitude to God for his continuing provision. Apart from fortuitous gifts from wealthy supporters like the Thorntons and occasional bequests, all George Lambert's income came from the pew rents at the church. There was painful resentment when he felt the deacons expected him to undertake a financial burden which it was not right for the minister to bear, though ultimately they were generous when increasing ill-health made him unable to fulfil his duties and in providing a pension of £30 a year to his wife after his death.

He worried over the costs of a large household during a long period of war when food shortages resulted in escalating prices. To increase his income he invested, with only limited success, in the whaling trade and, after taking due thought, purchased a lottery ticket, leaving the outcome to divine Providence. He bore the inevitable negative response without complaint. In his darkest hours, when he despaired of the success of his labours, he was well aware that he had neither the resources nor the freedom to embark on a different career.

His house in Mytongates, an extension of Mytongate, just beyond the site of a former town wall and not far from the Humber in an area which was still semi-rural, was a busy place. The formidable programme of reading, writing, meditation and prayer he set himself must have required enormous self-discipline in the early years when it was filled with noisy young children, particularly in cold weather when he economised by delaying the lighting of his study fire. It was a hospitable house with friends constantly calling and staying far longer than was convenient. He was ever aware of the passing of time and the work left unfinished when he was forced to spend hours in what he regarded as trifling chit-chat. Members of the church with spiritual and personal problems felt free to call for guidance and they were always received with sympathy.

By the standards of the time George Lambert lived into late old age but he did not achieve longevity without endless complaints about his many illnesses and his belief that he was at death's door, understandable in a period when what one now regards as minor problems could be life-threatening. The medical men of Hull often received summonses to the Lambert home. He took it all very seriously – humour has no place in his journal – and he could never have foreseen the wry smiles his catalogue of woes would produce in a reader. A number of such entries, sufficient to convey the tone of his diary and his personality, have been included in this edition, but many have necessarily been omitted, in particular the sad story of his inexorable physical decline which occupies much of the last volumes and which makes painful reading. Some of his illnesses would now surely be diagnosed as psychosomatic. In his spiritual life he set himself impossibly high standards and, though it was the convention of the time to confide one's unworthiness and sinfulness to the pages of one's diary, there is no doubt that he frequently suffered great nervous stress. The total commitment to every tenet of his faith which he demanded of himself was not easy to achieve and the realisation that his livelihood and the support of his large family depended on the public expression of that faith was never far from his mind.

He lived through the period which provides the tranquil, civilised background to Jane Austen's novels. For him it was a terrible time. The nation was at war, food was scarce, prices rose astronomically and the established order was overturned by revolution and the guillotining of a king and queen. His reading of the newspapers brought him no comfort. A reactionary government in England, disturbed by what had happened in France, saw Dissenters as a Radical threat and made moves to curb their liberty: a policy which George Lambert, a loyal constitutionalist, felt as a deep injustice. As a non-freeman he had no vote in Hull's parliamentary elections but he saw the advantage of the secret ballot as a curb on the corruption he witnessed. Long before legislation was passed he recoiled against the cruelty of the slave trade.

He was an active member of the Committee for the Abolition of Slavery and, although he made no reference in his journal to the visit to Hull of the freed slave, Olauduh Equiano in November 1792, the probability is that he was present at the meeting held then as, along with a number of eminent local figures, he was named as a subscriber to the sixth edition of Equiano's work, *The Interesting Narrative and Other Writings*, published the following year.

It would be easy to gain from the journals the impression that George Lambert was a melancholy, unsociable man, prone to introspection, tormented by his sexuality and always conscious of his unworthiness for the ministry. But a diary can be an outlet, often therapeutic, in which the writer releases the emotions and thoughts which have been submerged during the day. He was a serious man, a worrier, and he had to contend with many real problems. He also had a very happy marriage, he was at the heart of a large family, he dined out with friends and his life, within his own circle, was far from solitary. How far his colleagues and acquaintances were aware of his inner torments is doubtful. Quite probably most saw him as a successful, confident man, a powerful force for good, for whom they held a deep respect.

The long-awaited end came on 17 March 1816. He was 74. A lengthy solemn account of his death, written by a member of his family, was sent to Fish Street and is preserved in the Church Book.

He was an important figure in the town, several Anglican clergymen attended his funeral and a eulogistic, but in this case truthful, obituary appeared in the *Hull Rockingham*: 'A man with a more truly Christian spirit never lived. He loved all mankind.' A friend, the Rev Edward Parsons of Leeds, preached the funeral sermon and George Lambert was buried in front of the pulpit which he had occupied with such distinction for so many years.

The congregation subscribed £80 for a monument by the eminent Hull sculptor, John Earle. Erected on the north wall of the gallery, it recorded in Latinate phraseology and with appropriate formality the many virtues of a pastor who, it was hoped, would inspire his successors to follow his example both in their sermons and in their lives.

He lay there for less than a century. Hull continued to change and its population to move into the suburbs, away from the Old Town and from Fish Street, where the numbers declined from the great days of George Lambert. In 1899 it was closed and replaced by Fish Street Memorial Congregational Church, Princes Avenue. The old building took on a new role as a telephone exchange, the premises of the National Telephone Company. Later it was used as a warehouse but eventually become derelict and was demolished in 1984. By now the movement of population out of the Old Town was being reversed and the site was used for a new housing development.

6 Interior of Fish St. chapel north aisle 1904 (LSC2/10 Hull Local Studies Library)

A photograph exists of the gutted interior of the chapel when bodies were exhumed for reburial. George Lambert himself was re-interred in Spring Bank Cemetery. He had played a not insignificant part in Hull's history but he is not numbered in its pantheon of great men. It is a judgment he would have accepted with perfect understanding and total humility.

The golden verses of Pythagoras

Archbishop Leighton's translation[2]

[2] Robert Leighton (baptised 1612–1684), Archbishop of Glasgow, whose writings published after his death, 1692–1708, achieved some popularity.

We should not allow ourselves to go to sleep, till we have seriously resolved the actions of the day, and asked ourselves what have I done amiss? What good have I neglected to do? That so we may reprove ourselves for what has been wrong and take the comfort of what has been as it ought.

With reverence at thy own tribunal stand,
And answer justly to thy own demand,
Where have I been? In what have I transgressed?
What good or ill has this day's life expressed?
What have I fail'd in what I ought to do?
In what to God, to man, or to myself I owe?
Enquire severe, whate'er from first to last,
From morning's dawn, till evening's gloom has past.

Soul Memorials Vol 1 1769-1781

1769

I had invitations from ... [Cleckheaton], from Gloucester, Nottingham and Hull. I accepted the last. Preached for the first time in the New Chapel April 9 1769. Was ordained March 14 1770 and blessed be God have to the year 1780, in which I write this, been made happy, and I hope useful amongst them.

There are a few remarkable deliverances for me and mine which I shall here record, hoping that it may be useful to some of the children when I am removed.

1775

Friday, 21 July
My son Samuel[3] was this day delivered from the jaws of death almost by a miracle. Standing under the shafts of a cart which was upon a decline in Mr Taylor's yard, another boy pushing the cart, the shafts fell, knocked down Samuel, who fell with his breast against a piece of oak. The cart was set agoing and, humanly speaking, he must have been crushed under the wheel but by a small stone against which the shaft stuck just as the wheel came to his head.

Thursday, 27 July
Being reduced to a few shillings and in debt several pounds. This day the Lord sent in a present supply by an hand that I had no knowledge of before.

Saturday, 14 October
My wife bad of a sore breast, scarce recovered from a hoarseness myself, expenses high and only a small matter in hand ... handed in a supply by a friend, who presented me with two guineas.

[1776]

Friday, 18 October[4]
As the mason was paving the back yard Samuel pulled down one of the largest stones. Had it fallen on him death or a fracture must have been the consequence. But by a sudden spring backwards the end of the flag fell close to his toes without hurting him. What rendered the deliverance more remarkable was that another stone lay behind him on the ground, rather above the place where he stood, so that, had he struck against it, instead of jumping on it, his legs at least might have been crushed.

1778

15 July

Elizabeth Lambert[5] brought almost to the brink of the grave. The physician baffled. The case desperate. Her moan penetrating to the very heart. Yet when all hope was gone, He that had brought her to the grave brought her up again. . . .

23 July

Samuel Lambert unknown to us had been riding upon one of Mr Banks's[6] horses. Was thrown from it and found stiff on the turnpike road[7] leading to Anlaby. Was brought home, his head broke, very sick.

Wednesday, 28 October[8]

My son William[9] . . . this day fell downstairs without being much hurt.

1779

Nov [sic]

I was seized with an inflammation on my liver which brought on a dropsy. Had nothing before me but death.

1780

22 September

This afternoon my wife and I went as far as Kirk Ella to see Mr Woodall. On our return we found that both Elizabeth and Phebe[10] had fallen backwards out of the parlour window upon the hard stones. But neither fracture nor disordered reason ensued.

Friday, 29 September

This was the day for the meeting of ministers.

Saturday, 30 September

Have been hindered all day from that retirement which I wished to enjoy. Mr Popplewell[11] called on me on his way from Ashby de la Zouch to Beverley.

Tuesday, 3 October

This day my voice was so much affected by the cold that I was unable with the most violent exertion to make any sound above a whisper.

Wednesday, Thursday, Friday, 4-6 October

Much indisposed both in mind and body.

Tuesday, 10 October

Wholly engaged in company all the day. Had no time for reading, meditation or other delightful employments. I find much company (even tho' of good people) not always the most profitable.

Wednesday, 11 October

This morning I heard a very excellent discourse delivered at the High Church by Mr Richardson of York.

Monday, 16 October

Had some agreeable conversation this afternoon with two friends about the excellencies of Christ and in the evening upon my return home met with my brother W Ansley[12]. What a refreshment does it give to the mind to meet with dear friends and relatives at seasons; especially when we have been long separated from them.

Wednesday, 18 October

I have this day been at Beverley. Found my mind much upon the rove both on the road and while there.

Friday, 20 October

I have this day been detained from my usual employ in the study by the indisposition of my wife, the concerns of the family and the company of friends. We had some friends to drink tea with us. . . . I am rather uneasy in not having anything prepared for the Lord's day . . . I was much concerned about my poor wife this evening. The frequent complaints with which she has been exercised of late had me to fear that her constitution is much upon the decline.

Saturday, 21 October [written as 20 October]

I this day heard once more from my aged father[13] who I concluded by his long silence had been ill. O that I could hear that his eyes were opened to see a clear passage into that eternity that he is hastening to. I wish to find my heart more concerned about him and led forth in prayer for him.

Lord's Day, 22 October

I have this day been blessed with much liberty, enlargement and pleasure in the work of the Lord. . . . I hope the labour of the day will not be wholly lost. The people seemed very attentive. Some were much affected.

Monday, 23 October

As I rode to Cottingham this afternoon my mind was much employed upon spiritual subjects.

Thursday, 26 October

I had this day very agreeable conversation with Mrs Binnington.[14] She seems to be a person that needs much encouragement in divine matters.

Saturday, 28 October

In the evening I went to see Hugh Ross,[15] who, I was informed last night, was ill. Poor man – he has been greatly exercised with pain. He seemed to take it unkind that I had not called on him before. And tho' my conscience could vindicate me that I had not known of his illness sooner, it gives me great pain even to be suspected of want of affection or kindness.

Monday, 30 October

Mrs Ross spoke much of the benefit she found in attending under the last lecture. . . . In the afternoon called on some sick persons, and spent some time in conversation and prayer with them.

Tuesday, 31 October

This morning I rose early that I might have more time for private religion and study. And by the help of God I purpose to continue this practice. . . . Time has been lost in company. Much of it passed away in attending to the greatest trifles. And I find too much delicacy to interrupt visitants in my own house. I lend the ear, even while my heart is distressed.

Thursday 2 November

Mr Ross informed me that he had found the sermons which I had published peculiarly useful and refreshing to him during his confinement. I have had repeated testimonies of the same nature both from others and of those who are entire strangers to me. Blessed be God that I have so extensive an opportunity to speak both to friends when I cannot be personally with them and to bear a testimony in parts of this nation where I never was, yea and in distant lands. Some have been sent to Archangel, Sweden, etc. And in the Isle of Wight I have heard of their being particularly useful.

Friday, 3 November

No sooner had I just got entered upon my studies than I was called off by company, which continued in succession till about seven in the evening. Truly I may say with a good man, 'What a multitude of precious hours have been lost in unprofitable discourse.'

Monday 6 November

In the afternoon I rode to Cottingham. It was the most severely cold I almost ever remember to have been out in.

Tuesday, 7 November

Returned from Cottingham this morning. It was severely cold and much wind and hail.

Wednesday, 8 November

I was much entertained while a person was playing some of the deck tunes on a harpsichord. . . . I had but sixpence in the house, and several weeks to the quarter day. The Providence of God sent a person that I had never seen before who presented me with a ten pound note.

Lord's Day, 19 November

[Mr Ross] with several more of the members of the church came on to express how useful the sermons upon Psal 143.8 had been made to them and desiring that they might be published.

Monday, 20 November

This day opened with mercies. Almost as soon as I got downstairs Mr King[16] came to the door and stayed with me till near one o'clock. . . . I had been relating something both of my spiritual and temporal state to him, when, to my great surprise, he presented me with £20 as a donation from J T Esq.[17]

Saturday, 25 November

I have this day heard of the death of Captain Fletcher. A letter came from him this day week, appointing his wife to meet him at Liverpool. She set off yesterday in full expectation to enjoy his company. But today we hear he is lodged in the briney waves.

Lord's Day, 26 November

This was the day for the collection for the Charity Children.[18]

Monday, 27 November

When going to mount my horse to go to Cottingham Mr Popplewell[19] and Mr Tiger arrived [?] to the door and stayed with me more than an hour so that it was dark before I got out of the town. The horse proved very unruly, reared on its hind legs frequently. But Providence was my protector.

Wednesday, 29 November

My daughter Hannah[20] being scalded all over her breast thro' the carelessness of the girl provoked me very much. I find my evil tempers soon agitated, and, tho' soon over, yet they give me cause for painful reflection for a long time after.

Wednesday, 3 December

[Advice to his descendants] If they are brought under any serious concern about their precious souls, I would advise them to keep a diary and every day minute down their walk with God, for I own I have found it useful and wished I had begun it sooner.

Monday, 4 December

This morning I met with a great and unexpected trial. I was informed that some remarks from the pulpit had hurt the minds of some, and were much censured by one of the elders of the people. The two things objected were 1st that I had advised my hearers to take some part of the beginning of every day to converse with God by prayer, reading and reflecting upon what lay before then. The 2nd was that I had advised those that were able to keep a diary or at least a weekly account of the frame and state of their souls. It distressed me much that any objection should be made to such things, especially by those that I should have hoped had known better.

Tuesday, 5 December
Drank tea at Mr Carlill's,[21] prayed at parting but too much of the time was taken up in trifling conversation.

Thursday, 7 December
Had much liberty in proclaiming Christ as a free and full Saviour to one who is far gone in a consumption at the Charity Hall.

Monday, 11 December
I this day rode as far as Swanland. The day proved remarkably fine. Mr Jones accompanied me and the conversation was very agreeable. We had a mixed company to tea at home this afternoon, which rendered it not so agreeable.

Lord's Day, 17 December
I have many mercies to be thankful for this evening. . . . That my son Samuel has this day completed the tenth year of his age. That he has every member of body sound and every faculty of mind opening. That he can read the Scriptures and has made some proficiency in writing. . . . That my dear wife, tho' she had been lately much threatened, has been spared to me ten years after that great deliverance wrought for us.

Monday, 18 December
In the evening I went to Cottingham and preached the lecture.

Thursday, 28 December
I have been much discouraged today with a view of the state of our national affairs. Engaged in war with America, France, Spain[22] and on the eve of a Dutch war also. I am amazed to find such confidence in people after such evident tokens of the divine displeasure. . . . Yesterday a person sent in a very useful present in various articles with whom I have very little acquaintance and this day a lady who has been repeatedly kind presented me with two guineas, which will about make up the year's accounts.

Lord's Day, 31 December
The congregation is not declined in numbers – O that they may grow in grace. In my family no breach has been made and many gracious appearances for them. In my public labours I have in the general found much pleasure and profit.

1781

Monday, 1 January

Dined at Mr Gilder's[23] in company with Messrs Milner,[24] Harris,[25] Riddell[26], Jones[27] and Towers.[28] The conversation was very agreeable. I afterwards went to Cottingham and preached to a crowded assembly from 2 Tim 46.

Monday, 8 January

Read Mr Hartley's[29] address to the Association at York in which he gives a very affecting and I fear a very just description of our state as a nation. He concludes it, as follows: 'We have not a single ally in the whole world and every man's hand is lifted up against us.'

Monday, 15 January

I have been much engaged today with my wife's brother from Leeds. A circumstance turned up respecting the manner in which his father had disposed of our share of the effects at his death. That it was left to my wife and children. It gave me some concern, being different to what I had expected, and because, if I should be infirm, it may render me dependent on the children or if they prove undutiful may render my situation very uncomfortable. However, I at last got my mind composed.

Saturday, 20 January

I had a very bad night. Slept very little. Much disturbed while asleep. Thoughts of what lay before me very discouraging. A melancholy gloom hung upon my mind which quite depressed my spirits. I resolved to go to Swanland and propose a change with Mr Gill.[30] Had a very pleasant ride thither. But soon after I got in it came on a very heavy storm of rain and snow. Was wet thro' on my return to Hull, and very near being thrown when I had got within a few hundred yards of the town. The horse first stumbled, flew out on one side and set off on a gallop. Thro' mercy I recovered my seat and received no hurt.

Monday, 22 January

Visited the Dutch prisoners in their confinement, found my heart much affected for them, particularly for some who were much in years. They expressed great gratitude and seemed far much more cheerful than I could have expected.

Tuesday, 23 January

Engaged with a person from Barrow in going about the settlement of their place. I this day signed their writings as trustee for the chapel and took a copy.

Thursday, 25 January

I this day became a subscriber to the general library.[31] Took out the 1st volume of Bishop Hurd on the prophecies.[32]

Monday, 29 January

This day William cut his finger in a most shocking manner till all the top of it from below the upper joint being hung by a piece of skin. What will be the consequence I know not but it was with great difficulty we could get the blood stopped.

Wednesday, 31 January

I have taken up the chief part of this day in reading Shaw's Travels to the Levant, Holy Land etc.[33] They are both very informing and entertaining.

Tuesday, 13 February

I returned from Cottingham this morning to breakfast, found my family in peace which was a privilege worthy of notice, seeing some near them had been in distress and danger. The Humber had, by the height of the tide and force of the wind, broke down the jetty or pier facing my house, had burst its banks; and the water now in some houses above a yard, but by the turn of the tide it never came so near us as either to fright or endanger us. I went to see the desolation it had made this morning when I got home and indeed it was surprising to see how great stones had been carried by its force ten or more yards and the earth was washed away in some places into holes above a yard deep. O what a mercy to be preserved from the violence of those ragious [?] elements.

Wednesday, 14 February

I went this morning to the High Church.[34] Mr Stillingfleet[35] preached a very useful sermon.

Lord's Day, 18 February

About one o'clock this morning I was awaked with a noise and the smell of fire. It was so light in all the back part of the house that there was no need of candle. It was with difficulty that I got the family awake. When I came down found Mr Banks's malt kiln all of a blaze. What little wind there was was full upon our house, but happily it was very low. Between three and four I went to bed but got very little sleep. O what a mercy that we were not consumed.

Wednesday, 21 February

This being a day appointed for a general fast and humiliation.

Thursday, 22 February

In the morning bottled the wine.

Monday, 26 February

About 8 [?] o'clock set off for Cottingham. I had not gone above a mile and an half when I met a waggon loaded with hay. The horse I rode on went very quiet past the first horse, then stood. As soon as the wheel came opposite us the horse turned short round with the fore feet down towards the ditch. Not being upon my guard I lost my foot out of the left stirrup. It set out on a full gallop. It was a miracle of Providence that I was enabled to keep my seat. However, thro' mercy I recovered the stirrup and got safe.

Tuesday, 27 February

This morning before I left Cottingham I went to see Mr Ringrose[36] and had some very agreeable conversation on divine subjects. On my return in passing by a cart, the horse again took fright and ran away with me. It rained very hard, my hands were numb and cold; the more I endeavoured to pull it in, it ran with the greater violence; at last it ran against a horse that was in another cart, at the distance of half a mile from *that*, which it took fright at. When it came up to the other horse, with its nose it stopped as if it had been shot. Otherwise, probably both I and it had been dashed to pieces. I dismounted, walked about two miles and got home very wet.

Wednesday, 28 February

I went to see a Jew's funeral.[37] Conversed with them but found them remarkably ignorant. I enquired whether they had the same distinctions of sects as formerly or if they had any of the sentiment of the Saducees. The only answer I could get was that there always were both good and bad men but that all Israelites believed the resurrection of the body.

Friday, 9 March

After dinner we received a letter from Leeds informing that my wife's father had been visited with another fit and was thought to be in great danger. I am preparing to set off for Leeds in the morning. . . . My dear partner has been but poorly for some days past in her bowels, something of the same complaint she had about six months since. . . . Since I wrote the above we received a letter by the diligence[38] informing that Father Ansley died this morning about 11 minutes before one. Death has entered the family, the root is smitten and the branches will soon wither.

Saturday, 10 March

As the diligence was going over the narrow bridge before we got into the market place in York, as we were ascending, a waggon loaded with corn was coming off it. The wheel of the latter got within our wheel and had like to have tore our carriage to pieces. But we were preserved. It was the day the Judge came in. There was something very solemn to hear, the trumpets sounding, the expectation and preparation discovered and numbers habited in the most superb manner. My thoughts turned upon the Judgement day.

Monday, 12 March

Attended my Father Ansley to the silent mansion of the grave. The will was read. Blessed be God for the provisions made.

Friday, 16 March

This day I returned for Hull. About two miles on the other side [Market] Weighton the two diligences entered into a contention which should get first. The other was overturned and that which I was in run with violence against the wheel of a cart. Providentially no person was hurt, but it might have been of very serious consequences.

Saturday, 17 March

This morning I received a letter from Mr Dobson of Kidderminster informing me that their late Pastor, Mr Fawcett, was removed from them by death, and inviting me to pay them a visit as a candidate to succeed him. It is a populous town, a large meeting house, a numerous congregation and a genteel stipend. But the people of Hull have always carried to me with the strictest affection. I purpose weighing the matter further and laying it before the Lord in prayer before I fix either one way or the other. My mind has been much unsettled by this affair thro' the day. I have been [un]able to give my thoughts to what I wished to have them employed about.

Lord's Day, 18 March

As we were sitting in the evening, my wife reading, her cap touched the candle and was all in a blaze in a moment. It was so ordered that she had before taken out the pins and, being loose, she got it off with only scorching her arm a little. Her hair was on fire but extinguished by throwing her apron over it, It was a gracious Providence that she was not much hurt.

Monday, 19 March

The subject of a remove has employed much of my thoughts and conversation this day. In the morning I was enabled to leave the matter with God, ready to go or stay as he saw might be most for his glory. In the evening I laid it before the deacons and Trustees, assured them of my affection for the people but left it either to have a larger place to preach or to think of a change. They are to meet about it again next Thursday.

Tuesday, 20 March

Have been much employed this day in writing. Sent a copy of Father Ansley's will, list of plate, debts and cash with the advice of the attorney to Mr Sommerville. Letter to brother Will and one to Mr Dobson, in all full six sheets of paper.

Monday, 26 March

My wife and I went for Leeds where we arrived about 6 in the evening. Found friends well. One circumstance deserves notice. As we went from Weighton there were three in the diligence, and one, a young woman, rode on the box. Being remarkably cold and blustering it concerned me much to see a woman so much exposed. I proposed to those who were in the carriage to take her in. The person with my wife consented. Soon after she got in her conversation led us to conclude she had been acquainted with divine thing. She then informed us that she was first awaked and brought under a concern of soul by hearing me once at Hull. ... We continued at Leeds till Saturday, March 31.

Thursday, 5 April

I drank tea at Mr Todd's[39] who expressed great concern for my continuance at Hull.

Friday, 6 April

I this day sent a letter to the deacons and Trustees with some proposals relative to my staying at Hull. Three of them came on in the evening and expressed their approbation of what I had mentioned. There were some faint hopes that a new chapel may yet be brought about. But I wish to leave it with Him who I know will order all things well.

Monday, 9 April

This day I received the goods from Leeds that were sent by water. Was engaged all the morning in unpacking them.

Tuesday, 10 April

Was informed that the deacons and Trustees in a meeting the last night had agreed upon the building of a new chapel. Was after informed that it was doubtful.

Monday, 30 April

I have been engaged this day in conversing with some of the people, visiting the sick and reading. The deacons and Trustees came on in the evening and proposed advancing the support of my family by an additional collection but they thought it would not be possible to build a new place. My mind (tho' deeply affected with a sense of their generosity) was led to decline it, as it would render me a burden upon them and which same might prevent the success of my labours. I find a disposition rather inclined to cast myself upon God.

Wednesday, 2 May

I painted the red room.

Lord's Day, 6 May
In the ordinance was enabled to commit myself, my wife in her present circumstances, my family, my charge and the designs of a new place of worship to God.

Thursday, 10 May
This day the Trustees agreed for a piece of ground for a new chapel.

Tuesday, 15 May
The Church met this evening and agreed 1st to build a new chapel, 2ly they appointed a committee to conduct that business.

Thursday, 17 May
I this day began to read Gibbon's History of the Decline and Fall of the Roman Empire.

Saturday, 19 May
In the evening my wife was very poorly and expected that she should be in labour this night but about 10 o'clock it went off again.

Lord's Day, 20 May
A collection was made for the new chapel at Grimsby. We collected £6.14.1½.

Monday, 21 May
Attended a meeting in the evening relative to a plan for a new place. In the evening my brother William Ansley arrived from Leeds.

Tuesday, 22 May
I have been quite restless all last night and much disordered in my head and bowels. I heard the clock strike every hour except three. Poor Phebe has also been very bad. She seemed but restless all yesterday but has been in a high fever all the last night and thro' the day. I begin to be very apprehensive that it will be the smallpox. I have felt some uneasiness that she has not been innoculated.

Wednesday, 23 May
Phebe has again had a very bad night. I fear it will be too much for her. My mind cleaves very strongly to her. She had been a most engaging babe, remarkable for her amiable temper and vivacity and affection. She is become very engaging to us by her conversation. . . . The spots began to appear this day. She is very poorly and I think will be very full.

Thursday, 24 May
Have been much engaged with and about my dear Phebe.

Friday, 25 May

I received the letters from Kidderminster which will put a complete period to any thoughts of visiting them. They have not, I think, used me well but hope it will be over-ruled for good. I think it is much if they get a faithful gospel minister to settle with them.

Saturday, 26 May

The child exercises both body and mind.

Monday, 28 May

Much distressed by the fears [?] of one of the church relative to a new place. This evening they were to meet to purchase the ground for a new place of worship. Phebe has been very poorly but those who are judges seem to think her in a fair way.

Thursday, 29 May

I have been much indisposed today with the bad night I passed thro' last night in attending on Phebe. Am sure that I did not sleep above half an hour all night. This morning she seemed in a fine way to our apprehension. Her eyes opened. The pock turned on her face and the swelling abated. When the apothecary came on he expressed his fear from the last circumstance and wanted to place a blister on each ankle.[40] We sent for the physician who concluded there would be no occasion and thought she was in a fair way of doing well. It has given a great shock to my mind.

Wednesday, 30 May

I hope Phebe is in more promising circumstances. Many of the pustules are turned.

Tuesday, 5 June

Attended the committee in the evening and presented the form of a petition which was approved by them. Lord favour the design.

Tuesday, 6 June

Heard Mr Milner in the morning.

Lord's Day, 17 June

Mrs Grime came on this evening. She observed that last Saturday was fortnight she was much distressed. Her husband and one child in a French prison. Without bread for her and the child that was with her at home. In this condition she found herself much distressed. She took up the sermons I had published, read the second of them and found her mind much supported. On the Lord's Day went to chapel, was refreshed. When she went home she sat down to meditate on what she had been hearing. The child interrupted her by saying, 'Mammy, what are we to have for dinner?' The question affected her much. Her answer was God must provide. Soon after, an unexpected person entered her habitation with a large supply, one that had never brought her anything before and that knew nothing of her situation at that season. The relation of it affected me much.

Thursday, 21 June

I have been much distressed today by a letter, a part of which was shewn to me, to be convinced that a person who for more than eleven years has professed the most cordial and unshaken friendship has endeavoured to discourage the attempt for a new chapel and to misrepresent my conduct representing Kidderminster. I am happy not only in the testimony of my own conscience but in the consciences of all that have had to do anything in the affair. The deacons and Trustees have seen every letter that passed between the people of Kidderminster and myself so that I could not deceive them as was insinuated by the letter, nor had I any such design.

Saturday, 23 June

I was low in purse and have every day the prospect of an expensive time before me. But this day the Lord sent in a very comfortable supply by Mr Grundy who paid for his book. I have long expected it and at seasons was ready secretly to murmur but now I see there never was a time since it was due that it could have come more acceptably or was more necessary.

Tuesday and Wednesday, 3 and 4 July

I put these two together because I have not been in bed since Monday night. My wife was taken with labour pains from about 9 o'clock last night. This morning between five and six she, after a very hard travail, was mercifully delivered of a son.[41]

Friday, 6 July

This has been a very distressing day with me. In the morning I met with very insolent behaviour from a servant. For some time I was enabled to stand proof against it but at last it stirred my temper and put me into a great passion. It is impossible to say what I felt after it. To be sure, the provocation was great but if it had not been for my depraved nature it would have had no effect. Besides I have behaved often as bad to my great master and yet he has been gracious. Besides this I had a very unfavourable account from the school of my son Samuel. And this evening one of my wife's breasts has been very troublesome. I fear it will prove bad.

Saturday, 7 July

I have . . . been much alarmed with my wife, she having much fever.

Lord's Day, 8 July

My wife in a high fever.

Monday, 9 July

Have reason to hope that my wife is in a more favourable way.

Tuesday, 17 July

Obliged to walk from Cottingham having the rheumatism so bad in my shoulder and right arm that I could neither manage nor bear the motion of the horse.

Saturday, 21 July

Samuel, Hannah and Phebe very poorly and yet have found some degree of gratitude that it was much better with us than some other families, particularly one in the neighbourhood who have a child laying dead by taking poison that they had put to kill flies.

Tuesday, 24 July

My wife's breasts are very bad again. She was obliged to send it out to nurse.[42]

Wednesday, 1 August

Heard Mr Milner in the morning. Found my mind much upon the soar [?] while under the word.

Monday, 6 August

Mr Harris having got ordination in the Church of England has wrote his people word that he can no longer officiate amongst them. And one of the Trustees intends to move it in their meeting tomorrow evening to make it out to my people. There seems something singular both in the season and his proposal. . . . A violent fever rages. One man and his child is removed in a few days and his wife lays dangerously ill. . . . Conversing with an aged person this day concerning the state of the nation. He expressed a strong persuasion that some greater event would happen in the year 1788. The only ground he gave was that the Spanish Armada was in 1588, the revolution in 1688 and that he wished the same date to be observed in the present century by those who lived to see it.

Wednesday, 8 August

I afterwards heard that the Trustees of the New Chapel[43] in Dagger Lane had met and that the generality inclined to propose my succeeding Mr Harris. Only two objected, but nothing was fully determined.

Thursday, 9 August

I have this day been much engaged in meeting with the Trustees both of our own place and belonging to the Chapel in Dagger Lane. If we enter that place they expect £400 to be paid down for the enlargement and other decorations. There appeared something mercenary in the proposal at first view because the greater part of the expense had been paid already and much of it had been laid out on superfluous decorations. But I heard afterwards that they intended to apply the money to charitable uses.

Friday, 10 August

This day I received a letter from Mr Harris and afterwards had conversation with another of their Trustees. On the whole I secretly but sincerely wish that we may not have the place as I find every art is used to prejudice the public against us as Dissenters. In the evening I went to Mr Harris's lodgings and showed him the inconsistency of the excuse made in his letter. As the two things on which he there grounds the change of his mind viz the universal approbation the people shew to Mr Jones and the general dislike of giving up the place. Seeing his recommendation of Mr Jones to the people was previous to any knowledge or thought there could be on his part of the one or the other.

Saturday, 11 August
In the morning thoughts were much engaged about the New Chapel and my mind much averse to the thought of entering upon it. I had four objections. 1 That in the most favourable view it was very precarious whether it would answer. The expense would be great, certain and constant, the supply for to answer it uncertain. 2 ly Four hundred pounds sunk at once and the interest of [on?] 840 more to pay annually, besides other expenses was a great sum. 3 ly But, setting that aside, was it really consistent, nay might it not cause reflections to be cast upon us by our Dissenting brethren to expend perhaps £50 in order to pay for Books of Common Prayer, a surplice, a painted creed, the King's Arms etc 4 ly It is not improbable, as there must be an assistant, that discord in divisions might take place in time. ... I wished the Trustees to stop all progress about it. This day my son Samuel while out at play run a nail into his left arm at the bend. It bled much and yet seems to be dangerous as it is between the two veins. It is so much amongst the arteries and guiders that I am a little alarmed for the consequences.

... This evening after I had wrote the above Mr Gilder came on and set my mind at liberty, informing me that the Trustees of the New Chap[el] in Dagger Lane had met this evening and resolved to continue it upon its present plan in the hands of Mr Jones. I bless God for this. Also I account it one of my main mercies and an answer to prayer for my mind was so oppressed with the thought of going to it that I could not help making it matter of prayer that the Lord would prevent it. It is something singular 1st that I have found such a change in my own mind. At first I thought there might be the hand of God in the proposal, from the time in which it fell vacant and was proposed, but afterwards I felt my mind totally averse to it. 2ly That there should be such a change in their Trustees between their meeting on Wednesday, when there was a great majority for me, and tonight when it turned the other way. I am very thankful for the event: but think Mr Harris not only to have acted a contrary and disingenuous part but discovered an unfriendly, not to say persecuting, disposition.

Tuesday, 14 August
We have this day been obliged to remove George to another nurse as the woman we had was not in a condition to keep him any longer.

Wednesday, 15 August

This day took down two of the beds[44] which has so far taken up my time and exhausted my strength that I have nothing very particular to notice this evening.

Friday, 17 August

Mr Hinton called on me in the morning and sat some time, as did Mr Boyes[45] in the afternoon. He came to signify the desire of some that Mr Harris and I should have a meeting. I am sure I bore him no ill will, but as to professing friendship I cannot see how it can be expected to be sincere on either part. However, tho' I will not shun a meeting, I have no thoughts of seeking one.

Thursday, 23 August

Mr Burnett[46] informed me that his daughter had wrote him and that Mr Addington of Market Harborough was for removing to London and that the people had thought either of Mr Barnes [?] or me. I know none of the people there and the only thing from which they have had any such thoughts was from reading the sermons that are published. . . . For my part I am not elated with these things. . . . I have been under the very disagreeable necessity of administering correction to my son Samuel. I am sure it was worse to myself than to him. Lord, even parental correction is an ordinance of thy appointment; be pleased to succeed it with thy blessing. I have not done it in anger but in love, not for my pleasure but his profit, not so much for disobedience to me as sin against thee. O deliver him from lying lips and a depraved heart.

Saturday, 25 August

Crossed the water to Barton. Walked from thence to Barrow and from thence to Thornton, Thornton Hall and College.[47] The last is a fine old ruin. The entrance has been very magnificent. Part of the folding gates are yet standing. It has a very venerable aspect. But the inhabitants are forgotten, their mansion in ruins and the teeth of time is eating away the workmanship of those who have long since been made a repast of worms. . . . Returned to Barrow much tired having walked 15 or 16 miles.

Lord's Day, 26 August

During prayers several young men stood without, making a great noise, but they afterwards came in and behaved with much decency.

Monday, 27 August

Returned from Barrow to Hull. In coming over the Humber I was knocked down by the sudden change of the sail. Even the man who guided the vessel did not perceive the change of the wind; it was so instantaneous   Providentially I received no hurt but my wife's brother bled for some time at the nose.

Thursday, 30 August

About noon an express came from Barrow to inform me that Mr Brian of Sheffield and Mr Wren of York had met there and had demanded the chapel. That a rabble had rose upon it and broke the windows. Upon this I wrote to one of the Trustees desiring him by no means to give up the place to Wren and recommending peace. I am really concerned that men who profess to call themselves Gospel ministers should act in a manner so opposite to the temper and conduct of the Prince of Peace.

Saturday, 1 September

About ten o'clock Mr Wren called upon me and we had a long altercation about the chapel at Barrow. As he has taken possession of it and informed me that Mr Wilby was resolved to preach in it, I wrote to him immediately to dissuade him from it, fearing that it might breed a riot and that some might receive harm.

Thursday, 6 September

Have had many thoughts about the money we are to have by the order of our late Father Ansley. I feel some anxiety about its being placed out so as to be secure and to be improved for the advantage of the family. To think about it is necessary; but I am afraid of being too anxious about it. . . . In the evening I was summoned to a meeting relative to the thoughts of a new chapel. I went fully convinced that it was much needed, but apprehensive that it could never be got thro'. The Trustees thought otherwise. Mr Tong[48] set down £50 more and Mr Gilder £20 and Mr Jones £30. This brought the subscription to about £420. £700 more would be wanted. It was thought 150 might be collected more than what was subscribed in the town, 150 out of it, and if mortgaged for 400 Mr Tong was willing to pay the interest of 100. The meeting was very unanimous.

Tuesday, 18 September

Went by water to Grimsby, had a very pleasant passage.

Wednesday, 19 September

This being the day for the Ordination at Grimsby.

Thursday, 20 September

Rose about five in the morning and took a walk on the bank leading from the town to the Humber. The tide was rising and the day remarkably fine. . . . About one o'clock we set off for to walk to Clay Thorp. Were obliged to wade in mud, a kind of quicksand and water for above a mile to get to the sloop. Got to Hull about six.

Thursday, 27 September

Attended the meeting of the Trustees about a new chapel. It was resolved to meet the next Thursday and then enter into an agreement with the builders.

Friday, 28 September

In the evening attended the meeting of ministers. . . . Several useful remarks were made [on a passage of Scripture] and upon the whole much unanimity prevailed. . . . Mr Milner and I were the persons engaged in prayer.

Wednesday, 3 October

In the evening I went into the home of a neighbour, a Jew, to see the decorations they had made for their feast of tabernacles. The room was decorated with boughs, flowers and fruit and extracts from the Scriptures. I had some conversation with him but found him amazingly ignorant and found my mind much affected on account of the affecting state of the Jews.

Thursday, 4 October

Have been engaged in the garden most of the day.

Monday 8 October

Spent much of the day in visiting the sick. Rather alarmed with some bad smells I found in those rooms where I had to visit people in the flux[49] and fever.

Friday, 12 October

Received a letter from Brother Ansley advising to place our money in the Stocks.

Saturday, 13 October

Heard that a letter I wrote some time ago in confidence to a friend at London had been the instrument of much uneasiness to a person to whom it related. What I wrote was founded upon facts, but if the person has really seen his error and repented of his faults I should be very sorry to injure him.

Monday, 15 October

Dined at Mr Gilder's. Drank tea at Mr Atkinson's in Finkle Street. . . . In the evening attended the committee who met to sign the agreement with the builders for a new chapel.

Friday, 19 October

The tide was so remarkably high this morning that it got into many houses in the town and has done considerable damage.

Wednesday, 24 October

Mr Wilby of Barrow came to propose a collection for the new chapel they are building there. But I could not sign the petition because of the late unsteady conduct of the people there and the promise that I made some time since relative to Howden. To me it appears very precipitate but I sincerely wish it may prosper.

Saturday, 3 November
A letter I received this morning from my father made me very uneasy and unfitted my mind for some time for study. I could not help wishing it was more in my power to assist him in temporal comforts. He seems to think it want of affection but thou Lord knowest that it is want of ability. After tea I got it in some measure off my mind.

Thursday, 8 November
Called upon Messrs Gilder, Story, Winter. Dined with Mr Jones. Drank tea with Mr Carlill. Attended the committee and had some very free and agreeable conversation with Messrs Milner and King.

Thursday, 15 November
This morning as I was reading in my study news was brought me of the death of John Ingram, a poor man whom I have visited for some time past, and the last visit was enabled to be very open and faithful with him, which I never could find liberty to be before. He has left a widow and five children, I fear in very low circumstances. .... It is two years this month since I had a prospect of leaving my family in similar circumstances.

Friday, 30 November
Continually horrified with defiling thoughts. Unable to reason them away or divert the mind to other subjects.

Lord's Day, 2 December
I had some free conversation with my children in the evening and Samuel seemed much affected. Lord call my dear Samuel and claim him for thy own in a way of grace.

Monday, 3 December
Much troubled with frightful dreams in the night.

Thursday, 6 December
Have found myself very dull in my spirits and experienced great want of spirituality thro' the day.

Notes to Vol 1

[3] *21 July 1775.* Samuel Ansley Lambert, baptised 13 January 1771.

[4] *18 October 1776.* GL has been confused or careless in copying this entry into his new journal. He shows it as 1775, though the other details clearly indicate it should be 1776.

[5] *15 July 1778.* Elizabeth Lambert, born 4 September 1776.

[6] *23 July 1778.* Mr Banks had a malt kiln (see 18 February 1781). The 1791 Directory includes Alderman John Banks, Posterngate.

[7] *23 July 1778.* The Hull-Anlaby-Kirkella turnpike was opened in 1745.

[8] *28 October 1778.* GL wrongly dates this as 1775, though the other details indicate 1778.

[9] *28 October 1778.* William Lambert, born 19 November 1773.

[10] *22 September 1780.* Phebe Lambert, born 16 August 1778.

[11] *30 September 1780.* Rev Joseph Popplewell was a minister in Beverley 1780-90. John Popplewell was a chemist and druggist of Market Place, Hull. The Church Book shows a John Popplewell, auctioneer, excluded from membership.

[12] *16 October 1780.* brother: elder brother-in-law (Christian name unknown). GL refers to another younger brother-in-law as 'Brother William Ansley'.

[13] *21 October 1780.* GL's parents were William Lambert (1703-89), married 1736 to Anna Green (d 27 January 1767).

[14] *26 October 1780.* Jane and John Binnington were both entered as members in the Church Book.

[15] *28 October 1780.* Hugh Ross, whose son, John, was baptised in 1771.

[16] *20 November 1780.* Rev John King, vicar of St Mary's church, Lowgate: always known as the Low Church in contradistinction to Holy Trinity, the High Church.

[17] *20 November 1780.* The Thorntons were great supporters of GL, both financially and in religion. Originally from Hull and retaining many Hull links, they had moved to Clapham and were mainstays of the Clapham Sect, an influential Evangelical element in the Church of England. J T, ie John Thornton (1720-90), a Director of the Bank of England, purchased advowsons and installed Evangelical incumbents, was a friend of John Newton and William Cowper, and spent £2-3,000 on extending knowledge of the Gospel. His sister, Sarah, married William Wilberforce's grandfather, Robert, and his youngest son, Henry, married Marianne, daughter of Joseph Sykes. William Wilberforce's uncle married John Thornton's aunt. A vessel named *Clapham* was principally owned by Jeremiah Wright, but Benjamin Wright of Clapham, James Shrapnell Bowden, a Hull merchant, Charles Hobhouse of London and William Rust, Hull goldsmith, were also subscribing members.

[18] *26 November 1780.* Charity Children: Charity Hall, rebuilt by 1702, was on the north side of Whitefriargate.

[19] *27 November 1780.* See note 30 September 1780.

[20] *29 November 1780.* Hannah Lambert, born 21 September 1775.

[21] *5 December 1780.* The Carlills were closely involved in Fish Street chapel from its beginning. John Carlill, sugar baker, was a trustee of the chapel. Carlill, Gilder, Kirkbridge & Co were High Street merchants. Bassano, Carlill & Co were sugar refiners of Wincolmlee. Thomas Carlill was the owner of the *Isabella*. The Church Book contains the names of a number of members of the family who were also members of the Fish Street congregation. John Carlill junior (see 18 September 1788) would presumably be the merchant of that name who, like other members of the family, had shares in whaling ships.

[22] *28 December 1780.* 21 January 1779 Spain declared war on Britain, besieging Gibraltar.

[23] *1 January 1781.* John Gilder, merchant of Mytongate, with shares in whaleships, subscribed £140 to Blanket Row chapel when it was formed in 1769. A staunch supporter of Fish Street (see tribute 24 February 1813), serving 41 years as deacon, a great friend of GL and involved with him in whaleship shareholdings.

[24] *1 January 1781.* Rev Joseph Milner, headmaster of Hull Grammar School from 1767 and lecturer at Holy Trinity church from 1768, was a fervent Evangelical and the acknowledged leader of the movement in Hull. When the previous vicar of Holy Trinity, the Rev Charles Clarke, died in July 1797, his brother-in-law William Wilberforce came to stay with his sister in Hull and canvassed the aldermen for Milner's appointment (Stubley 10). He was elected vicar of Holy Trinity in August 1797, but caught a chill on his way to his institution in York and died on 15 November 1797, aged 52. See ODNB.

[25] *1 January 1781.* Mr Harris, minister of the New Chapel, Dagger Lane (Ebenezer Chapel), with whom GL had a disagreement over the possible acquisition of that chapel in 1781 (see 6-17 August 1781), though in the event the decision was taken to build Fish Street chapel.

[26] *1 January 1781.* Edward Riddell (d 1811), one of the 11 members of Dagger Lane Chapel who, dissatisfied with the Rev John Burnett, seceded to Blanket Row. He prayed at the opening ceremony on 9 April 1769. One of the first deacons and

a strong financial supporter. Prominent in Evangelical circles (see Darwent 205-7). His memorial in the graveyard of the old Sculcoates St Mary's church, Air Street, stated that 'after a life of active service in the Church of Christ [he] entered into his rest Sept 18 1811 in the 80th year of his age'. The firm of Riddell & Son, architects, builders and brickmakers, did much work on the Dock Company estate, developed after the opening of The Dock in 1778, giving Hull fine Georgian suburbs outside the town boundary. See Ivan and Elisabeth Hall, *A New Picture of Georgian Hull* (York 1978/9). Fish Street chapel was built by Hammond & Riddell for £734. Edward's son, Thomas (1764-1810), became an obsessive critic of GL and caused him much stress.

[27] *1 January 1781.* Josiah Jones, of Quay Street, a prominent member of Fish Street chapel, was one of the 11 who in 1769 seceded from Dagger Lane to Blanket Row, subscribing £42. At GL's ordination on 14 March 1770 he 'gave an account of their formation into a church'. One of the first deacons. A Guardian of the Poor.

[28] *1 January 1781.* Mr Towers, not otherwise identified, had a mill (see 25 April 1786). Mary and Sarah Towers are both inscribed as members in the Church Book.

[29] *8 January 1781.* David Hartley 1731-1813, Whig MP for Hull 1774-80. Opponent of the American War of Independence. Introduced proposals for the abolition of slavery.

[30] *20 January 1781.* Rev George Gill, from Heckmondwike Academy, was ordained at Swanland, 7 June 1775. The charge was given by GL. He left Swanland for Market Harborough about 1782, after marrying Miss Watson, a Swanland heiress [J G Patton, *A Country Independent Chapel* (Hull 1943), 35] He was succeeded by the Rev Richard Leggatt. When the Rev Edward Dewhirst, minister at the Cottingham chapel, became a Unitarian, the congregation hesitated to eject him because of his sincerity, but GL, Gill and the Rev Richard Leggatt were called in to supply services for those who still believed in the Trinity [E B Smith, Zion, *A History of the United Reformed Church, Cottingham, 1692-1992* (Cottingham, 3rd edn 1992, 7-8] GL published his sermon preached on the death of Mrs Gill. See 19 September 1784.

[31] *25 January 1781.* Hull Subscription Library was founded in 1775, housed at first in a rented room but moved to larger purpose-built premises in Parliament Street in 1801. J N Crosse, *Account of Hull Subscription Library* (Hull 1810).

[32] *25 January 1781. An Introduction to the Study of the Prophecies concerning the Christian Church, and in particular concerning the Church of Rome* by Bishop Richard Hurd (1720-1808), (1772, 5th edition 1778). See ONDB.

[33] *31 January 1781.* Thomas Shaw, *Travels or observations relating to several parts of Barbary and the Levant*, (Oxford 1747).

[34] *14 February 1781.* High Church: Holy Trinity church, Hull.

[35] *14 February 1781.* Rev James Stillingfleet, d 1826, Rector of Hotham for 56 years.

[36] *27 February 1781.* The Ringroses were shipowners, later related to the Voases and the Wilsons. Samuel and William Ringrose, gentlemen, lived in Cottingham. See Allison 15.

[37] *28 February 1781.* The Jewish synagogue was in Posterngate.

[38] *9 March 1781.* diligence: a public stage coach.

[39] *5 April 1781.* John Todd, gentleman, of West Street, was a prominent member of Fish Street Chapel. In 1769 he subscribed £25 when the congregation moved from Dagger Lane to Blanket Row, and he was on the fund-raising committee to pay off the Fish Street mortgage in 1799. He was a signatory to the petition of 1803 pleading for Dissenters to be exempt from training in arms on the Sabbath. D Todd was a shareholder in the whaler, *Molly*.

[40] *29 May 1781.* Blistering, usually in the form of a blistering plaster containing cantharides, was used to draw infection to the surface, where it would be expelled through the seepage from the burst blister. It was also used as a counter-irritant to draw existing irritation away from the original site.

[41] *3/4 July 1781.* George Lambert, born 4 July 1781.

[42] *24 July 1781.* Wet nurse: a woman paid to suckle the child of another.

[43] *8 August 1781.* New chapel in Dagger Lane also known as Ebenezer Chapel, opened 1781 by the Baptists. In 1781 it passed to the Countess of Huntingdon's Connexion.

[44] *15 August 1781.* Taking down the beds: probably dismantling the heavy hangings.

[45] *17 August 1781.* GL enjoyed the hospitality of Hull merchant John Boyes at his Anlaby residence on a number of occasions. Boyes built Anlaby House 1795-6 [Allison 10]. He rented a pew in St John the Evangelist's church. There were other Hull men named Boyes, one of whom may be referred to in this entry: Bethel Boyes, gentleman of Mytongate, Bryan Boyes, merchant of Mytongate, Thomas and Robert Boyes, merchants and furriers, Mytongate without. The Boyes had a marital link with the Ringroses.

[46] *23 August 1781.* Rev John Burnett. Pastor at Dagger Lane Chapel from 1767, but dissatisfaction with him on his adoption of Presbyterianism led to the recession of a group and the formation of a separate church in Blanket Row. Though GL differed from him in theology, they remained friends and he preached Burnett's funeral sermon.

[47] *25 August 1781.* After the dissolution of the monasteries, including Thornton Abbey, an Augustinian foundation of 1139, the 'college' (probably an almshouse) was demolished and 'a most stately home' built from the material. It 'fell quite down to the bare ground without any visible cause'. [N Pevsner and J Harris, *Lincolnshire*, (2nd revised edition 1989)]

[48] *6 September 1781.* Daniel Tong. A leading whaler-owner. One of the 11 men who in 1769 seceded from Dagger Lane Chapel as it moved towards Presbyterianism and built a new chapel in Blanket Row. A major financial supporter of Fish Street chapel. Darwent, 118, quoting Hadley, states that, when he suffered financial ruin, the members of Fish Street chapel failed to give him the moral support he deserved.

[49] *8 October 1781.* Flux: an abnormal discharge of blood or excrement from the body.

Vol 2 1782-1783

1782

Tuesday, 1 January

I was sent for to pray with a poor woman in dying circumstances: a poor habitation and slender provision; her husband in the ague and she sitting upright in a chair, in which condition she had been labouring for breath for six days and nights.

Thursday, 3 January

Our youngest child we have been obliged to take from nurse today. I hardly ever saw so poor an object – reduced almost to skin and bone, his eyes swelled up to such a degree as to be quite closed and burnt up with a fever.

Lord's Day, 6 January

I also received two letters, the one from Mr Mackey at Dunkirk where he is detained prisoner. I found my heart much drawn out for him. The other from Mr Bruce of Grimsby informing me that things are rather uncomfortable with them.

Monday, 7 January

I have been brewing today. . . . My son George has never opened his eyes for four days and has been blistered today behind each ear. I have been much concerned lest the humour which has fallen in his eyes should deprive him of the blessing of sight.

Tuesday, 8 January

George continues very bad of his eyes and is blistered for it behind the ears.

Friday, 11 January

I spent the morning in my study without success and, as it was a very clear frosty day, in the afternoon I took a walk to Newland Tofts[50] and drank tea with Mr Puckering. We had some very agreeable conversation upon the future and present success of the Gospel.

Monday, 14 January

Dined at Mr Binnington's. The conversation turned upon the news of the day viz our loss of Eustatia,[51] St Martin's and another island. . . . This nation may be crushed and probably will. . . . As the member of a particular community and the parent of six children I cannot help being concerned but as a member of the great system I am unmoved, firmly persuaded that whatever is is right and best, because God sees it so.

Thursday, 17 January

Mr Gill being ill I rode to Swanland. The frost was very severe. I found him very bad of a complaint in his eye; advised him to apply to somebody of skill and returned soon in order to send a surgeon to him.

Wednesday, 23 January

Spent the morning in reading Williams' *History of Denmark*[52] – a remarkable evidence of the depravity and cruelty of human nature.

Monday, 28 January

I met with one thing that affected me much today: a person mentioned my *sleepy congregation*. Lord, am not I the cause? However, this I can say, that I do as well as Thou art pleased to help me.

Thursday, 31 January

I this day heard of the disorderly walk of one of my people which gave me very great concern, especially as he was one of the first that invited me to Hull.

Monday, 11 February

I have been just as long in the world today as I once was in the wilderness. Forty years the Lord has been leading me to prove me and shew me what was in my heart and I have found it to be very deceitful.

Wednesday, 13 February

Dined at Mr Gilder's with Mr Milner, had some very agreeable conversation with him upon union with Christ. After dinner walked with him to the Garrison[53] and continued the conversation upon several interesting subjects.

Monday, 18 February

My wife observing Mr Carlill to look very poorly yesterday at chapel and being informed that he had something of a lethargic complaint desired me to go and see him. I found him in bed in a violent sweat and breathing very hard. Mrs Carlill endeavouring to wake him, he just opened his eyes and spoke to me, then turned on his back and said it is a complete work. She apprehended that he was much better, but as soon as he had spoke he was on a doze again and throwing his arms about. I signified my desire to have a physician called in; she consented. I proposed going for Dr Williams.[54] But before I had left the room two minutes he expired. I have lost a steady and valuable friend; and there is something very affecting in the season of it as his mind was much fixed upon a new chapel and his help would have been very considerable. . . . He has been an ornament to the church in which he stood connected eight years and seven weeks.

Tuesday, 19 February

My mind has been a good deal depressed with the state of things amongst us, our valuable members dropping off and none coming in their place.

Thursday, 21 February

I had a pretty long conversation with young Mr Carlill and have very great hopes that in time he may fill the place of his valuable father. He is of a very reserved disposition and is sensible of it but hope in time there may be more freedom. I looked at the new building but was much affected in the thought that while it rose its greatest promoter was laid low and which I cannot but notice as a very singular dispensation the very day that the new chapel was begun he died.

Saturday, February 23

Mr Jones brought on the salary and sat some time. . . . It is reduced about 2 pounds below the last quarter, which is discouraging as things are.

Monday, 25 February

Engaged most of the morning in paying the bills etc of the last quarter.

Wednesday, 27 February

I have been much exercised with temptation today and almost bore away with the torrent.

Thursday, 28 February

I have lost another valuable friend today in the death of Mr King, vicar of the Low Church. He was a man of a most amiable spirit, the most tender feelings and sincere piety I almost ever met with. It was thro' his persuasion and under his inspection that I published the sermons which I hope have been rendered very useful. The world, the church and the town have sustained a very great loss. Few, if any man, could have been found to fill the place he did at the time he was called to that parish. But under his amiable conduct prejudice subsided and love increased. . . . Drank tea at Mr Wright's[55] and was led to see the hand of Providence eminently displayed in his instrumentality. As my last salary was lower than common, and expenses ran higher I felt some concern how the family was to be supported. This day Mr Wright made a present of a five-guinea note.

Thursday, 7 March

This day my brother-in-law William Ansley left Hull. I accompanied him to the boats and took my leave of him. He has been in my family about three quarters of a year. O but I fear that there is no saving change. My heart has often yearned over him and been distressed on his account.

Tuesday, 12 March

Returned from Cottingham. But I think I was never out in such a hurricane in my life. I could not keep upon the horse but was forced to dismount and walk. With being so much in the wind I have been very poorly most of the day.

Thursday, 14 March

In a letter this day received from Mr Thornton was enclosed a £20 bank note. . . . I have been much behind in my accounts, have been expecting something from the effects of my wife's father. But when disappointed at one door God has opened another.

Friday, 15 March

Have been detained all day by Mr Smith. In the evening I attended him to the boats, in his way to Barrow.

Tuesday, 19 March

Mr Gill came to me soon in the morning. Breakfasted and dined with me. It gave me great concern to find he was resolved to remove from Swanland. In that case I have not one minister to change with but shall be left alone.

Wednesday, 27 March

Peter Dixon also called on me to desire that I would baptise his child while he was at Greenland. I told him that on account of his neglect of public ordinances and family worship while at home that I should not do it on his account unless I found something more satisfactory respecting religion from his wife than I did in him. It was very disagreeable to me but I am glad that I was enabled to reprove him with faithfulness and in meekness.

Saturday, 30 March

As I came thro' Fish Street I observed the people crowd to the windows of the new chapel, and upon going in found that the scaffold had broke down as they were lifting up one of the main beams, that five men were fallen and three very much hurt. They were carried away in chairs, all complaining by signs of their breasts but unable to speak. Thro' mercy none of them had broke any bones. It is very singular that I have always had a dread of this and have taken all the pains I could to caution them against danger.

Monday, 1 April

Visited the men that were hurt at the chapel and several others.

Thursday, 4 April

Had some very agreeable conversation with Mr Ride, one of the persons that got hurt at the chapel.

Saturday, 6 April

I this day received a letter from my aged father informing me that he was in good health and that Mr Haydon, late minister of the Anabaptist[56] meeting at Tewksbury, was dead.

Thursday, 18 April

Received a letter from Brother Ansley and wrote one to my father in consequence of it. It represents my father's income as in a very precarious state which I am very anxious to have thoroughly examined into.

Monday, 22 April

Walked in the afternoon to Cottingham and preached there in the evening. ... It was a remarkably fine day and every bird seemed to strive which should warble the sweetest note.

Thursday, 2 May

Mr Barker[57] called on me who is come to settle at the Low Church.

Thursday, 9 May

As I had to go a collecting for the chapel to Beverley today I was enabled to seek a blessing from God on myself and my endeavours. ... We were very kindly received and gathered £7. The only disagreeable [sic] was to hear the complaints of the minister against the people and the people against their minister. But this led me to a grateful sense of that favour of Providence towards me. Truly the conduct of my people has been constant evidence of their sincere regard. I am much fatigued this evening thro' the uneasy horse I rode on.

Monday, 13 May

About ten this morning set off for Swanland. When I rode about two miles and half the horse was very near throwing me into a ditch. I dismounted, attempted again, but all in vain, he would not pass a waggon. I mounted again but found I could not hold it in when I had turned its head towards home. I got off and walked back. In the afternoon walked to Cotingham.

Wednesday, 15 May

Spent part of the day in the garden. O to feel the refreshing showers of grace in my own soul.

Monday, 20 May

Great news has been received today from the West Indies of Admiral Rodney having taken and destroyed 6 men of war, 1 first rate, 3 twenty-fours, one 64 and one 70. 400 were killed on board the *Ville de Paris*. May these things terminate in the producing of a desired peace.

Thursday, 30 May

[Journey to London.] Mr Towers and I crossed the water; had a very disagreeable passage and were three hours in making of it. We took the coach about 11 and got to Lincoln in the evening.

Friday, 31 May and Saturday, 1 June

I include these together as by travelling all night they seem as one. We had very rainy weather. Arrived safe in London about ten o'clock. When we had got there we knew not where to turn and it rained very heavily. We called on Mr Rivers who very kindly took us in. The influenza prevailed all over the town and we apprehensive of taking it.

Lord's Day, 2 June

From this time I cannot be very particular. Mr Towers fell ill of the influenza and in two days after myself. It has left me very weak. During my continuance in London I have been very kindly received by the ministers. … I am now (June 22) returned to my family in safety and found them in health tho' they have all been poorly and Elizabeth by falling into the ditch before the house had like to have been suffocated. In the journey we have had several gracious appearances. There being 22 passengers within and without, the coach once broke down. Several times the harness failed and when near Barton the horse on which the post boy rode fell as we were coming down hill and another horse trod on them but no harm ensued.

Tuesday, 25 June

This day my son William had like to have been suffocated by falling into a ditch but providentially a man coming by saw him and pulled him out by the leg.

Thursday, 4 July

I have often thought that as my family was large and expenses exceeded my income that Providence might send something by the lottery.[58] I bought half a ticket [indecipherable] in the Irish lottery and thereby cast the lot in the lap, but this day I received advice that it was drawn a blank. I feel the loss. However, my view in the trial was upright and hope the disappointment may not be without its uses.

Monday, 8 July

Preparing for a journey. Tuesday set off with Mr and Mrs Tong. Got to Spittle, next day to Newark, the day following to Nottingham. Preached there twice on the Lord's day. Collected fifteen guineas and an half. Set off from Nottingham on the Monday, reached Chesterfield, the next day Sheffield, but all was in a state of confusion thro' the imprudence of the minister. Messrs Greaves and Venner each gave me two guineas. Got to Rotherham on the

Wednesday and spent the evening with Mr Jonathan Walker. Reached Thorne on Thursday.

Friday, 19 July
Set off from Thorne about six and thro' mercy got safe home about six in the evening.

Lord's Day, 21 July
Violently hot. Rode to Beverley and preached both parts of the day. Have not found much liberty in the work of the day. A great hardness [?] appeared upon the face of the congregation which seemed to have some influence on myself.

Friday, 26 July
Have been much taken up with various calls from the study. Particularly about three in the afternoon I was sent for to visit Mr Burnett who was taken with the gout at his stomach. His groans were violent, he desired me to pray. Conversed a little and expired about half an hour after. ... Yesterday he was preaching and concluded the service about the same hour that on this day he closed his life. This is the second gospel minister that has been removed from Hull within this year. ... Attended a meeting of the Trustees in the evening, when all things were fixed relating to the opening of the new meeting.

Saturday, 27 July
In the afternoon was called down [from the study] and found George choking with a crust of bread which had got fast in this throat. I forced my finger down the passage which gave him present deliverance.

Lord's Day, 28 July
Preached the last sermon in my old place.

Monday, 29 July
Engaged most of the day at the new chapel.

Wednesday, 31 July
The new chapel[59] opened.

Lord's Day, 4 August
For the first time I have been privileged this day to preach the gospel in a new place and to a large congregation.

Monday, 5 August
Samuel Thornton Esq[60] called in the morning and presented me with a £20 bank note towards the new place.

Lord's Day, 18 August

I have not eat above an ounce of bread all day, violently afflicted with flatulences in my bowels. After service I took an emetic and was obliged when it was over to lay down. . . . During the exercise of the vomit I sustained a great loss. One of my fore teeth which had been loose for several months came out without either pain or the loss of any blood. I fear I shall find it very prejudicial to my speaking in future.

Saturday, 7 September

Returned from Scarbro' where I have been in order to bath.[61] Have not found that benefit from it that was hoped. Was much affected on my return to find my son George dangerously ill of an inflammation at his lungs. His sufferings are great.

Lord's Day, 8 September

This has been a day much to be remembered. I hardly ever was more unfit for preaching and yet seldom more helped. We have every moment expected the removal of my dear little boy.

Monday, 9 September

I have been much engaged today by the kindness of many friends calling to see the child. Thro' mercy there is a strange alteration which gives me some flattering hopes that he may get thro' it. But be that as it may, it is a great favour that it is so much better in his breathing which before was really frightful.

Wednesday, 11 September

George rather worse of the violent hoarseness that has fallen upon his lungs. I have been reading Watson's account of the Spanish Armada in his life of Philip the 2nd.[62] A singular interposition of Providence in behalf not only of the British nation, but the Protestant religion. Humanly speaking, had that succeeded, Popery had once more spread its darkness over all the nation.

Wednesday, 25 September

Sent a letter to my father with a five guinea note included. I would bless God that I have an opportunity to evidence filial duty to an aged parent.

Wednesday, 2 October

The militia being reviewed before our house, this morning drew my attention.

Friday, 1 November

As usual I retired to my study in the morning, was soon called off by company and detained till two in the afternoon at which time my wife was taken with labour pains and in about half an hour delivered of a fine boy[63] before the assistance requisite could be in the room. Thro' mercy all was well and she got thro' very favourably.

Monday, 18 November
I have wrote nothing since last Thursday, but what I have gone thro' since that season will I trust be never forgotten by me. On Friday morning I was taken with a violent spasm in the back which deprived me of the use of all my limbs for near half an hour. The pain was so exquisite that my groans were heard at a great distance. I was blooded[64] and blistered immediately and carried by two men in a chair to my chamber, never expecting but to be brought down a corpse. But God has graciously blessed the means and seems to promise a restoration.

Wednesday, 11 December
I had to attend at the library, being appointed one of the committee.

Saturday, 21 December
Being a very fine morning, the children were walking backwards and forwards before the door. Near the gates as a truck was going by Phebe was thrown down and the wheels went over both her thighs. They were much bruised; the skin fridged [sic] and the flesh swelled but blessed be God no bones broke.

Wednesday, 25 December
Heard Mr Barker at the Low Church from Heb 2.16. It was a good sermon and well introduced with a description of our state by the Fall.

1783

Tuesday, 7 January
I have found my mind very much alarmed in visiting several persons in the fever which is become so common and very fatal. Lord preserve me not only from the infection if it be thy blessed will, but from the undue fear of it. Drank tea with Mr Carlill. Attended the vestry meeting for signing away the old chapel.

Wednesday, 8 January
The number of sick persons increase so much upon me that I know not how to get thro' them; and what affects me much is that my wife seems to [be] beginning in the same way she was a little above two years since. ... Something turned up which gave me great uneasiness, but if spared till tomorrow I intend to search into it more particularly.

Thursday, 9 January

Enquired into the case that gave me so much concern last night and find that the Trustees expect my paying either the whole or part of the interest of the money on the place. I thought the request very unreasonable considering the family I have to support. But shall rather submit to inconveniences than cause any uneasiness.

Wednesday, 22 January

A dispute having commenced between the physician and surgeon relative to the orders of the former not being punctually observed by the latter when my back was bad. The whole morning has been taken up with them and the rest of the faculty, who judged upon the case at the Infirmary. Dr Baynes[65] said that it was a psoas abscess[66], and almost a miracle that it did not prove fatal.

Wednesday, 5 February

Most of this day has been spent with Mr Williamson of Howden in conversation relative to the settlement of their place in the hands of Trustees.

Saturday, 8 February

Received letters from my father and Mr Galland. I had been long uneasy about the former, but have occasion to be thankful that my fears have been without foundation.

Saturday, 15 February

I have this evening finished my preparatory work for the day that is approaching. It is no small privilege after a minister has been settled so long with a people to be furnished with fresh matter.

Saturday, 15 March

Our youngest child John being very poorly I went this forenoon to see him and found him very much stuffed at his breast.

Lord's Day, 16 March

This was the day for the collection for the Infirmary. ... The congregation was not quite so large as usual; but we collected £14.1.5½d. Several were absent whom I expected to be there. Several of the members have been very irregular in their attendance of late. Three there are who hardly ever attend – and one who for one sermon she hears from me attends three at another place; and one who, not a twelve month ago, would have give half they were worth rather than that I should leave the town. These things are discouraging.

Monday, 17 March

A very solemn and affecting Providence happened this morning about three o'clock in Bishop Lane. A violent fire broke out and consumed the house, and a man and his wife perished in the flames.

Friday, 21 March

Very much affected in reading the account of the earthquake which was given in the papers today. It happened February 5th, another February 9th. Messina destroyed. Palma and Semina[ra] are no longer in existence.[67]

Saturday, 22 March

I received a letter from the Trustees of the Infirmary[68] today returning thanks for the sermon and the collection made last Lord's day at the Infirmary. But it was a sufficient recompense to me that I had an opportunity to recommend so laudable a charity and that the recommendation was so cordially received by my people. They have proved (considering their great exertions of late in the building a new meeting house) that their faith brings forth the fruits of love.

Thursday, 27 March

Have had my mind much disturbed with the reflections cast upon one of the deacons which has arisen from the journeymen joiners demanding an advance of wages. I hope a few days will prove that there is no foundation for the severity even of some of the brethren who should be slow to hear and slower to propagate such reports.

Monday, 14 April

Have drawn up a petition to the Trustees of Lady Hewley's[69] Charity. It seems to be much encouraged and the interest to be strong, but the event I shall leave with him who knows what is best for me and will certainly order it.

Tuesday, 22 April

In returning from Cottingham this morning I was very near being thrown from my horse. Obliged to leave it at the Turnpike House[70] and walk home. I grow so very timorous that I am hardly fit for any horse and as to walking am soon fatigued, from which I fear that I shall be forced to give up going to Cottingham.

Thursday, 24 April

Went to Beverley in company with Mr and Mrs Jones. I think this may be numbered with my last days. I have been like a dry branch all the day.

Monday, 28 April

A young man who had been apprentice to a watchmaker in the north, being out of his time, was going up to London by shipping. A Dutch privateer came up with the ship and took it. He with another young man was taken on board the enemy's ship. A day or two after, the *Resolution* cutter came up with them, engaged and took them. When he got on deck he saw the Lieutenant dead, the Captain surrounded, several of the men bleeding, the young man that had been taken with him slightly grazed with a ball as he went up. He was greatly alarmed expecting to be sent into eternity every moment.

The ship being taken was brought into Hull. The young man enquiring for a place of worship was directed under my ministry. The word was abundantly blessed to him. He was led to admire the Providence which cast him into this place and left the place to go for London with tears in his eyes. Expressing not only gratitude for God's grace to him but pleading that those who remained under the ministry might find it as profitable to them as God had rendered it to himself. What is rather singular, I heard nothing of this till the young man had left the town but had it from one of the members at whose house he lodged during his stay at Hull which was about three months.

Wednesday, 7 May
Heard Mr Milner preach in the morning. . . . It was a subject calculated for much usefulness and was heard by me with pleasure which I trust will be accompanied with profit.

Friday, 16 May
A letter from Wakefield relative to Lady Hewley's Charity. The account was that they had ordered one payment but fixed nothing relative to the continuance of it. Perhaps I have been placing too much confidence in the persons who have been engaged in the application.

Wednesday, 28 May
As I had a little time to spare I went to hear the sermon at church previous to the laying the first stone of the new Infirmary. Great expressions of joy have been made on Sir Henry Etherington[71] engaging in that work. . . . I have been much affected with detecting my son Samuel more than once today in a deliberate falsehood. . . . I am at a loss how to act in my dealings with him so as to evidence a proper displeasure, yet not to harden him by too much severity.

Tuesday, 10 June
Our son George has been very ill and much swelled under his chin. I fear it may be of bad consequence. In the evening I had a very zealous Antinomian[72] called on me. We had a very long dispute but I apprehend to very little purpose.

Thursday, 12 June
I have been at Welton today. Set off about six in the morning. Spent most of the day in the agreeable walk there in company with my good old friend Mr Gill.

Thursday, 26 June
In the evening I got to Welton and after supper had a very solitary walk.

Friday, 27 June

Much of this day has been spent in company with Mr Jobson junior. We have walked a good deal and had some very pleasing and I hope profitable conversation. I have found myself happy in his company. . . . Welton is a delightful situation, but it has been rendered more so by his company.

Thursday, 3 July

I have this day passed from the pleasing solitude of retirement to my usual hurry in a town. Dined with Mr Spyvee[73] and drank tea with Mr Wright[74]. Have found my temper a little discomposed by the behaviour of one of our servants; but kept from passion.

Wednesday, 9 July

The beds were taken down today which took up much of the day and was very fatiguing.

Friday, 11 July

In the afternoon I walked as far as Sutton in company with Dr Baynes and Mr Garwood. The time passed very agreeably, and the conversation was upon interesting subjects. . . . In the paper today there was the longest and most numerous accounts of the damage and deaths caused by the lightning on Wednesday sevenight[75] that I ever saw. It filled above one column of the paper.

Lord's Day, 13 July

Mrs Thornton from Clapham was present [at chapel], came into the vestry, kindly enquired after my family and presented me with a guinea.

Monday, 4 August

I have been employed most of the day at the chapel as the deacons were much engaged and had fixed upon this day for letting the seats.

Wednesday, 13 August

Was detained most of the afternoon in waiting for the physician to attend my son William who has some symptoms of a fistula[76], but hope it may prove a boil. In the evening I was detained in hearing an unhappy dispute between two of the members.

Thursday, 14 August

After dinner I took a walk with some friends to Newland Tofts.

Monday, 18 August

A meteor or ball of fire was seen to pass over the town this morning and alarmed many people.

Tuesday, 19 August
The account of the expulsion of the Morescoes out of Spain is very affecting and discovers the power of a false zeal and the intolerant spirit of Popery.

Wednesday, 20 August
I was rather discomposed as I was going into the pulpit by a person informing me that Mr Green had changed his lecture and was going to preach at the same time we did. Such conduct has greatly the appearance of opposition.

Friday, 29 August
I this day received 6 pounds from the York fund.[77]

Monday, 1 September
I have been under a singular operation today viz the cleaning my teeth and fixing one in the front that hindered my speech.

Tuesday, 2 September
Our house has been almost like an hospital. My wife and one of the servants bad of the rheumatism in the face.

Saturday, 13 September
I have been much affected this morning with the account of a young man who has long attended with us and professed (and I believe really) to have received much profit, being under great soul distress, concluding there is no hope or help for him. In the evening one of the members came to express their great concern they have been under from the apprehension that they had lost their only daughter in a sloop that perished last Saturday, and, tho' relieved from that, they still fear she might be at sea.

Wednesday, 17 September
It is so very sickly a time that I am hurried from chamber to chamber without hardly any interval. Many die, and I am continually walking thro' infected air. Hitherto God has preserved me, but I cannot banish fear from my breast and secretly wish that I could be excused from many places that I am called to enter.

Lord's Day, 21 September
After sermon I gave out the following hymn which I composed yesterday [a six-versed hymn].

Monday, 22 September
Engaged thro' the morning in visiting the sick, in the afternoon went for Cottingham but was sadly mounted; very heavy rain came on so that I was obliged to take up at Newland. After tea got to Cottingham, preached and walked home in the evening.

Friday, 26 September
In the evening just as I was going to the study my wife was seized with labour pains, and about 9 in the evening delivered of another boy.[78]

Saturday, 27 September
One of my children like Moses has been drawn out of the water this day viz Elizabeth.

Thursday, 2 October
I never was so disagreeably circumstanced. The family large and the whole management of it laying upon me. Many sick and some of them at a great distance that the whole of my time is employed in hurrying from thing to thing and place to place and all quite out of the line for composing the thoughts for those duties which I wish to be most in. In going to and from the Garrison to visit a poor woman I was so fatigued as to be scarce able to get home.

Saturday, 18 October
Did not begin the 2nd sermon till after 3 o'clock but had finished it by eight. I have wrote so much today that it has made my right hand swell very much.

Tuesday, 21 October
I have been greatly alarmed this morning; as soon as I went into my wife's chamber I found her very ill and had been so all the night with violent cramps in her stomach and bowels. I was very apprehensive that it was the disorder which now prevails and dreaded the consequences on account of her weak state. But upon taking some rhubarb and magnesia she was better.

Thursday, 23 October
In the afternoon went to Drypool, Stickney's Mill[79] and Wincolmlee.

Friday, 31 October
This afternoon our child[80] was baptised by Mr Mildren.

Tuesday, 4 November
I this day received a guinea bequested by Mrs Hinton [his 'good old friend' of Cottingham had died 18 October]. Also was much struck with the peculiar kindness of a lady who presented me with a five-guinea note.

Thursday, 6 November
About two in the afternoon I took the boat for Barton. Arrived at Lincoln about twelve at night. Set off from thence the next morning about five and travelled night and day till I got to London about 9 in the morning on Saturday.

Tuesday, 11 November

Went to the merchants' lecture. . . . From the lecture I went to the coffee house where the ministers met and got them to sign the case.

Wednesday, 12 November

Like a poor pilgrim I have been wandering about most of the day till I am so weary that I can hardly stir. In the morning I went to Clapham, stayed about an hour and walked to London, then to Broad Street and from thence to Hoxton Square. Hitherto I have only got signatures to the case and have not finished that. I begin to fear that I shall do very little for the service of the cause I come upon[81] and the expenses are already very great.

Saturday, 15 November

My time is now taken up in going from place to place to present the case. I find it will be very tedious as it is difficult to find the persons I apply to at home, and the days are short. Some have received me favourably, while others have refused to look at the case.

Lord's Day, 16 November

This morning I was called to preach at Mr Bell's meeting in Artillery Street. But so small a congregation I hardly ever saw. In the afternoon I preached for Mr Hilton's Old Gravel Lane, Wapping; but having no time for retirement or to look over the notes of my sermon I found it very dry and uncomfortable work. I long to be with my old flock.

Thursday, 20 November

In the morning I went to Wapping; returned much fatigued. Dined with the Book Society in the most spacious room I ever saw and with the largest company. Soon after dinner (which began about four o'clock) I returned. Such large companies are no way agreeable and never profitable to me.

Saturday, 22 November

I have been passing thro' some very solemn scenes today which brought to mind a variety of occurrences. After walking about in Westminster Abbey for some time where the valiant lay conquered and the great are abased, I took a turn to the burying ground of St John's where the dust of my dear mother is deposited. From thence I took a walk to the house where she finished her course. After a variety of reflections I resolved to take a turn to Chelsea and view the house where I was born. Oh what a scene of changes! How soon will the place that now knows us know us no more! Perhaps my children may some time gaze upon the place where my dust shall rest.

Tuesday, 25 November

About noon went to see the balloon discharged. It was a globe composed of gummed silk and filled with inflammable air. It was kept down by cords and remained several hours in that state floating backwards and forwards. When let loose, tho' ten feet in diameter, it rose gradually into the air till it became no larger than a dot and then disappeared.

Tuesday, 2 December

I have met with but little encouragement today and was severely handled by one person about using notes. Indeed, I can hardly preach either without or with them.

Saturday, 6 December

After travelling about all the morning I went to dine with Brother Ansley and met his brother Will.[82]

Saturday, 13 December

On Monday last I took the coach to Gloucester. Arrived there about one on Tuesday. Got to Tewkesbury a little after three, had the happiness to find my father well. Spent the Wednesday and Thursday with him and entered London again about 12 this day.

Tuesday, 23 December

This has been a very wearisome day. Applied to many places but either they were from home or not inclined to attend to the case; only one person has served it. Engaged to dine and drink tea in company where there was nothing but general trifling conversation. My spirits were very low till I got a letter from home which encouraged me a little.

Wednesday, 24 December

Have been more successful today in my applications than the preceding.

Notes to Vol 2

[50] *11 January 1782.* Newland Tofts. Newland, a rural area north of Hull, was then part of the parish of Cottingham and not incorporated within the town boundaries until 1882.

[51] *14 January 1782.* George Rodney, the most enterprising of the admirals of that period, was posted to the West Indies 1780, captured the Dutch island of St Eustatius, 3 February 1781. It fell to the French De Grasse in November 1781. See 20 May 1782.

[52] *23 January 1782.* John Williams, *The rise, progress, and present state of the Northern Governments viz the United Provinces, Denmark, Sweden, Russia and Poland etc* 2 vols (1777).

[53] *13 February 1782.* Garrison: the Citadel, formed from the remains of the town wall, on the east side of the River Hull.

[54] *18 February 1782.* Dr Williams. J A R Bickford and M E Bickford record no Dr Williams of this date in their directory, *The Medical Profession in Hull 1400-1900*, but there was William Williams, chemist and druggist of Lowgate, who may have been popularly accorded the title of doctor. A 20th-century Beverley pharmacist was known as doctor by older residents.

[55] *28 February 1782.* Samuel Wright Esq of Mytongate. A wealthy property owner after whom Wright Street was named and also an underwriter. Initially an important supporter of Fish Street but later uncooperative.

[56] *6 April 1782.* Anabaptists were opposed to the baptism of children. Promoters of their beliefs in Hull caused much worry to GL.

[57] *2 May 1782.* Rev John Barker (b 1748) was vicar of St Mary's, Lowgate, 1782-1816, presented to the living by Samuel Thornton.

[58] *4 July 1782.* Lotteries, then the only form of organised gambling available, were held in England 1627-1826, apart from 1699-1709. They were widely and persuasively advertised in newspapers.

[59] *31 July 1782.* Fish Street church. See description in Sheahan 545.

[60] *5 August 1782.* Samuel Thornton (1754-1838), son of John, a wealthy merchant banker, elected MP for Hull along with his cousin, William Wilberforce, in 1784 (though Wilberforce resigned to take up his seat as MP for Yorkshire), serving until 1806. A great benefactor of GL.

[61] *7 September 1782.* Seabathing (and drinking sea water) for health reasons was growing in popularity. GL bathed at both Hornsea and Scarborough. Although he refers to a bath in his house (10 March 1805) and there were purpose-built baths in 19th-century Hull, the nearness of his house to the Humber, his seasonal bathing and a reference to hurting a foot all indicate that he bathed in the Humber. He also drank sea water, with mixed results.

[62] *11 September 1782.* Robert Watson, *The History of the Reign of Philip the Second, King of Spain, etc* (2 vol 1777)

[63] *1 November 1782.* John Lambert, born 1 November 1782, baptised by the Rev Joseph Popplewell. An earlier John Lambert, born 9 December 1772, had died and his name was re-used for a later-born child.

[64] *18 November 1782.* Bleeding was used for many complaints and often for conflicting reasons, but basically to remove what was seen as an excess of potentially diseased blood.

[65] *22 January 1783.* Dr S Stanhope Baynes, one of the first three physicians at Hull General Infirmary 1782, practised from his home in Trinity House Lane 1782-1800. He was a committee member of Hull Subscription Library 1789-99 (Bickford 9).

[66] *22 January 1783.* Psoas abscess: an abscess which forms in the fascia near the psoas muscle in the lower back and works its way round and down inside the body until it usually presents as a fistula in the upper thigh leaking pus, a very serious condition before antibiotics, often the result of a tubercular infection.

[67] *21 March 1783.* See *York Courant* 18 March, 25 March, 1 April 1783.

[68] *22 March 1783.* New Infirmary. A hospital, funded by subscription, was opened in a house in George Street in 1782 but moved to the new purpose-built premises in what is now Prospect Street in 1784.

[69] *14 April 1783.* Lady Hewley. Sir John Hewley (1627-1710) and his wife, Sarah, of York and Bell Hall, Naburn, were very influential Nonconformists. After her husband's death she established the Hewley Trust for the support of 'poor godly' preachers and their widows. (ODNB)

[70] *22 April 1783.* The Hull-Beverley turnpike was opened in 1744. The first tollbar cottage out of Hull was at Newland.

[71] *28 May 1783.* Sir Henry Etherington Bart, d 1819, aged 88, was a member of a family which formed part of the Hull merchant aristocracy with a mansion in High Street. His wife was a sister of John Porter, another of whose sisters married John Thornton. Etherington's country residence was Ferriby House, North Ferriby. 'He was eccentric, good and benevolent, and the patron of every charitable and religious institution in the town.' (Sheahan 803)

[72] *10 June 1783.* Antimonian: a believer that Christians are by grace set free from the need of observing any moral law; linked with the Lutheran doctrine of Justification by Faith.

[73] *3 July 1783.* The Spyvees were one of the leading families of merchants and shipowners. They were linked in business and marriage with the Coopers. The

firm, Spyvee & Cooper, had premises in Lime Street, not far from the Sugar House. A Spyvee was a subscriber to the building of Fish Street chapel.

[74] *3 July 1783.* B Wright, a deacon, was on the fund-raising committee to pay off the Fish Street mortgage in 1799. On 13 May 1792 a Benjamin Wright purchased a pew for £14 in St John the Evangelist's church. B Wright had shares in the whaler, *Clapham*. Wright, Bowden & Wright, merchants, had their counting house in High Street.

[75] *11 July 1783.* Sevenight (sometimes sennight): obsolete expression, here meaning 'a week last Wednesday'.

[76] *13 August 1783.* Fistula: an abnormal passage between a hollow organ and the body surface or between two hollow organs.

[77] *29 August 1783.* York fund - Lady Hewley's Charity (see 14 April 1783).

[78] *26 September 1783.* Joseph Lambert, born 26 September 1783.

[79] *23 October 1783.* In the late 18th century Robert Stickney was a miller, at Blockhouse Mill, opposite Dansom Lane, a four-sail mill (Fowler 11).

[80] *31 October 1783.* Joseph, born 26 September 1783, baptised by Mr Mildrum (sic) according to the Fish Street register.

[81] *12 November 1783.* GL was collecting subscriptions to the Hull chapel.

[82] *6 December 1783.* 'Brother Will': ie Willliam Ansley's own brother-in-law, another Will.

Vol 3 1784-1785

1784

Lord's Day, 4 January

I have been preaching three times today, for Mr Bennett[83] in the morning, Dr Addington in the afternoon and in Mr Thornton's family at Clapham in the evening. Spent the evening very agreeably and did not go to bed till about one in the morning.

Monday, 5 January

Breakfasted with Mr Samuel Thornton. Returned to London.

Tuesday, 6 January

Drank tea and settled some temporal concerns with Mr Ansley.

Thursday, 8 January

After packing up and settling all things for my journey about five in the evening I entered the coach, travelled all night in a severe frost and reached Lincoln about nine the next night. As much snow had fallen and the roads were very much interrupted by it we resolved to leave Lincoln about eleven. We did so and travelled in the most severe night that ever I remember. Found the roads very bad, often apprehensive of being thrown over. But thro' the care of Providence we got safe tho' very weary to Barton about eight the next morning. On coming there we found the Humber so much froze that the boats had not been able to pass as usual for several days. However, as a skiff or open boat was about to make the attempt, I resolved to adventure. When about the middle of the river we were so closed in with the floating ice that for some time they were unable to stir one way or another. Very disagreeable ideas began to present themselves. At last by a violent effort of all the men we began to get disentangled and thro' mercy arrived this morning (Saturday 10) safe and found the family all in comfortable circumstances of health.

Monday, 19 January

I dined out. Baptised two children and attended a meeting of the Trustees for the chapel in the evening when I delivered up the money I had collected in London.

Monday, 9 February

In the afternoon I set off for Cottingham, but there being a great fall of snow I turned back; and in the evening went to the vestry to settle about the poor being relieved [in the severe weather conditions].

Friday, 13 February

I and my family have been liberally provided for, while I have heard this day of one perishing for want of food and fuel. Coals are got to the enormous price of 2/6 a bag. We are very low but not left without fire. This long frost is very alarming both with respect to the poor and in regard to the brute creation. The birds die very fast, fodder is much wanting for the cattle owing to the scarcity of hay the last year.

Monday, 16 February
I did not go out till the afternoon. Visited the sick and drank tea at Mr Towers's. My family is at present almost like an hospital. One servant is bad of a sore throat and has not been out of bed since Saturday. John is very ill and my wife but poorly. But thro' the goodness of Providence we have fire, food and physic, which are three very important articles at this season. The frost seemed to be going today but this evening it is returned as violent as ever.

Tuesday, 17 February
This morning died Jane Spofford. She has been in fellowship with the church above ten years and, tho' poor, a very honourable member. Her second marriage was very imprudent, and the poor woman felt the effects of it to her death. The day before she departed I was with her, when her husband was railing and saying all the spiteful things he could of her. Wretched company for a dying hour.

Thursday, 4 March
Received a letter from London informing me that Brother Ansley had been ill some time and continued very poorly, that his brother William Ansley was very ill and not likely to continue many days. Poor young fellow. He has lived a very dissipated life for several years. May these warnings be noticed and improved by myself and all concerned.

Monday, 8 March
A letter received from London this morning informed us of the death of brother William Ansley. He was removed on Friday morning, the 5th inst. The account shocked us much. Poor young man, when he first went to London everything was promising both for time and eternity. After (I fear thro' a disappointment in love) he took to drinking, shunned his relations and was unfit for business and seemed to turn his back upon everything that is good. Sister Ansley writes thus: 'This morning it pleased the Almighty to call to himself our brother William – he died about 7 o'clock – was perfectly sensible and composed – he passed two nights in great pain and misery – was at seasons engaged in the most fervent prayer. I hope he is happy. Poor man, I believe he never injured any one but himself.' He was born May 12 1755. Aged 28 years and 10 months.

Friday, 19 March
A very melancholy accident happened. As a cart loaded with corn was going over the North Bridge it broke down. The cart, horse and a man fell into the water and both of them were drowned.

Saturday, 20 March

This day the Mayor and Alderman went in form to lay the first stone of the new gaol[84] which being within sight of our windows drew in many spectators and has prevented my application to study as was wished.

Tuesday, 30 March

The mind[s] of the people are now engaged about the election which is to come on tomorrow. This is all the theme – who are you for? – or who do you think will get it? May I give diligence to make an election of far greater importance sure.

Wednesday, 31 March

There has been nothing but noise and confusion today. Many were led up to vote for representatives of the nation who were unable to stand by themselves; or I presume to speak for themselves when they come to the hustings. It is affecting to see things in such a state. Self-interest, the influence of others or the fumes of liquor have the principal weight in most, if not all, of our elections. Was the power of electing made more extensive and done by ballot there would be more consideration, less confusion. No one would be tied to any party, nor could the lower class be influenced in the time of election to vote on the side of the greatest number from the hope of future gain.

7 Gaol, Castle St, artist B Gale, engraved by J Taylor (Tickell's *History of Hull*)

Thursday, 1 April

This day the contest ended. Messrs [William] Wilberforce[85] and [Samuel] Thornton were returned and chaired. The concourse of people was very great; some disturbance was produced by the rabble after the members were gone out of the Market Place but it was soon ended. The numbers that voted were for Wilberforce 807, Thornton 751, [David] Hartley, who declined in the morning, 337. I am very glad it is over, for such affairs engross too much both of one's time and thoughts.

Wednesday, 7 April

I bottled part of the wine.

Saturday, 17 April

The day proving very fine, the physician ordered me to walk out. The chief part of the morning was taken up in providing a man and horse to go in search of a supply for tomorrow.

Monday, 19 April

Robert Clark from Cottingham came to inform me of the death of Mr Ringrose[86]. It seems probable that my preaching at Cottingham will now be over. Every person is dead who was either inclined or able to receive the ministers or pay the hire of their horses.

Monday, 10 May

A good old woman called to take her leave of me this morning who is going to settle in Lancashire, was awaked under my ministry at Cottingham when she was 72 years of age; her intellectry [sic] is very strong and her conversation much like the Christian; her expressions of joy at being sent to Cottingham at that advanced age, as well as her concern at being now removed, were very lively and affecting.

Friday, 14 May

About 2 in the afternoon my aged father got safe to Hull and was remarkably well after a journey of near 200 miles and at so advanced an age, being turned 81 years.

Monday, 17 May

I have been the whole day employed in fixing things for my father in his lodgings.

Tuesday, 18 May

This day has been as yesterday spent with my father, except so much as was necessary to write some letters and baptise a child.

Wednesday, 19 May

Ever since my father got to Hull I have lived a strange kind of a trifling life. Sauntering about from place to place is the whole of my employ. I must make an alteration, for it is neither pleasant nor profitable. It unfits me for duty and produces a strange indolent disposition which would be excused from everything.

Thursday, 20 May

My spirits have been a good deal depressed by a person who was one of the first instruments of bringing me to Hull reducing his subscription near four pounds in the year and propagating a false report respecting what I give towards the interest of the money that is upon the chapel. It is true he is easily refuted and has been so by many witnesses, but that is not altogether sufficient I find to remove the trial from my mind.

Friday, 11 June
I do not recollect a day in which things have run so cross for a long time. Was not able to fix upon a text till near tea time. . . . Had but just entered my study when I was rung down to Mr Leggatt[87] and his spouse, who were just arrived, and after sitting a while desired me to walk with them to the Garrison. The prospect is dark respecting the next Sabbath, having not finished the introduction to one sermon.

Monday, 14 June
I have made little progress in anything today: partly thro' various hindrances and the business going on in the Town; viz the choice of a new Member of Parliament in the room of Mr Wilberforce.[88] Tho' there was no opposition yet it made some hurry.

Lord's Day, 27
I have often of late had a great deal of concern respecting my wife. She has grown very thin and discovered great signs of weakness. At present she complains of great soreness and pain in her side and at her breast. I dread a consumption and fear a remove.

Wednesday, 7 July
A variety of things have concurred to distress my mind and ruffle my temper. The two boys instead of going to the chapel went to bath and did not come in till about ten o'clock. I was much alarmed and thought it my duty to correct them. Wish I could have done it with a more calm spirit but when I had given the eldest a stroke or two with the cane he declared he would write and do everything as bad as he could, which made me lay on with greater severity than I intended.

Friday, 9 July
I rode to Anlaby with Mr Towers, his sister and my wife, dined and drank tea with Mr Boyes. In the interval walked to Hessle and spent about half an hour with Miss Briggs.[89]

Monday, 26 July
About eight in the evening it began to rain very fast. Mr Carlill and several friends drank tea with us. We sent a servant to Drypool for to fetch some things who met with some vile fellows who robbed her and otherwise abused her. Mr Carlill returned with her. It thundered and lightened dreadfully so that he stayed with us all night. It was near two in the morning before I closed my eyes for sleep.

Tuesday, 27 July
I have been very much engaged with company and my thoughts very much exercised about the affecting event which has taken place in

the family. In the evening some reports reached me which tended to shew that our servant had been but too much to blame, tho' the men had proceeded much further than she expected or intended. We were under great apprehension lest she should do some violence to herself, and did not get to bed till morning. After dinner we had a violent storm of thunder. The lightning killed a cow but a little way from our house and scorched the hedges.

Thursday, 29 July
This being the day appointed for a general thanksgiving for the restoration of peace[90] we had service in the morning.

Tuesday, 3 August
Have been very uneasy in my mind on account of something disagreeable turning up from a letter I wrote several years ago. It was extorted from me and I was as tender as I possibly could of the character to which it related, without betraying the confidence placed in me by the person applying. However, disagreeable as it is, I meant well and hope Providence will prevent any bad consequences.

Monday, 9 August
It was fully my intention to have gone into Lincolnshire to have spent two or three days, but as I was going to the boats a person came for me to baptise a child which was ill.

Monday, 16 August
I set forward for Lincolnshire upon a visit to Holton [cum Beckering]. The passage over the Humber was very boisterous. But thro' mercy I got safe.

Tuesday, 17 August
At Saxby upon a visit walked about and in the evening preached to a very attentive audience.

Wednesday, 18 August
In the evening I rode to Barrow and preached a lecture, but had little liberty in the work. However the people professed to be much benefited. After the service I returned to Saxby, much fatigued with the exercise of the day.

Wednesday, 1 September
This day the new Infirmary was opened. I went to the church to hear a sermon preached on that occasion by Mr Stillingfleet.

Thursday, 2 September
My wife, Mrs Burn and myself went to Swanland upon a visit to Mrs Leggatt. The day proved very fine and the country people were very busy in cutting down their corn. It has been a very threatening time for some weeks past for the harvest.

Lord's Day, 19 September

I have been at Swanland paying the last token of respect to the late Mrs Gill [gave two discourses]. . . . The relatives requested the latter discourse to be published.[91]

Tuesday, 21 September

Engaged in transcribing part of the funeral sermon which I preached on Lord's day at Swanland for the press.

Wednesday, 22 September

Morning and evening I have been writing for the press. Went in the forenoon to the church and heard Mr Milner.

Friday, 24 September

Last night and most of the day I have had a great deal of pain thro' the stump of an old tooth which some years ago broke off rather within the gum. It greatly unhinged my mind for study.

Monday, 27 September

My wife has taken a journey into the country to try what the air will do for her.

Tuesday, 28 September

We have been taking down the beds and have been much hindered by other concerns.

Thursday, 30 September

After dinner I took a walk to Anlaby to see my wife. She appears much better for the country air. I did not get home till near eight in the evening. But being a delightful moonlight night it rendered it peculiarly agreeable.

Monday, 4 October

I have been engaged all the day in domestic concerns; except towards the evening when I attended a meeting of the Trustees for the choosing of a clerk.

Tuesday, 5 October

I have been much distressed most of the last night with a complaint something similar to the nightmare. It has left me very languid all the day. . . . I find myself almost afraid of going to bed, apprehending the return of the complaint which was so distressing last night. I have been pleading with God to prevent it, for sensible I am that not a thought can cross the mind without his permission.

Wednesday, 6 October

In the morning reviewed, corrected and sent away the funeral sermon for Mrs Gill to be published. After dinner I found myself much indisposed with a violent pain in my back which alarmed me much lest it should come to such a head as before when I was brought so near to the grave.

Monday, 11 October
This has been the fair day at Hull.[92] A season for the amusement of children and the gratification of gluttony. I have seen very little of it except what I could not avoid.

Thursday, 14 October
Dined at Mr Spyvee's. Walked with him to Sutton to see Mr Pead[93] interred. He was buried in a vault. . . . I was much pleased with the whole service and should like to be buried in the same manner and the same anthem sung upon the occasion. What is the reason I cannot say but there is something so disagreeable to me in the sound made by throwing the earth into the grave when the coffin is in it as I cannot describe.

Saturday, 16 October
In the study most of the day and composed a sermon, after which I reviewed the proof sheets of the sermon which I have in the press. In the evening I began to prepare another sermon by way of introduction to that already printed, but am yet undetermined whether to send it or not.

Wednesday, 20 October
Sent the second sermon to York to the printer. Dined at Samuel Wright's Esq.

Friday, 29 October
I have this day come to a resolution to place some money in the Greenland trade.[94] Have long wished for an opening, which has now presented itself.

Monday, 8 November
Have been much employed about the sermons which came from the booksellers this day. One hundred copies were sold at the Vestry besides some at home.

Thursday, 11 November
Much troubled in the evening with the toothache.

Monday, 22 November
Have been fully engaged all the morning with friends calling upon us and looking over the copy of a deed for the settling of Howden meeting.

Friday, 17 December
This day my eldest son concluded his fourteenth year.

Tuesday, 21 December
In the evening I read till I could understand nothing for the noise of the children. I wish I could improve time more but the weather is so

severe that I cannot bear in the study without a fire; and in the hurry of the family nothing can be done with profit.

1785

Saturday, 22 January
I took a walk as far as French's Gardens.[95]

Tuesday, 25 January
In the evening attended with the ministers at Mr Milner's. . . . Eight ministers were present and the conversation very agreeable and profitable.

Tuesday, 1 February
I went to Wincolmlee to baptise a child.

Thursday, 10 February
In the morning engaged with the ministers about the hymn book . . . and in the evening attended the church meeting. . . . Two persons were ordered to be admitted, one was proposed and two who had left the town disorderly and with disgrace were ordered to have their names erased from the Church Book.

Tuesday, 15 February
In the evening I went to see Walker's[96] transparent arrer [left incomplete] and was much delighted both with his description and the prospect.

Monday, 28 February
When I got home in the evening I was obliged to go as far as Paradise Row.[97]

Tuesday, 1 March
I have spent the chief part of the day in company with the ministers in the revising of the supplement. In the evening we had company till bed time. I grow weary of the work I have undertaken, and secretly wish that I had never undertook it; for the alterations must be considerable and, after all, it is impossible to make it what one would wish.

Tuesday, 8 March
From ten in the morning till after four was taken up in revising the supplement. . . . It gives me pleasure that we have at length got thro' the supplement; it has taken up a great deal of time, some thought, and may probably expose us to some censure from those who were partial to the original collector or to the general sentiments contained in the generality of the hymns that are excluded, but upon the whole I trust we, and the more judicious part of our

congregations, will find it more agreeable and beneficial in the conducting of that part of worship.

Tuesday, 29 March
[Letter] from Mr Ansley respecting Samuel's going to London.

Tuesday, 12 April
Have spent most of the time in reading Pascal's[98] Letters Vol 1st. In it he expresses the principles of the Jesuits in a most clear, full and faithful manner. I have been greatly shocked by quotations from their writings calculated to destroy both morality and revelation. Perjury, falsehood, adultery, murder, in short, every vice is countenanced by them, and renovation, repentance and love to God wholly set aside. Blessed be God for an open bible and the exposing of such awful delusions by the Reformation.

Thursday, 21 April
I went out this morning with a view to visiting the sick but calling at Mr Jones's they insisted upon my going with them to Welton and the carriage was at the door. I could obtain no excuse. The day proved remarkably fine.

Tuesday, 26 April
Engaged in preparing for Samuel's going to London.

Thursday, 28 April
This morning about 6 I went over the water with Samuel on his way to London. He parted in tolerable spirits. This is the first time I have been put to that trial. It is uncertain whether I may ever see him again. He is launched into the wide ocean of this world.

Monday, 2 May
Sat at the request of a friend for a picture.

Wednesday, 18 May
In the morning wrote and sent off a letter including a bill valued £8.18.0 to Mr Fuller[99] for the Academy. About noon received an exhibition of £15 from the Trustees of Lady Abney's will.[100] How little was this expected.

Monday, 23 May
As the chapel was going to be whitened, I got up before five this morning to collect and parcel the books.

Wednesday, 25 May
Papered a room.[101]

Tuesday, 31 May
This day from six in the morning till eight this evening has been taken up in papering a room.

Wednesday, 15 June
Heard Mr Milner's lecture at the church.

Thursday, 23 June
I received a letter today from Samuel. Blessed be God for his care over him while removed at such a distance.

Friday, 24 June
I have been studying for the benefit of the Infirmary today.

Lord's Day, 26 June
I have been preaching this day for the benefit of the General Infirmary at this town.

Monday, 27 June
I have not been very well today, drank tea at Mr Rust's,[102] attended the singing meeting.

Monday, 25 July
I devoted this morning to pasting the waste and commonplace books.

Thursday, 28 July
Was taken up this morning in attending upon the consecration of the new burial ground.[103] Had a very good opportunity of seeing the whole solemn farce.

Monday, 1 August
An odd genius has been with me this morning pretending to be the prophet Elias. As I was going out had little time to hear his nonsense. He is no way deficient in impudence. But his end in travelling about, as I learn he is doing all over England, I did not learn. Only he said his Master Jesus Christ would appear very soon.

8 Holy Trinity burial ground, Castle St. 2008

Tuesday, 2 August

This day arrived the ship *Benjamin*[104] from Greenland in which I have a part. She has only brought one fish and it is generally supposed that it will be a losing voyage but I find my mind not only composed but in some degree thankful, 1st that the ship is arrived. Had that been lost, which has been the case with some, my family had been great sufferers. 2 ly, that none of the hands have been injured while several of other ships and one whole crew in the same trade have been sent to the bottom. 3 ly, if we sustain loss that it is no greater.

Friday, 5 August

I received a letter from Brother Ansley settling some accounts, also another from Samuel. It is a great privilege that the accounts are very favourable, both respecting his health and diligence.

Tuesday, 9 August

I rose early and should have gone into Lincolnshire but through misinformation was disappointed in my tide. In the afternoon I went to see a kind of a young whale which the sailors call a bottlenecked Grampus.[105] It measured about 24 feet and was killed at South End.[106]

Wednesday, 10 August

Have been at South End to see another Grampus which has been left by the tide near Wintringham.

Tuesday, 23 August

Dined at Mr Wright's with the Revd David Brown[107] who is going out to India to preside over a large school there. The children are about 500, of both sexes, and are to be trained up to such occupations as they seem best qualified for. He seems very happy in the idea and flatters himself with the hopes of success in initiating them into the knowledge of Jesus Christ.

Saturday, 3 September

I could not fix upon a subject till after dinner. Began a discourse but was soon called off by the coming of Mr Sykes[108] and his wife. It is now near eleven at night and I have but just retired from company.

Tuesday, 6 September

Being very wet I have not been from home all day. Bathed in the morning. Devoted most of the day to reading.

Tuesday, 27 September

Received a letter from Hackney near London informing of the death of an old friend, John Gibson Esq.[109], and that as token of his regard he had left me ten pounds.

Friday, 4 November

While I was out a person informed me of the death of Mrs Thornton of Clapham. I [was] much affected with the tidings. She was the instrument of procuring me lately a very liberal donation, and I have formerly received many benefits from the hand of God thro' the channel of that family.

Friday, 11 November

Reading the paper in the morning, fixing upon a text and forming the outline of a sermon on it took up the morning.... The study has been left vacant most of the day.

Thursday, 1 December

Spent the afternoon with Mr Beatson[110] in applying for subscriptions for the book of tunes sung in the several congregations at Hull which he is about to publish.

Lord's Day, 4 December

Last week a child of one member was removed by the smallpox.... As upon my return from chapel our daughter Hannah seemed to have been under some serious impressions, I took her aside and conversed and prayed with her.

Monday, 5 December

Engaged both morning and afternoon either with company at home, or going with Mr Beatson to make applications for subscriptions for the tune book.

Wednesday, 7 December

This day John Atkinson has lost his last child in the smallpox; the other died last week. James Bromby has a daughter taken to her bed of the spotted fever[111] and another of my hearers has been seized with the palsy and deprived of speech. [Much sick visiting at this time. He was also ill.]

Saturday, 31 December

[Survey of the past year]. No breach has been made upon us, except by the remove of my eldest son, who I hope will be mercifully provided for: accounts of him have been pleasing and flattering.... I was very anxious to lay out some money in a ship, hoping the advantages arising from it might be very useful in my family, but there I met with a disappointment; however the Lord has handed in from two quarters from which I had no expectation, which was equal to it. I refer to the exhibition of £15 from Lady Abney's money and £10 left to me by John Gibson Esq of Hackney.

Notes to Vol 3

[83] *4 January 1784.* Dr Bennett, a prominent Congregational minister and father of another one, Sir Risdon Bennett.

[84] *20 March 1784.* New Gaol. A new building in Castle Street replaced the inadequate one in the Market Place.

[85] *1 April 1784.* William Wilberforce topped the poll (807 votes) with his cousin, Samuel Thornton (751) gaining the second seat. David Hartley was defeated, with 337 votes.

[86] *19 April 1784.* The Ringroses were important merchants and shipowners, later linked with such major merchant and shipowning families as the Voases and the Wilsons.

[87] *11 June 1784.* Rev Richard Leggatt, a student from Lady Huntingon's college, was minister at Swanland 1783-5, when he moved to Cottingham, where he served until 1790, then leaving for London. Under him the Cottingham congregation re-united.

[88] *14 June 1784.* 'the choice of a new Member of Parliament . . .' Wilberforce had been elected both for Hull and Yorkshire. He chose to sit for the more prestigious county constituency and Walter Stanhope was elected without a contest in his place as MP for Hull.

[89] *9 July 1784.* Miss Briggs was probably a member of a Hull family of shipowners and merchants (see 27 December 1787 and 28 September 1812).

[90] *29 July 1784.* Possibly the Peace of Versailles, 20 May 1784, whereby Holland ceded Negapatnam to Britain.

[91] *19 September 1784. The Living Believer's view of his course; and the Dying Believer's confidence in his Lord, being the substance of two sermons preached at Swanland . . . Kingston upon Hull, September 19, 1784* [on death of Mrs Hannah Gill] (York 1784).

[92] *11 October 1784.* Hull Fair was still held in the Old Town but its exact location cannot be identified.

[93] *14 October 1784.* Benjamin Pead, described as citizen and ropemaker of London but late of this parish [Sutton], died 11 October 1784 [Sutton-on-Hull Memorial Inscriptions (East Yorkshire Family History Society)]. In 1755 John Thornton induced Pead to join with him in oil-milling, including establishing a soapworks. The firm formed was Thornton, Pead & Co.

[94] *29 October 1784.* Greenland trade. The whaling trade, a risky enterprise which could produce great profits or losses. Investors, like GL, usually bought fractional shares in a ship to minimise risk.

[95] *22 January 1785.* French's Gardens became the site of Mason Street and Sykes Street.

[96] *15 February 1785.* Probably a reference to Adam Walker (1731?-1812) who gave illustrated lectures on astronomy, originally using a machine, the orrery, which showed the relative positions and motions of the plants with respect to the sun and to one another.

[97] *28 February 1785.* Paradise Row, since renamed Carroll Place in honour of Lewis Carroll (Charles Lutwidge Dodgson), whose grandfather, Charles Lutwidge, lived in nearby Charlotte Street.

[98] *12 April 1785.* Blaise Pascal (1623-1662), a Jansenist (ie a Catholic Puritan), wrote critically of the Jesuits in *Les Provinciales*, translated into English and published in London in 1657: a book which would appeal to GL, who was strongly anti-Catholic and particularly disliked the Jesuits.

[99] *18 May 1785.* Probably Andrew Fuller of Kettering. See 4 October 1799.

[100] *18 May 1785.* Lady Abney's Will. Sir Thomas Abney (1639/40-1722), merchant and mayor of London, and his second wife, Mary (d 1750) were great supporters of Nonconformity. Lady Abney succeeded him as a notable Nonconformist benefactor. (ODNB)

[101] *25 May 1785.* Block-printed wallpapers had been available since the 16th century. Expensive hand-painted Chinese wallpapers were imported by the East India Company.

[102] *27 June 1785.* William Rust, clockmaker and silversmith, jeweller and goldsmith, settled in Hull in 1783-4 His business, based in the Market Place, prospered and he also invested in property development and whaling. He and his family played an important part in GL's personal and religious life. In 1790 he was elected a deacon at Fish Street, and in 1804 he became a trustee of the church. He was active in the Hull Missionary Society and in much charitable work, a founder and first chairman of the Port of Hull Society, later the Sailors' Families Society, known locally as Newland Orphan Homes. [Information supplied by Mr Alan Marshall of Kirkella.] He owned shares in a number of whaling ships. See Darwent 207.

[103] *28 July 1785.* The new burial ground for Holy Trinity church in Castle Street.

[104] *2 August 1785. Benjamin*, a ship of 306 tons, made its first voyage 1782.

[105] *9 August 1785.* Grampus: Probably a bottled nose whale (Hyperoodon ampullatus); maximum length 9 metres (30 ft), which ranges from Spitsbergen to Spain.

[106] *9 August 1785.* South End: the edge of the town bordering the Humber.

[107] *23 August 1785.* Rev David Brown (1763-1812) was educated at Hull Grammar School and was in India from 1786 until his death. Although an Anglican, he was highly regarded by Dissenters.

[108] *3 September 1785.* Joseph Sykes (1722-1805), a powerful High Street merchant, an Evangelical member of the Church of England. His daughter, Marianne, married Henry Thornton, MP.

[109] *27 September 1785.* John Gibson, mason of Manor Street, recorded as a member in the Church Book.

[110] *1 December 1785.* Rev John Beatson, for 24 years pastor at Salthouse Lane chapel, died 23 April 1798. One of the leaders of Hull's cultural society and President of Hull Subscription Library 1788-91.

[111] *7 December 1785.* Spotted fever was usually typhus.

Vol 4 1786-1788

1786

Monday, 16 January

Drank tea at a place where a person engrossed all the conversation. I was obliged to pay a painful attention for near three hours and an half. Patience is a virtue which is sometimes put to the stretch.

Monday, 23 January

In the morning I sat some time in the study before breakfast without fire, which brought on a violent pain in my stomach, alarmed me very much and obliged me to keep house all day.

Wednesday, 25 January

I have so much company at home and so often to visit abroad that when I come to reflect how the day has been spent it appears a vast unfilled blank. I am sensible much time is murdered in empty, unmeaning visits. To engross the conversation is ill manners and to sit silent to let all the unmeaning prattle run thro' the ear is tiresome and what grieves me as much as anything is: that when the chit chat ceases a minister is desired to engage in prayer with his mind disagreeably disarranged by all the toilsome service he has been reduced to for a considerable time.

Thursday, 2 February

Have visited several of the sick in the course of the day; among others a youth only 15 years of age, in the last stage of a consumption. It was remarkable to hear his conversation tho' unable to lift his head or move out of the position in which he was laid.

Tuesday, 7 February

I have been again called to visit a family in the spotted fever.

Tuesday, 7 March

In the afternoon bottled the wine.

Friday, 10 March

I received a letter from London outlining the account with Brother Ansley. A mistake of seven pounds ten shillings which stood against me fluttered me very much, tho' certain that the error lays with him. I could not rest till I wrote to him, and hope it will soon be set right. But after the loss I have sustained by the *Benjamin* (which I desire to submit to as the hand of Providence about £25) I cannot well stand it, nor can I account it duty to my family to sit down contented without endeavouring to set all things right.

Friday, 24 March

Received a letter from London stating the account between me and Brother Ansley: this took me up till near four in the afternoon.

Thursday, 30 March

I have been as usual engaged most of the day from home, except so much of the forenoon as was taken up with one of the members who has some trifling difference with another. I advised him to propose a meeting and conduct it in a Christian temper.

Friday, 31 March

I have been privileged to hear today from my son.

Friday, 14 April

This may have been a *good Friday* to some but, not to say it has been a *bad*, I think it no way improper to say it has been a very *unprofitable* one to me. Company from morning to night without interruption. Really people are very inconsiderate and friends act very unfriendly. Whether they allow time or not to prepare, they expect to see us in our pulpits at the appointed hour. Lord, thy people hinder; do thou help.

Tuesday, 25 April

I was obliged to go as far as Mr Towers' mill to visit a person in a fever.

Thursday, 4 May

We have had workmen jobbing about the house which has taken up some attention.

Saturday, 6 May

One of the children has been very feverish today, which makes us apprehend the smallpox.

Wednesday, 17 May

Have been at the chapel about some shades to the great windows.

Saturday, 20 May

I have been very much unhinged and distressed in my mind today by a letter received from one of the members requesting me to give up six pews for the accommodation of poor people. It is intimated that many of the members are much dissatisfied. I am sure it is unreasonable when I am certain there are not less than 170 or 180 seats unlet in the place. Besides, I have no power to order things at pleasure. The letter intimates as much as that I make great advantages from the place. I wrote the following answer but did not send it: 'I am concerned to hear that there are any complaints amongst the people. It affects me much that any should suppose that I am influenced by avarice. If those who complain suppose that I have been making an estate or have even supported my family with what has been raised from the chapel, they are mistaken. Was it in my power to provide for my family and yet follow the ministry without any pecuniary help from that quarter, there would not only be free seats but a free chapel so far as it concerned me. Had the application been [sic] to me been to give up to the poor the money raised by the pews you mention, your friend might have been satisfied tomorrow morning even upon this short notice. But I do not apprehend myself to have any right to make laws or alterations concerning the place. The Trustees are certainly the proper persons for to apply to in that business and there is little doubt but they will comply with your request. However, with your approbation I will collect them together and lay your petition before them on Monday evening. I remain yours GL.'

Lord's Day, 21 May

Our house is like an hospital at present. George is beginning of the smallpox, Hannah and Phebe have sore throats and fevers to a considerable degree and I find a slight touch of the same complaint myself.

Tuesday, 23 May

George appears as if he would be very full of the smallpox.

Wednesday, 24 May

Joseph is coming out with the smallpox and appears as if he would be remarkably full.

Thursday, 25 May

George and Joseph continue very poorly.

Lord's Day, 4 June

I scarce ever found myself less able to exert my voice in the work of the Ministry. The day very hot and faint. The doors and windows of the meeting all open. The bells (being the King's birthday[112]) very troublesome and myself very weak.

Monday, 5 June

I have been to Beverley today in company with Mr Towers. The day proved very fine and the conversation very agreeable. Mr Parker introduced us into his walks[113] which were peculiarly pleasant.

Friday, 9 June

I have found my frame very much relaxed all day, my mind very much indisposed for study, and greatly deranged by the conduct of a servant who, after living with us more than fifteen years, would go away without any previous warning on account of a sailor she has lately got acquainted with and who lately sold his wife[114] to another man. I desire to be thankful that my tongue was under such a guard that I was preserved from speaking unadvisedly with my lips. I feel a great concern for the poor woman as she has been a very faithful servant to my family.

Monday, 12 June

I have been bathing this morning and find myself much relieved by it. This evening there was a meeting of the Trustees relative to the Settlement of the choice of Trustees in future. Also to deliberate upon enlarging the Vestry. Mr Tong proposed to give ten guineas and Mr Carlill five towards it, but Mr Jones proposing only one it is likely it will entirely drop.

Tuesday, 13 June

The garden employed my time this morning. I have not been able to attend to it for some time past and the weeds have made considerable progress.

Wednesday, 14 June

Spent the morning in weeding the garden.... In the evening walked as far as the Spring Gardens.[115]

Wednesday, 21 June

About eleven I went on board the boat [en route to London]. About noon took chaise with Mrs Mackley and Miss Collier of Scarbro' and immediately proceeded on the way to Bourne with intention to sleep there. When we came to the inn, finding the people gone to bed and very much out of humour at being disturbed, we resolved at about midnight to proceed on our journey.

Thursday, 22 June

Soon after we had left Bourne it began to lighten very much. The flashes were very dreadful and with one the driver said he was so much affected that he could see nothing for a short time after. About 3 in the morning we got to Peterborough, and about an hour after proceed[ed] in a light coach for London, where we arrived safe this evening about seven and had the pleasure to meet my son in good health.

Friday, 24 June

Drank tea with Colonel Markham, brother to the present Archbishop of York.[116]

Monday, 26 June

Went to Rotherhithe and from thence to Greenwich with Mrs Mackley and friends. Took a view of the Hospital and park. Returned to dine with Mrs Hardcastle. Crossed over to Wapping and returned to Broad Street much tired.

Tuesday, 27 June

Attended the lecture at Broad Street. Went to the coffee house. Delivered several letters I brought from Hull.

Thursday, 29 June

To the Museum. Dined with Mr Bainbridge at four and trifled away the rest of the day in worldly company. My situation is very disagreeable and connections painful.

Friday, 30 June

Attended some trials before Lord Loughborough at Guildhall. Went over the British Museum.

Wednesday, 5 July

Went after breakfast to Clapham. Had some agreeable conversation and a pleasing walk with Mr Thornton. After dinner he took me in his carriage thro' North Wood and showed some of the most agreeable prospects I ever saw. From thence we went to Black Heath, drank tea at Mrs Wilberforce's.[117] Heard Mr Venn[118] expound and went to prayer, after which Mr Thornton set me to town. This has been the most agreeable day I have had since I left Yorkshire.

Thursday, 6 July

In the morning I took a place in the coach, bid farewell to several friends, after dinner packed up and about five took my seat in the stage coach and left London.

Friday, 7 July

I have travelled all night and day with very profane and disagreeable company. Reproof was in vain and therefore silence was the disapprobation I discovered. About nine this evening I got in safely to Lincoln.

Saturday, 8 July

Set off from Lincoln as the clock struck seven. Got to Barton about three and was more than two hours and an half upon the water. On my return home I found all in health. . . . How sweet is rest and how welcome home to a weary traveller.

Wednesday, 19 July

I have been with several of the sick today and I fear more time than profit attends that business. I feel something formal creep into that work, and observe a very great abuse of it, for now, when a minister visits a sick person, instead of having opportunity to speak close to his conscience, or enquire into the state of his soul, the chamber is thronged with persons who crowd in as spectators

Monday, 24 July

I have been engaged thro' the day in the business of the family, particularly in taking down the beds and putting the wine in casks, and am so tired that I know not how to hold up while I write this.

Wednesday, 26 July

In the evening Messrs Riddell and Carlill. Our conversation turned up respecting a member who, after being joined to the church a few months, has left us in a very disorderly manner [complaining of errors of religious practice and theology].

Thursday, 27 July

[Long letter from John Whitton, the member who has resigned, setting out his theological position with a preamble explaining his stance:] 'Having for some time past perceived an essential difference between your sentiments and mine, and being now convinced of our entire disagreement in every part and principle of Christianity, I am constrained to withdraw myself from your Society, and from henceforth am no member of the meeting in Fish Street whereof you are pastor, and consider myself perfectly at liberty to attend my God in any other place where his voice is heard, and his grace powerfully displayed and felt.'

Friday, 28 July

[Long letter of reply including:] 'Your letter was not delivered to me last night till after the church meeting or it should have been read. Your conduct in this affair to me appears both unchristian and exceeding disorderly. The whole of your letter, with this answer, shall (God willing) be laid before the church the first opportunity, who *alone*, not I, have the right to approve of your withdrawing. However, when that business comes before them, so far as my consent as an individual is required, you may depend upon having it; for, in my opinion, a person who will deliberately write and publish such notorious falsehoods against another, as the charges you would fix upon me and the doctrine I teach, is absolutely unfit for religious society. But I humbly trust both myself and religious sentiments are too well known by all the ministers in this town for my character to be essentially injured by the gross calumnies you have, or may continue to propagate against me.'

Since I wrote the above Mr Whitton has been on at my house and, after a great deal of conversation, he acknowledges that if he was mistaken he is concerned that he should have wrote as he did, but there was something very guarded in all that he said. At his request I promised not to expose his letter, which I am since sorry for, as I know not how it can be done. However, let me be pressed as I may, I am resolved to keep my word until I have first spoke to himself. I have done little or nothing preparatory for the Sabbath. My mind has been too much exercised about other things.

Lord's Day, 30 July

This evening the *Benjamin* from Davis Strait arrived, in which I have a part, containing 135 butts of blubber and about 2 or 2½ ton of bone, the product of three fish. Blessed be God for all his benefits.

This I would receive as Peter did the piece of money in the mouth of the fish.

Monday, 7 August

My wife and I took this day a ride to Cottingham to spend the day with Mr Egginton.[119] It proved remarkably pleasant particularly in the evening on our return, and what perhaps rendered it still more delightful was my lately reading of Cooper's 2nd Volume of poems.[120]

Thursday, 10 August

I dined at Mr Rust's. After dinner went to a funeral at the Quakers' meeting. A woman spoke for a considerable time and afterwards went to prayer, but the most incorrect, unmeaning and I thought unintelligible stuff that I ever heard.

Saturday, 12 August

About noon I bathed, and after dinner found myself very sleepy.

9 William Rust; a founding father of The Port of Hull Society for the Religious Instruction of Seamen, 1821; now the Sailors Families Society. (Darwent)

10 Bracket clock c.1800 by William Rust; active as a clock, watchmaker and goldsmith c.1790-1823. (J E S Walker *Hull & East Riding clocks & watches*)

Thursday, 17 August

I have been to spend the day at Cottingham. Mr Gilder was so kind as to take my wife and me in a postchaise to dine and drink tea with him there. But I did not enjoy the day owing to violent pain I was in all the last night with the rheumatism on my wrist [?].

Monday, 28 August

I got up about four this morning to brew, in which I have been engaged most of the day.

Lord's Day, 7 September

One Mr Mills, a minister near Wolverhampton, called upon me with a petition from his people, and a letter recommending the case from Mr Parsons of Leeds. . . . A great part of this day has been spent in transcribing a sermon. I have often been pressed earnestly to publish another volume of sermons; have therefore resolved to write out a few that they may be ready should I either be removed, or spared to see the propriety of publishing of them.

Tuesday, 3 October

I have been brewing today; but everything went cross. The copper would not act as usual, and we have had company without intermission.

Lord's Day, 8 October

We have had a very awful morning. When I got up in the morning the waves were dashing over the bank of the Humber in the most alarming manner. I never recollect to have seen it so before. Several sloops were dashed to pieces and some men lost their lives. In going to chapel my wife was taken off her feet, Hannah blown down to the edge of the water in the Bush Dike[121] and Phebe drove against some pails but happily no other damage was received but a violent blow upon Phebe's eye, which has made it very black and wounded the corner of the lid a little. My mind was greatly agitated at not seeing them at chapel and forboded the worst. I preached in great confusion.

Thursday, 19 October

I was much pleased in hearing that a gospel minister in the establishment, one who I have very high opinion of, is likely to go over with the convicts who are to be sent for Botany Bay, one of the places discovered by Captain Cook.

Thursday, 26 October

Called upon Mr Gilder who paid me for the bone belonging to the ship *Benjamin*.

Wednesday, 1 November

Had application from a very reputable family for a pew in my meeting place. Blessed be God for any prospect of increase and that some who were my greatest opposers upon coming to Hull are now stated hearers.

Monday, 13 November

On a committee this morning on the choice of mistresses for the spinning schools.[122]

Wednesday, 15 November

In the forenoon Mrs Hide, who is chosen mistress to one of the spinning schools, called upon me. In relating a variety of trials which she had experienced since she last left Hull one circumstance she related affected me much as I was more particularly concerned in it. She related that being cast by Providence for some time to reside in a little village near Brightelstone [Brighton], she went thither every Sabbath on foot to hear the word, tho' six miles. After some time she became acquainted with several of the people who worshipped there. Among others she one day fell in company with a gentleman of considerable property, and remarkable for his liberal support of the cause and poor of Christ who, hearing her speak of Hull, he observed that he believed by report few places by account were more distinguished by Gospel privileges than that place; and enquired further if she was acquainted with any of the Minsters who preached there. On her making mention of my name he remarked that, tho' he was unknown by person to me, that the volume of sermons that I had published had been remarkably blessed to his profit more than any book he had read.

Thursday, 16 November

After the meeting I was obliged in consequence of a request from the deacons to lay before the church the letters that had been passed between Mr Whitton and me some time since on account of the same turbulent spirit manifesting itself. The altercation was protracted to a considerable length but at length he withdrew himself from the church. He is a man of very insinuating address and great subtlety. I fear he will do considerable injury.

Monday, 27 November

I have had a great deal of company today. From one of the members [Hugh Ross] I have had a great deal of trouble today. He has long endeavoured to prejudice several of the people against my ministry. Today he owned it and asserted that the glory of Christ was hid and there was nothing of the Gospel in my sermons, that the ministry was chaff. I cannot say but such charges affect me; but I feel very happy under a consciousness of their falsehood. . . . However, the same day several have been with me declaring how precious the word preached was rendered to them only yesterday.

Thursday, 30 November

After the close of the meeting the same troublesome member who brought such charges against my ministry on Monday last came to the table pew. My spirits were greatly affected and discomposed as soon as I saw him. He talked in a very mystical manner for some time. I fear there will be much uneasiness with him. I am sure it troubles me much. The variety of trials I have met with of late press so hard upon my mind that I should certainly retire from the ministry was it not for a large family and no probability of support for them. My way is at present hedged up and I would not wish to force it.

Friday, 1 December

I have been very much depressed in my spirits all the day. When I would have diverted my thoughts from the disagreeable subject which presses so hard upon my mind, I have found it impossible. Have turned over the Bible again and again but have not been able to fix upon anything. Either it would point too much at the person who has caused me so much trouble, or it would not sufficiently display the present truth which I wish to demonstrate. I own it is exceeding weak and foolish to be so much troubled when my conscience tells me that what is laid to my charge is false, the greater part of the people are not only satisfied but affectionate, and the man who is the cause of all is a very weak positive foolish person. But I cannot help it.

Saturday, 2 December

One of the members came on complaining that he had not lately found the ministry what it used to be formerly. . . . The intimacy of the person who came tonight with the man who caused me so much trouble on Monday and Thursday last leads me to think that is owing to his influence, but he behaved in a Christian spirit; so that I was enabled to bear it.

Monday, 4 December

On my return found several waiting to converse with me. Had some in one room and some in the other till near ten at night. The busy man with whom I have had so much trouble is most assiduous in his vile pursuit to blacken my character.

Monday, 11 December

In the evening there was a meeting of the church relative to some things asserted by Mr Ross [See his charges 27 November]. For a long time he persisted with the greatest obstinacy; but at length owned that pride, ignorance and want of judgement had led him to assert what he had, and that he had been acting a very vile part. The change was so sudden and his sentiments and language so very different that I can hardly believe a reality in anything that passed. However, his acknowledgement was admitted to be sufficient.

Tuesday, 19 December

Called again and again on Mr Jones and found him to my apprehension in dying circumstances. It is much if he lives over the night as he appears quite insensible. Should he be removed I shall lose a very sincere friend who has stood very steadily by me for near 18 years and who was one of the first instruments of my coming to Hull.

Wednesday, 20 December

My time has been much taken up with Mr Jones today. I have been four times at his house. Before 8 in the morning, from eleven till near two, at four, and near 9 this evening. The second and last time I saw him and found him very full of comfort in his own soul. He expressed great gratitude to God for the ministry he had sat under for more than 17 years. Said that he then felt the comforts of it, and as a dying man wished to set his seal to the faith of it. In my own apprehension he is better, and will probably recover; but I desire to receive his testimony in the light in which he viewed himself when he gave it.

Lord's Day, 31 December

[Review of the past year, including:] The congregation has increased rather than diminished; the salary has been larger than before and the ship I have a share in has done well.

1787

Thursday, 4 January

I have this day received for the oil belonging to the *Benjamin*. I desire to be very thankful for the comfortable [sic] sent in by that channel, would receive it as immediately from the bank of the Almighty.

Monday, 22 January

Applied part of the morning to the work of transcribing for the press.

Friday, 26 January

Settled the insurance of the ship with Mr Egginton.

Tuesday, 6 February

Have had the stone cutters at work today.

Wednesday, 7 February

Have been engaged amongst the workmen most of the day.

Tuesday, 13 February

Settling the pew book most of the morning ... and attended the singing meeting.

Wednesday, 14 February

We have been obliged to have workmen today to take down and rebuild our kitchen chimney which was very near falling.

Saturday, 7 April

The chimney in our kitchen smoked so much that we were obliged to have workmen, which hindered me much. However, I have finished another sermon.

Wednesday, 11 April

A minister preached for me this evening who happened to be in the town. ... The discourse was chiefly made up of extracts from Shakespeare, Young, Addison etc. I fear it was labour in vain. It was merely acting a part and supplicating applause without the ability to obtain it.

Saturday, 9 June

I was sent for to a person who was quite frantic whether with liquor or passion it was not in my power to say. They desired me to pray but I declined, observing that it did not appear a proper season for it.

Monday, 11 June

Walked in the morning and bathed. ... Have had to perform in the course of the day the disagreeable work of conversing with a member on something very disagreeable observed in their conduct.

Wednesday, 13 June

Drank tea with Mr Rennards,[123] Newland; upon mounting my horse to return home it began to be very wild, upon which I walked home. Riding has brought on the heartburn to such a degree that I feel myself very poorly.

Monday, 2 July

In the morning went to Mr Watson's school to enter the children.

Monday, 23 July

Detained with my father in the afternoon who has been very bad of a stoppage of water.

Friday, 27 July

About seven was obliged to attend a church meeting. ... Mr Ross withdrew. He was present and charged me with despising the poor and with forcing the church to admit persons contrary to all order. I have my testimony with God and in the church that I never did the one or the other. He has been dissatisfied for some time. ... I have ever behaved to this man in the most friendly manner, often relieved him and once given him half a guinea to put him in a way to support his family. However, it was never given as a bribe, and had I held back any truth or propagated any error it would have been duty in him to have opposed. But to my knowledge this has not been the case.

Monday, 30 July

Have been engaged today in taking down three of the beds; feel myself uncommonly weary after it.

Tuesday, 31 July

Have been brewing, taking down and putting up two beds, and have baptised three children.

Friday, 3 August

Have been taken up also in fixing about the Greenland trade. Came to the resolution to retain but a sixteenth in the *Benjamin* and to hold the same share in the *Minerva*.[124] Mr Gilder agreed with Mr Christopher Briggs to take the other 16th in the *Benjamin* at the price I gave for it.

Saturday, 11 August

I have had very few hindrances today, except a woman who came about a parcel of dreams which I could say nothing about, except guard her against delusions and point her to the word.

Monday, 13 August

Bathing and writing in the morning. Walked in the afternoon and baptised a child. Read a little after tea and amused the children with a microscope.

Friday, 31 August

Mr Gilder engaged us to visit Cottingham today. We went about ten, and are just returned at near nine. It has proved a very favourable day. The country people very busy about their harvest.

Monday, 3 September

This morning I was upon the committee at the Hall upon the choice of a mistress for one of the spinning schools.

Tuesday, 11 September

[Long account of previous night's illness when he thought he was dying].

Monday, 17 September

I have been engaged this day in examining and rectifying the Chapel Register. Had to call upon several persons to enquire the age of their children, having only the day of their baptism.[125]

Wednesday, 19 September

Mr Spyvee and Mr and Miss Cooper[126] drank tea with us.

Monday, 1 October

I have passed thro' the day but in a manner which I can scarce describe. Visited a sick person. Called on several friends and drank tea with Mr Wright in Mytongate.

Wednesday, 24 October
[Long account of a reformed sinner, Peter Dosser,[127] a member of the congregation].

Monday, 29 October
In the afternoon I went with William to Mr Levitt's when he was bound apprentice.

Wednesday, 7 November
Have been looking over some papers and preparing some sermons to send to the printer.

Friday, 9 November
Received a proof sheet from the printer.

Thursday, 29 November
Engaged most of the morning at the chapel about the removing some persons to make way for Mr Egginton's family.

Friday, 30 November
This morning as soon as I was shaved I had to baptise a child on the dock side near the far end. I then went to see Richard Smith who had been much hurt the previous day by the fall of a piece of timber. I found him much bruised and swelled but no bones broke. On returning home I read the newspaper to my father.

Friday, 7 December
As the gardener came to plant the hyacinths etc. I was engaged all the forenoon.

Tuesday, 11 December
I just got out to Mr Levitt's[128] in the morning to pay him the money that he was to have with W[illiam] Lambert.[129]

Thursday, 27 December
Settled about the ship *Benjamin* in the morning, conveying one half of the property I had in her to Mr Christopher Briggs.[130]

Friday, 28 December
Mr Gilder came on about the ship *Minerva* which took me up some time. . . . I have been informed today that a few members who have withdrawn from the Baptist Church are for setting up a new sect under the denomination of Sandemanians[131] and that Hugh Ross, who some time since withdrew from our church, intends to join them. Probably more in time may follow his example.

1788

Monday, 7 January
I sat this morning for my picture by the particular desire of a friend. I felt very awkward and was very tired.

Wednesday, 9 January
Sat for the picture this morning.

Thursday, 10 January
Miss Robinson called in the afternoon to take leave, going to the East India's. Conversed with a disorderly member.

Friday, 25 January
I have lost this day.

Monday, 28 January
Received some disagreeable tidings concerning the bills being returned for the bone belonging to the *Benjamin* which, if they not be taken up, will take at the least 25 more out of my pocket, and I apprehend I shall sustain over 50 loss by it already.

Wednesday, 30 January
Dr Baynes called on me about noon and ordered me to be blooded immediately, expressing some fear of a stroke of the palsy ensuing.

Friday, 22 February
My father being ill I have been very much hindered thro' the day. About noon he fell down in a kind of fit, and was blooded in the afternoon.

Saturday, 23 February
My father continuing very much indisposed has employed my thoughts and takes up much of my time today. To me he appears to sink very fast. Nor should I wonder if another fit was to come on if it put a period to his life in a very little time.

Tuesday, 26 February
My father tho' much better requires great attendance.

Wednesday, 12 March
I took a walk upon the Turnpike this morning and found it remarkably fine.

Saturday, 22 March
In the afternoon I baptised a child. The circumstances attending it were very affecting. The father was hearing me last Sabbath morning. Taken ill on Tuesday and died yesterday about 4 o'clock. His wife was delivered about 8 and he removed out of the bed to make way for her. After that I was sent for to a person who was in hysterics.

Wednesday, 2 April
In the morning I bottled the wine. After dinner turned over a bed in the garden.

Monday, 7 April

This evening Mr Riddell came on to my house and hinted at his intention to take himself out of the church because his son-in-law Rhodes[132] was not admitted into it. I wished him to consider. Some deep laid scheme seems to be in hand.

Monday, 21 April

In the morning before breakfast walked with the children from near 6 till 8.

Wednesday, 30 April

In the evening had a very agreeable walk with Mr Milner.

Saturday, 3 May

As soon as I got up this morning one of my fore teeth dropped out. It has been loose for a very long time. I fear it will be a great disadvantage to me in speaking.

Tuesday, 6 May

I had an artificial tooth fixed in the vacuum from whence one dropped on Saturday.

Thursday, 15 May

I have reason not only to bless God for my own and my family's preservation this day, but especially for his care over my son George who in his rambles this day fell over head into some water and I suppose very narrowly escaped with his life.

Monday, 26 May

Left Hull about 7 in the morning. Crossed the water in order to take horse at Barton. When mounting, the horse flew back, broke the bridle in the hand of the person who held it, [bounded?] from side to side of the lane, forced me against a wall, began to rear. I threw myself off and escaped to the astonishment of all unhurt. After some time I got on another horse, rode to South Welton where I dined at Mr Sarjent's, a most amiable family. After dinner rode to Caistor where I arrived in the evening in health and safety, tho' much tired.

Monday, 2 June

Dined at Mr Levett's and went over the boats for Barton, where Mr N Levett and myself took a chaise for Scunthorpe and arrived there in safety in the evening.

Tuesday, 3 June

Walked about the fields till about 11 … after dinner set off from Scunthorpe, got to Barton about 5. Drank tea, and arrived at Hull about 7.

Lord's Day, 8 June

Preached for the benefit of the Charity School. . . . Collected above twelve guineas.

Tuesday, 10 June

Spent the morning in the garden which had run into a very disordered state for want of looking over.

Tuesday, 17 June

In the morning I transcribed a sheet of Dr Owen's[133] works to complete a volume. . . . Walked to Sculcoates Church.[134] Drank tea with Captain Leak and spent the time very agreeably.

Tuesday, 24 June

Obliged to go and visit a sick person at Wincolmlee and returned by a walk round Spring Gardens and by Mr Portas's[135] Garden.

Monday, 30 June

Read a letter to Dr Priestley[136] from an undergraduate of Oxford, a smart but not very solid piece.

Monday, 7 July

After dinner walked with the family to Sculcoates and spent the afternoon at Mr Egginton's mill.

Monday, 10 July

In the morning walked to Mount Airy,[137] from whence I enjoyed one of the finest prospects of the country that I have seen for a long time.

Tuesday, 15 July

In returning in the evening I was seized with a strange confusion in my head as I was coming thro' the Market Place. My sight failed me, so that I grew quite dark. Staggered, and, had I not got against a man who supported me, I must have fallen. But I soon recovered my sight and got home, tho' very much fluttered. I rather fear it has been a fit, but am uncertain. What a mercy is it to my family that I was not brought home dead, which, had it been a little stronger, or, had I fallen, might have been the case.

Thursday, 17 July

I was very ill in the morning and so much affected in my head that I expected to fall every moment.

Friday, 18 July

This evening I took an emetic by the order of the physician, which operated the most violently that I ever remember to have met with any. I know not what to do as I have nothing prepared for the Sabbath and no supply.[138]

Wednesday, 23 July

My wife was taken exceeding ill. I got up and sat by her till between 2 and 3, when I went to bed again but got very little rest. . . . Have had several friends to see me. Some tell me half the church are for going into the water.[139] Others that one person has got no good my [sic] for attending for several Sabbaths. . . . It has happened, according to my apprehension, at a very uncomfortable season when I am so exceeding weak in body, so low in my spirits and so unable for to go about. I only went into King Street this evening and was taken several times as if I should have fallen.

Thursday, 24 July

A person came on to inform my wife that the servant she had hired and who was to have come last Tuesday had not been heard of and, as the boats were come from that place, was not to be expected; this put us much about as we shall be left destitute of a servant. While we were discoursing upon this Mr Gilder came on to inform me that a ship was arrived from Greenland and had brought news that the *Benjamin* was clean[140] – consequently that the advance money and insurance would be lost. Thro' mercy I was enabled to hear the tidings with composure. . . . I paid Mr Hunter the £100 with interest that I borrowed of his father.

Thursday, 31 July

In the morning I paid the bookbinder's bill.

Friday, 1 August

There is so much hurry about adult baptism. . . . There is a young man of the congregation who goes about discoursing of it in every company.. I am afraid that like the Judaizing teachers about circumcision he will do a great deal of harm. I feel myself very much discomposed about it, especially as I am unable to get amongst the people. My head is too much indisposed to study anything upon the subject and yet attend to what I may, the conduct of the forward youth is uppermost. People mean it well in telling me about it, but at present it is very prejudicial to my health. I went to see William this evening who is ill of a sore throat and was very near falling as I turned into the Market Place.

Monday, 4 August

Heard the children belonging to the schools in the morning. Have this evening had a blister put upon my back.

Tuesday, 5 August

I got no rest all last night thro' the blister on my back. It has run very much and was dressed this afternoon.

Wednesday, 6 August

The blister has been very sore but I have been so low and fluttered in my spirits that life was almost a burden.

Friday, 8 August

After dressing of the blister this evening it was so painful that I was obliged to send again for the apothecary. He found it so much inflamed that he was obliged to apply a different dressing, which gave me great relief.

Monday, 11 August

I find my mind so distressed what with one thing and another that, was there an opening, I should almost think it was a call for me either to leave Hull or the ministry.

Thursday, 14 August

This morning taken up with visits, waiting for the binder and bathing.

Saturday, 16 August

Mr McLean, a Sandemanian Baptist, I find is come to the town and is to begin to establish a new interest tomorrow. Thus one sect is creeping in after another to make way for the removal of the Gospel from this long highly fast town.

Thursday, 19 August

I rose soon after four in order to go over to Barton. Thro' various impediments it was after high water before we got there. Had the pleasure to meet my eldest son from London. Much grown and in good health.

Thursday, 21 August

I was rather alarmed this morning when I went to the necessary this morning [sic] by parting with blood.

Friday, 22 August

The bleeding returned again this morning. It makes me very faint.

Wednesday, 3 September

This day I have been at Hornsea with Samuel. The day proved remarkably fine. We set out soon after ten and got back about 7. I feel myself very much wearied.

Friday, 5 September

After a very restless night I got up about 6 and accompanied my dear Sam to Barton on his return to London. I endeavoured as much as possible to suppress my feelings and to secret [sic] my thoughts. But it is deeply impressed upon my mind that I shall never see him more in this world. I hardly think without a change that I can be long out of my grave. I consider it as a privilege that he is likely to be on a way to get his bread and I have been enabled since my return to plead earnestly for him with the Lord that he would be a father to him and take him under the wing of his Providence.

Saturday, 6 September
Have been ordered to take bark[141] today.

Saturday, 7 September
The bark which I have taken has been under God the most favourable mean that has hitherto been applied.

Wednesday, 17 September
I have of late been very much pressed with the apprehension that I must give up the ministry.

Thursday, 18 September
A letter was received from Mr John Carlill and read to the church in which he dissolved his union. I confess it has been a very great trial to me. His father was the grand instrument in the hand of Providence in rearing the present place in which I preach. I had great hopes of having much support and comfort from the son, but I am disappointed.

Saturday, 20 September
Obliged to go to market thro' the indisposition of my wife.

Saturday, 27 September
After dinner a person came on about some reflections that she had cast upon my ministry and saying that she was a Baptist in sentiment but should say nothing about it now, but make some future hurry in the Church. She utterly denied it and I supposed that from the solemn manner in which she spoke it must have been false. Scarce had I sat down at my desk when she returned with the person who had asserted it of her, who confirmed it to her face. It is a strange affair. However, I was glad to hear it and get to my work in which I have more pleasure than in vain wranglings.

Tuesday, 30 September
This morning walked with Mr Jones upon the Humber bank till after one. Read the newspaper to my father.

Wednesday, 1 October
Detained by the barber all the morning. Bathed.

Friday, 3 October
Scarce had I got into my study when Mr and Miss Hainworth was introduced to me by a letter from Mr Bottomley.[142] I went with them to see the Trinity House, the Dock etc. After dinner visited Mrs Atkinson at the turnpike house.

Tuesday, 7 October
Set off in the diligence this morning about 6 in company with Messrs Riddell and Tong. Got to Leeds about half after 7 in the evening.

Wednesday, 8 October

Met Mr Bottomley in the street as soon as I was up. Took chaise and went to Hopton where there was a lecture. . . . But the road was so bad that Mr Moorhouse was in the pulpit before we got there. After dinner various business was attended to and finally the case of the Academy which Mr Walker[143] declared his purpose of declining as soon as it could be done with convenience. Did not get to Leeds till near 12 at night.

Thursday, 9 October

Left Leeds this morning at 7 and reached home at near 9 this evening. . . . The carriage was so much crowded that I feel myself very much fatigued.

Friday, 10 October

Obliged to fill up the report and pay the duty[144] upon the chapel register to Mr Aldby, and being the Fair day a great many people have called which has taken up the whole of the day.

Tuesday, 14 October

Assisted Hannah in writing [a letter] to her brother Sam.

Tuesday, 28 October

In the afternoon drank tea at Mrs Hunter's with a mixed company. The conversation turned chiefly upon the manner in which the fifth of November is to be celebrated. I was very miserable the whole time and happy when there was an opportunity to withdraw.

Wednesday, 5 November

As soon as breakfast was over I went into the town with the children to see the procession of the day and in the evening the fireworks. It has been a day of hurry and confusion. A great concourse of people were assembled from it.

Monday, 10 November

Being this day appointed one of a committee for endeavouring to abolish the slave trade, I sat down in the evening to run over Clarkson[145] and Ramsay[146] on that subject. The account is shocking to humanity.

Monday, 17 November

Engaged in brewing. . . . In the evening there was a prayer meeting for the recovery of the King.[147]

Tuesday, 9 December

One person I had to call upon in the new buildings behind the Infirmary, the street being unpaved it was hardly possible to get to it.

Monday, 15 December

Much snow thro' the day. Have been but little from home except to buy William a great coat and to attend Mrs Witty's funeral.

Notes to Vol 4

[112] *4 June 1786.* The birthday of George III is still commemorated at Eton.

[113] *5 June 1786.* Mr Parker's walks: their location has not been identified, but Beverley historian Berna Moody has pointed out that New Walk, Beverley, was developed as a fashionable promenade in this period. Possibly GL saw this development.

[114] *9 June 1786.* 'Sold his wife': regarded as a method of divorce in a period when only the wealthy could take advantage of a private Act of Parliament to end a marriage.

[115] *14 June 1786.* Spring Gardens were off Spring Street.

[116] *24 June 1786.* William Markham (baptised 1719-1807), consecrated as Archbishop of York 1776.

[117] *5 July 1786.* Mrs William Wilberforce (1777-1847) was formerly Barbara Spooner, daughter of a Birmingham banker.

[118] *5 July 1786.* The Venns were influential members of the Evangelical Clapham sect, though with strong Hull links. Rev John Venn (1759-1813) was the son of the Rev Henry Venn, curate of Clapham, who was probably the preacher GL heard.

[119] *7 August 1786.* The Eggintons were merchants and moguls of the Hull whaling trade with interests in many ships. They owned a mill in Sculcoates. Gardiner Egginton lived at Aston Hall, North Ferriby, and Joseph, his twin brother (d 1830) was a Hull merchant, alderman and mayor. In 1769 Gardiner was a subscriber to Blanket Row chapel. Joseph had a pew in St John the Evangelist's church, which he purchased for £17, with an annual rent of £20.

[120] *7 August 1786.* William Cowper's *Poems* were first published 1782. Cowper (1731-1800) was a cousin of the Rev Martin Madan. See Appendix A.

[121] *8 October 1786.* A wide ditch which had run alongside the town walls was, at least in part, known as Bush Dike (or Busdike).

[122] *13 November 1786.* Spinning Schools. By the end of the 18th century three spinning schools were maintained by subscription, each for 34 girls, clothed and educated for domestic service.

[123] *13 June 1787.* Joseph Rennards of North End (the area near North Bridge) was an Assistant Governor of the Poor.

[124] *3 August 1787. Minerva.* Built in Norfolk, Virginia, 1765. Before 1797 she made whaling voyages to the Southern Fisheries rather than the Arctic - which were more usual for Hull whalers. In 1833 sold to Newcastle.

[125] *17 September 1787.* GL entered dates of birth as well as baptism.

[126] *19 September 1787.* Samuel Cooper, an important business-man, connected with the Spyvee family both through business and marriage, was a ropemaker, merchant and a mogul of the Hull whaling trade. He is said to have lost his wealth when paraffin oil replaced whale oil. With premises in Lime Street, Hull, he later made Tranby Lodge, Hessle, his residence, but, as his fortunes declined, he moved to Welton.

[127] *24 October 1787.* William Dosser was a malster of Blanket Row and James Dosser a brewer of Finkle Street (D 1791).

[128] *11 December 1787.* The Levett (or Levitt) family featured prominently in GL's family and professional life. William and Norrison Levett were grocers and teamen of Market Place. GL's son, William, was apprenticed to Norrison Levett, who in 1799 was on the fund-raising committee to pay off the Fish Street mortgage. A number of members of the family had shares in whaling ships.

[129] *11 December 1787.* A premium was paid for an apprenticeship, sometimes part being returned as wages.

[130] *27 December 1787.* Christopher Briggs was a merchant, shipowner and insurance broker of Bowlalley Lane, and a shareholder in whaling ships.

[131] *28 December 1787.* Sandemanian: a sect developed by Robert Sandeman (1718-71). 'He attacked the so-called popular preachers to the evangelicals, for adding works to faith and for not following the example of the apostles.' ODNB

[132] *7 April 1788.* Probably Josiah Rhodes.

[133] *17 June 1788.* Dr John Owen (1766-1822) was administrator of the British and Foreign Bible Society. One of his daughters married the eldest son of William Wilberforce.

[134] *17 June 1788.* Sculcoates church. The medieval church of St Mary, in what was still the village of Sculcoates, was rebuilt in 1759 in classical style. it was later demolished and replaced by the new St Mary's church in Sculcoates Lane (1916). Only the churchyard with a number of memorials survives in Air Street.

[135] *24 June 1788.* The Portas Family had nurseries. James Portas was a deacon, mentioned in the register of baptisms, and a member of the fund-raising committee of 1799 to pay off the mortgage.

[136] *30 June 1788.* Dr Joseph Priestley (1733-1804), theologian and natural philosopher. Of Independent persuasion, he was minister at Mill Hill chapel, Leeds, 1767-73, (see footnote: 21 July 1791).

[137] *10 July 1788.* Mount Airy: a landmark at South Cave.

[138] *18 July 1788.* No supply: no deputy. Elsewhere it often means supply of food.

[139] *23 July 1788.* Going into the water: joining the Baptists?

[140] *24 July 1788.* Clean: no catch.

[141] *6 September 1788.* Peruvian or Jesuit's bark was the source of quinine, powdered and used to reduce fever.

[142] *3 October 1788.* Possibly Richard Bottomley, gunsmith, of Scale Lane, or George Bottomley, pilot of Blackfriargate (d 1791), but more likely the Rev Samuel Bottomley of the Heckmondwike Academy, who was at Swanland in 1770 and later moved to Scarborough.

[143] *8 October 1788.* Possibly Samuel Walker (d 1796), Tutor at Northowram Academy 1783-1814.

[144] *10 October 1788.* A duty of 3d was payable on each birth and burial. The Fish Street baptismal register shows the dates when GL paid this duty.

[145] *10 November 1788.* Thomas Clarkson (1760-1846): leading abolitionist, *An Essay on the Slavery and Commerce of the Human Species, particularly the African* (1786).

[146] *10 November 1788.* James Ramsay (1733-89): abolitionist, *Essay on the Treatment and Conversion of African Slaves in the British Sugar Colonies* (1784); *An Enquiry into the Effects of Putting a Stop to the African Slave Trade* (1784)

[147] *17 November 1788.* George III had had serious bouts of illness in 1788.

Vol 5 1789-1790

1789

Saturday, 3 January

A friend in the neighbourhood who is to be town tomorrow offered to preach for me in the afternoon and desired to partake of the ordinance. I respect the man very much and was deeply sensible of the kindness of his proposal. However, knowing that there had been some variance between him and [one] of the members of the Church, I thought it prudent for peace sake at home, to mention it first. The person behaved well, but declared that he could not in conscience sit down with him, till he had removed some very strong objections from his mind, or made some concessions. I got a brother to persuade the minister to withdraw his proposal and was obliged to fly to my old sermons for supply. . . . It was impossible to keep warm with a fire in my study and, sitting close to it, I have felt much for the poor.

Thursday, 8 January

The many hindrances I have met with of late in the work of preparation for the pulpit led me to resolve to begin a day sooner. Accordingly I had a fire made in my study, but had scarce sat down before I was called down to a friend who stayed till noon. I applied a little after dinner. But was soon called to company who were come to spend the afternoon.

Friday, 9 January

Have been studying a sermon upon the subject of the slave trade, upon which I have been desired to preach and to have a collection on the next Sabbath.

Tuesday, 20 January

Have been engaged in brewing.

Friday, 30 January

Mr Portas also came on to do something at the garden which took up the afternoon, and he afterwards stayed tea.

Thursday, 5 February

Received a letter from Mr William Sedgwick informing me that he had altered his sentiments about baptism and desiring to dissolve his relation with the church. I was not much surprised at it as his acquaintance and a strong attachment and temptation lays on that side.

Saturday, 7 February

Called upon one of the members whose son was killed yesterday by a fall from the ship's mast.

Wednesday, 11 February

In the morning I went down to the Soap House to see Mr Thornton senior.[148]

Tuesday, 17 February

I this day received a very pleasing letter from a young man about 15 years of age. He had been brought up under a Socinian[149] ministry, but coming upon liking to a shop in Hull where in the event he did not settle, the Lord is as pleased to bless his word delivered by an unworthy minister for his awakening and conversion.

Friday, 20 February

I received a letter from Mr Welsh of London, proposing for me to take 3 or 6 young men to train up for the ministry. He to allow £20 a year for the board of each, £10 for education and £5 for washing etc. But I have so many engagements and am so poorly in health that I must decline the offer.

Friday, 27 February

A friend came on this evening who told me how indefatigable the Anabaptists are in endeavouring to make proselytes. It is a very trying time, and what will be the end of things I know not. I wish to be kept in a proper spirit and temper. But am almost at a loss how to act, whether to be still, or whether I should enlarge upon such exhortations as those [quoted in Biblical sources]. Their conduct and spirit has fully convinced me that they are influenced by the very spirit of the old Judaizing teachers and their deluded followers and that the circumstantial for which they contended as an essential being changed, they are in all respects like them. Like dogs they fawn, snarl, bark, bite, scatter and devour.

Friday, 6 March

I went to Mr Levett's to see my son William who appeared but poorly last night; found him in bed and in a high fever. About 2 got Dr Baynes to him who prescribed for him. I wished him to be removed home but Mr L thought he had better not.

Saturday, 7 March

I again visited William. The medicines had been given, but no way to promote a perspiration. I am very uneasy lest he should thro' neglect suffer. ... I visited him again this evening but found no visible alteration. In the course of the day George has also been seized with a fever and sore throat.

Lord's Day, 8 March

In the afternoon I was seized with a hoarseness and fearful that I could not proceed, but by sending for the medicine it was mercifully removed. ... William and George continue very poorly.

Monday, 9 March
The last night I sat up with William; he had a very favourable night and was much better in the morning. But in the course of the day fell off and is much worse. He was bled last night and now is ordered to be blistered. My wife is to sit up with him tonight. I called upon a few sick people.

Tuesday, 10 March
I went on to see William about seven in the morning. Found him much worse and that he had got very little rest all the night. The greater part of the day I have spent with him. The Dr ordering him a medicine which he desired me to be very particular in giving. I stayed till the blister was dressed when we got him a nurse. In the evening I went on again and found him rather upon a sweat.

Wednesday, 11 March
This morning about seven I went to Mr Levett's, found William asleep and the nurse informed me that he had been much refreshed with sleep. When he awoke I found him in a fine perspiration. Called several times in the course of day and found him better.

Thursday, 12 March
With William soon in the morning and found that he had enjoyed a good night and was much better.

Friday, 13 March
In the morning I went as usual to William and found him much better.

Saturday, 14 March
In the morning Phebe was taken very ill which detained me for a considerable time. In the afternoon Hannah and Joseph complained of their heads and sore throats. I went to see William and Mr N Levett.

Thursday, 19 March
Reading the *Monthly and Critical Review* in the morning and evening. The latter has made their remarks on the volume of sermons which I published last. They have been far more gentle than I expected or even desired, for their disapprobation of religious books is rather a recommendation of them. What they say is as follows: 'In our 48 volume part 7 we examined a former volume of sermons by Mr Lambert. These are distinguished by the same perspicuity, the same piety and the same peculiar phraseology; the language of a sect. The singular unaffected spirit of religion which pervades these discourses commands, however, our respect, and ought to command our recommendation.' By *the language of a sect* I suppose they mean to convey the same idea that they did in their review of the first volume. Where they say 'the language is plain, perspicuous and on many occasions evangelical but intermixed with

that formal kind of phraseology which distinguishes the religious presbyterian from the man of the world' I glory in the distinction.

Monday, 23 March

Attended at the Town Hall as a member of the committee on the slave trade. Letters from the members and from the chairman of the committee in London were read. Afterwards addresses to the King and Queen were introduced, debated, altered and signed.

Thursday, 26 March

Walked as far as Mr Portas's garden.

Lord's Day, 29 March

My son William was this evening giving me a relation of a very wonderful deliverance for which I praise God, and would record it for his future notice. As he and the two other apprentices with a labourer were removing a hogshead which was too large for the hole thro' which it was to pass, after jumping upon it as it hung suspended for a considerable time, he ran downstairs. When the cords broke, the windlass flew several yards and the hogshead fell. Had he been under it, which he but just escaped, he must have been crushed to death, it weighing I think he said 14 hundredweight.

Thursday, 2 April

About 8 in the morning went to Barton to the opening of the new meeting house there.

Friday, 10 April

Have done very little else but attend upon my aged father thro' the day. Found him very much indisposed in the morning and has continued so thro' the day.

Saturday, 11 April

We have supposed my father to be dying all thro' the day. He lay sweating and slumbering. About 3 they sent for me, apprehending him dying. But this evening he appeared more composed. [Continues very ill over following days].

Lord's Day, 12 April

The physician this evening expresses his apprehension that a mortification in the bladder will take place in my father's case.

Thursday, 16 April

I this day found my father exceedingly weak in the morning. Crying for mercy. He asked me what he must do to be saved. I pointed him to various passages for encouragement.

Friday, 17 April
Have passed thro' a very restless night with my poor father. He was incessantly pushing down the bed clothes and laying his arms out of bed. As I was giving him a bit of light pudding he said, 'Blessed be the hand that feeds me.' At another time I asked him if he knew who I was. 'Yes,' said he. 'My son – and a good son you have been to me.' I this evening took my leave of him, not expecting to see him again alive.

Saturday, 18 April
Have been with him most of the day till the great change took place about 20 minutes before 2 in the afternoon. . . . I was enabled to plead for him in his last moments and found liberty in doing it. . . . I hope he is safe. . . . Dying of a mortification it was thought provident to provide several necessary articles as soon as possible. Have been employed since in giving the requisite orders.

Monday, 20 April
My wife and I with our children etc attended him to Sculcoates where he was deposited according to the wish he expressed in a deep and dry grave. I had him laid in the church. It was a very solemn scene.

Wednesday, 22 April
When I was thinking how I was to answer all the necessary expenses of putting the family into mourning etc. Mr Gilder called with a second division of the money raised by the sale of the stores of the ship *Benjamin*. It came very opportunely and being quite unexpected I could not but view the hand of Providence in it. I have been attempting to prepare a sermon for the thanksgiving day which is to be tomorrow [for the recovery of George III].

Monday, 27 April
I have found it a very trying day having my poor father's things to remove from his late residence to my own.

Friday, 1 May
I have been in my study the greatest part of the day, transcribing the sermon I delivered on the day of thanksgiving as several of the hearers have expressed their desire to see it in print.

Monday, 4 May
Revised the sermon on the Thanksgiving for the press. . . . Conversed with Mr Prince about printing.

Thursday, 7 May
The annual lecture being at Cottingham. . . . After which an address to His Majesty upon his recovery was drawn up.

Friday, 8 May

The forenoon taken up in going to the different ministers for them to sign the address to His Majesty.

Tuesday, 12 May

The Thanksgiving sermon being published today I have been closely engaged.

Thursday, 14 May

Correcting the sermon in the morning which has a word printed wrong in it.

Friday, 15 May

Wrote several letters and packed up several parcels of sermons to accompany them.

Lord's Day, 17 May

John was taken very ill in the morning just as we were preparing for chapel, which fluttered me very much, but is better this evening.

Monday, 18 May

We were much alarmed this morning about John. He was taken very ill about 9 o'clock. Said he could not see and was very heavily afflicted. We sent for Dr Baynes who said it was a fit of the Kataleptic kind. For a considerable time he lay to our idea dying and it was near noon when he began to revive. Physic was ordered but he was obliged to take a large quantity before a passage could be obtained. He appears much better this evening.

Tuesday, 19 May

I have got two load of gravel into the garden today, which engaged much of my attention. Whether I overdid myself I know not, but I have been very bad of the headache all this evening. To such a degree that I could not hold up my head.

Monday, 25 May

After ten Mr Levett came on to propose taking me in a single horse chaise to Bridlington, otherwise I was to have gone early this morning.

Tuesday, 26 May

About five this evening Mr Levett, myself and my daughter Hannah in one chaise, Mr and Mrs Rust and their daughters in another, set off for Bridlington. Arrived about half past eight at Driffield, where we lodged the night. No accident and many mercies in the course of this day.

Wednesday, 27 May

Got no sleep thro'the night. Left Driffield about six and at about half past eight arrived at Bridlington Quay.[150] Breakfasted and obliged to hurry up to the town and immediately to the Chapel. . . . In the evening I was called unexpectedly at the particular desire of several persons to preach a lecture. Had not above ten minutes notice.

Thursday, 28 May

Got up about 5 this morning. Walked up from the quay to the town but returned to breakfast. Moving about all the forenoon . . . left Bridlington between two and three, and reached Hull a little after nine. Have been mercifully preserved in this journey tho' very near being overturned by running upon the curb stone upon a bridge. If we had gone over the fall had been great and we must have gone into the water.

Lord's Day, 31 May

I this day received a very kind and affectionate letter from my much honoured and valuable friend John Thornton Esq, containing £20 for myself and £10 for the poor.

Wednesday, 17 June

Revised part of an essay on the slave trade written by a friend. Wrote to Mr Dilly the bookseller upon the subject.

Thursday, 18 June

Dined with Mr Spyvee and afterwards drank tea with Mr B Wright at their country house.

Monday, 22 June

I this day sent 10 guineas to my printer for the last volume of sermons. Hope that in time I shall be able to get him paid.

Lord's Day, 12 July

I read more in the family than usual. This evening William being at home and fond of hearing of wars, I read the history of Judas and Maccabeus and afterwards the first Dialogue in Social Religion. I was tired with the exertion in reading, sooner than they were in hearing.

Lord's Day, 19 July

Mr Mason preached again this morning.

Thursday, 23 July

I last night eat some plumb tart and a little new cheese to my supper. About half past one this morning I awoke very ill. Broke out onto a profuse sweat all over me. Apprehended that I was dying. The wind soared from my stomach in the most astonishing manner as I once heard a person who was dying of the gout at his stomach. I took various things and kept parting at seasons with pieces of the cheese and the skins of the plumbs. What was emitted from my stomach was in a state of the greatest fermentation. About four I began to settle and got to bed, but got very little sleep after that, and that afforded me no refreshment.

Thursday, 30 July
In the morning before breakfast I made the wine which had been preparing before. Got it into casks.

Thursday, 13 August
In the evening settled with the printer the balance of his account for printing the volume of sermons. Have also had a great deal to do in settling some people in seats at the Chapel.

Thursday, 3 September
Ever since Monday, August 17, I have been at Scarbro'. In which time I have bathed 12 times, preached 5 and lost two heads of families out of the congregation. I this day returned. Set off from Scarbro' about 10 and got to Hull a little after 8. Was privileged to find my wife and family well.

Saturday, 5 September
Was very much affected at two to hear that my kind friend Mrs Burn had lost her son Gilbert. He was one of the first children that I baptised[151] and this was the last voyage he had to make during his apprenticeship. He fell from the mast on to some of the rigging and from thence into the sea as the ship was in full sail.

Monday, 21 September
Got up about five and bathed at 6.

Tuesday, 22 September
Bathed about 7.

Wednesday, 23 September
Bathed about half past 7 this morning.

Thursday, 24 September
The expenses for Samuel run high but have to be exceeding thankful that the accounts are so pleasing and that in the last year he had £25 allowed for his services.

Friday, 25 September
As I had bathed the four past days I this day took some sea water. Have been not very well before and since.

Monday, 30 September
In the evening saw the fireworks which were exhibited in the Market Place.

Saturday, 10 October
In the morning took some sea water as I was taken very poorly last night.

Wednesday, 14 October

We were much alarmed this evening by the Transports[152] making their escape out of the gaol. It happened soon after it was dark.

Wednesday, 21 October

I have been much indisposed thro' the day with a pain all over my limbs, something I rather think of the rheumatism, whether from going out last night after being confined thro' the day or whether from bathing I cannot say.

Monday, 26 October

After dinner went to Sculcoates to see the stone laid upon my father's grave.

Thursday, 29 October

Having being much confined in the course of the days past, I took a walk this morning on the Humber bank.

Monday, 16 November

I was very much alarmed this forenoon by my wife falling down stairs. She was coming down with a bowl of flour in one hand and some dirty cloths in the other when her foot slipped and she fell. When I got to her she lay like a person dead. Her left eye was closed and swelled under it large as a walnut. I was much afraid that the eye was out. I sent for a surgeon who bled her. She is very much bruised but thro' mercy no bones are broke.

Thursday, 3 December

Heard a lecture in Dagger Lane. The gentleman who preached was from York. I think I have not heard so strange a discourse for many years. He was a violent Supralapsarian[153] in sentiment but without common abilities. The whole consisted of naïve bold assertions and unconnected sentences. The Gospel suffers much from such imprudent preachers of it.

Wednesday, 16 December

I this day went to Beverley to consult with Dr Sampson respecting my complaint. The coach was at the door before I could get to speak with him and I was obliged to come away without his having time to write but he promised to write by the post.

Thursday, 17 December

In the forenoon I walked upon the dock[154] side for the benefit of my health.

Friday, 18 December

In the forenoon I walked upon the banks of the Humber.

Monday, 21 December

Rode as far as the Turnpike House[155] in the morning. But the horse taking fright in returning. I got home as soon as I could.

1790

Friday, 1 January

I have now entered upon a new year like a traveller upon a journey in which he knows not what may befall him in the way or whether he shall ever reach to the end. ... I walked upon the Beverley Turnpike till it was dinner time.

Tuesday, 12 January

Called upon several friends in the morning and got a single turn upon the dock side.

Wednesday, 13 January

The forenoon taken up with the committee at the library.

Tuesday, 26 January

We have been brewing today which has taken up part of my time. ... After dinner I went on to William and fetched him home, being very ill of a cold with symptoms of a fever.

Friday, 29 January

About nine this morning I went for the physician who has prescribed for him, but he has been very full of pain thro' the day.

Monday, 1 February

My time has been very much taken up with Messrs Williams, Leggatt and Smelley who called upon me relative to the business of the Test and Corporation Acts.[156]

Saturday, 20 February

At noon took a walk, and after dinner sat down to compose a second sermon. But in the evening my wife was taken very poorly, and I was obliged to leave all and run for the nurse and midwife but she afterwards settled.

Thursday, 4 March

Walked to Mr Portas's garden in the forenoon.

Tuesday, 9 March

Have been brewing, and bottling the wine.

Friday, 12 March

The bricklayers have been building up [the] chimney in the back kitchen, but I have not been much with them.

Lord's Day, 21 March
As I had just begun the sermon in the forenoon a young person was taken with a fit which discomposed me much. I apprehended that he was taken out dead till after the service.

Wednesday, 31 March
Drank tea this afternoon with Mr Rhodes. Conversation turned principally upon the repeal of the Corporation and Test Acts and upon the Bristol Tontine.[157]

Thursday, 1 April
I have this day put into the Bristol Tontine in the names of two of the children.

Wednesday, 7 April
A very dreadful fire broke out in Blackfriargate which I feared would be of very awful consequences as the wind was very high and it was some time before the engines could be got.

Thursday, 8 April
I this day received a letter from Samuel at London which gave me some concern as he seems dissatisfied with his present situation; and of all persons has reason to be most thankful.

Tuesday, 13 April
My wife has been poorly all day till about 7 this evening when she was very mercifully appeared for in the hour of extremity and delivered of a daughter.[158] May the addition to our family be a blessing and the Lord be honoured in it. She had many fears beforehand, but had a very favourable time.

Thursday, 22 April
I was obliged to go out, tho' very unfit for it, as far as North End.[159]

Tuesday, 27 April
In the forenoon Mr Williams baptised our daughter Maria.

Monday, 3 May
As I rested very poorly last night about 5 this morning I got up and took a long walk. I[t] was a most delightful morning, the larks were singing and everything appeared in what Milton calls Nature's Morning Prime.[160]

Monday, 10 May
Attended with the Committee to examine the children placed out at school. There have been 31 taught in the course of this year, and it gave me pleasure to find the progress they had made.

Tuesday, 1 June
Took down 3 of the beds.

Wednesday, 2 June
Took down the other two beds after I had bathed in the morning. Called in Dr Bridges[161] in connection with Dr Baynes about William's knee. They have ordered a blister upon it.

Monday, 21 June
This being the day of the General Election, I have done very little but ramble about. There has been no opposition[162] but a great deal of bribery and corruption. May I give all necessary diligence to make my own calling and election sure.

Tuesday, 22 June
After dinner we had one of the most violent storms of thunder, lightning, rain and hail that I ever remember to have seen. The last was as large as a common nut.

Friday, 16 July
Took down the green bed and afterwards helped to pull the furniture in pieces in order to its being dyed.

Thursday, 6 August
I was called to Miss Mary Brown who has been next door to us for the benefit of the air for some time past. Found her very ill and labouring for breath. Have been with her most of this day. About 8 this evening she grew very sleepy and expired in that situation without sigh, groan or struggle. Her complaint was a dropsy in the chest brought on I apprehend by grief of mind thro' a versality of mind respecting the man she should have. She was going to be married to a very worthy person. Then thro' persuasion of a sister drawn to fix upon another whom she passionately loved and of whom she was disappointed by his youth and being removed abroad.

Thursday, 19 August
Yesterday morning Mr Levett and I set off for Cave. Got there about 9. After breakfast walked out. In the afternoon drank tea with Mr Dalton of North Cave; had the most delightful walk back to Mr Levett's in as fine an evening as I ever saw. Got very little rest in the night. This morning rode to Hotham to visit Mr Stillingfleet. His gardens are admirable indeed. Returned by North Cave to Mr Levett's to dinner. About five set off for Hull. Called at Kirk Ella and drank tea with Mr Wright and after a pleasant ride got home about half past 8 and found all well, but myself rather fatigued.

Monday, 30 August
Bathed in the morning. Called upon several friends in the forenoon. But I was so lame with a hurt I got in my foot while in the water on Friday that I was glad to get home.

Lord's Day, 12 September
Mr Levett fetched me to William. He had been poorly for a day or two past, and had got a tooth drawn. They apprehended that he had been in a fit. I found him very delirious. Returned home and by the advice of my wife got him removed home in a coach. He continues very insensible.

Monday, 13 September
I account it a great mercy that reason is restored to my son.

Tuesday, 14 September
William had another fit this evening.

Wednesday, 29 September
Jane Taylor, who has lived twice with us, this latter time upwards of two years, this day left our family and another came into it. I am concerned that the former has improved no more while in the family, and this I expressed to her in as tender a manner as I could before we parted. May the change be in mercy to her and to the other who has entered.

Tuesday, 5 October
A little before 7 my wife set out for Swanland in a single horse chaise with Mr Riddell.

Saturday, 9 October
Wrote to my wife and to my son Samuel.

Friday, 15 October
About 4 this afternoon my wife arrived from Swanland in good health and in comfortable circumstances.

Tuesday, 19 October
In the forenoon I walked a little on the Humber bank and found some pleasure in my mind while musing by myself.

Tuesday, 26 October
I sat the second time with Mr Porter for my picture.[163] It takes up much time, and, was it not to oblige several friends, I should not have consented.

Wednesday, 27 October
Sat for the last time for the portrait.

**11 George Lambert; probably portrait by W.Porter (fl.1788-1802, London)
Ferens Art Gallery; pastel 51 by 40 cm**

Saturday, 30 October
I have been engaged most of the day in applying to friends for assistance in the case of Pickering.

Lord's Day, 31 October
[Full collection for Pickering chapel – £26].

Wednesday, 3 November
Mr McGeorge preached the lecture. . . . The language he used was good but I did not think that he entered much into his subject. . . . The orator may amuse the ear, but the Christian minister has to do with the judgment and hearts of his audience.

Saturday, 6 November
George continues very ill of a fever.

Monday, 8 November
George very ill but we hoped rather better till this evening when I did not like the symptoms and sent for the apothecary. But he gives hopes of his recovery.

Wednesday, 10 November
I have this day heard of the death of my valuable friend Mr Thornton. Blessed be God for all the favours I have received thro' him as an instrument. His death will be much felt both in the church and world for his liberality was confined neither to party nor nation but diffused thro' the world.

Thursday, 25 November

A very affecting Providence happened yesterday. One of my hearers who had been detected in stealing from his master (but on account of his wife who is a member), suffered to go unpunished, as he was working on board of a ship fell into the hold and died in a very short time after. How true the remarks of Solomon that he that being often reproved and hardeneth his neck shall suddenly be cut off and that without remedy.

Wednesday, 15 December

This day opened with a very heavy trial thro' my son William's imprudence. I know not how to act between a detestation of sin and the duty of a parent. May he see his folly and guard against such imprudence for the future.

Notes to Vol 5

[148] *11 February 1789.* See 14 October 1784.

[149] *17 February 1789.* Socinians: A Unitarian sect, founded by Italian reformers, Lelio Francesco Maria Sozini and Fausto Paulo Sozini.

[150] *27 May 1789.* Bridlington Quay (Key in GL's spelling) was the shore-side fishing village some distance from Bridlington Town. The advent of the railway in 1846 transformed Bridlington Quay into a flourishing seaside resort and it became more important than the original town.

[151] *5 September 1789.* GL baptised Gilbert Burn 25 March 1770.

[152] *14 October 1789.* Transports: GL means criminals sentenced to transportation, a system which began in 1787. Hull prisoners would be taken to a collecting point near London for the journey to Australia.

[153] *3 December 1789.* Supralapsarian: Believer in the form of Calvininism which maintained that the fate of individual men was predestined before the fall of Adam.

[154] *17 December 1789.* The first dock, known simply as The Dock (1778), was renamed Queen's Dock after Queen Victoria's visit to Hull in 1854.

[155] *21 December 1789.* Turnpike House. Either the Turnpike House at Newland on the Beverley Turnpike, or the Wold Carr Toll Bar on the Anlaby Turnpike.

[156] *1 February 1790.* The Corporation Act (1661) and the Test Act (1673) required all holders of public offices to receive communion in the Church of England and to take oaths of Supremacy and Allegiance to the King.

[157] *31 March 1790.* Bristol Tontine. A tontine was a speculative investment, each investor naming a person or persons who, it was hoped, would live a long time (as GL did his children); those who had selected the longest-living nominees shared the proceeds. Tontines were used in Bristol to raise money for the many developments of this period.

[158] *13 April 1790.* Maria Lambert.

[159] *22 April 1790.* North End: the area near North Bridge.

[160] *3 May 1790.* Possibly a reference to 'The morning shines, and the fresh field / Calls us; we lose the prime . . . ' (*Paradise Lost*, Book 5)

[161] *2 June 1790.* Daniel Bridges was one of the first three physicians at Hull General Infirmary from 1782 to his death in 1792. Also a flourishing oil miller.

[162] *21 June 1790.* Samuel Thornton and Aubrey, Earl of Burford, were elected unopposed.

[163] *26 October 1790.* Portraitists were often peripatetic. A W Porter, essentially a miniaturist, exhibited in London, 1788-1802.

Vol 6 1791-1794

1791

Tuesday, 4 January

I this day received the affecting tidings of the death of Mrs Sommerville, my wife's sister.[164]

Wednesday, 12 January

This evening proved quite a storm. I lost my hat going to Chapel, got very wet on my head and, having to turn back for another, was late at the lecture.

Monday, 7 February

This has been a day of great trial for me. Mr Rhodes having sent a letter addressed to the Church, desiring communion with them, but at the same time denying the doctrine of the Trinity, I had mentioned it to several of the members, who had observed that, upon the admission of such principles into the Church, they should withdraw. To propose a person of sentiments so opposite to my own and when I knew that, was he received by a majority, it would cause a considerable rent in the Church, I told Mr Rhodes that I neither saw it my duty to do it, nor would. He resented it highly and was very warm. I afterwards received a letter from Mrs Rhodes informing me that they should withdraw from the place, that her father Mr Riddell talked of dissolving his relation to the Church, and a message was sent by them to the Chapel that their pew might be let. May the Lord support me in this day of trial. I am sure I have no resentment against the man; yea, I esteem him. The preservation of Truth, and the peace of the Church is, I can appeal to God, the whole that I have in view.

Lord's Day, 20 February

My mind has been very much agitated of late about Mr Rhodes's case. I wrote to Mr Bennett for his advice and the opinion of the lecturers at Broad Street; they have decidedly given it against his admission.

Monday, 21 February

Mr Riddell called upon me this forenoon and stayed till near one o'clock. I read him the copy of the letter I sent to Mr Bennett and the answer I received respecting the case of Mr Rhodes. The answer was quite determinate against his being admitted. We had a long conversation about the subject; he took it far better that I expected and we parted in a very friendly manner.

Lord's Day, 6 March

One member was charged with falsehood and I confess things appeared dark against him. Another with secreting things that her husband had stolen from another but who pleaded and I hope was innocent. A third, who is a man in good circumstances, was detected in stealing the provision from a neighbour's cattle and in doing this repeatedly and almost constantly. He was once in a very promising state and very regular and exemplary in his attendance under the means of grace but since he married a woman of no very good fame he became very remiss. I had spoken to him upon the subject and he pleaded the distance of his residence and the cattle he had to attend to etc. On this occasion he confessed the fact but was so overpowered with shame or grief that he could hardly say yes when a friend proposed to go and pacify the injured person who had applied to the Justices and only waited the result of our meeting whether he should prosecute him or not. A fourth who professed to receive his first serious impressions under my ministry and who has been several years in the church goes to hear at another place in the morning and never comes with us to the Lord's Table.

Wednesday, 9 March
Dined with Mr Wright in Mytongate.

Lord's Day, 20 March
Before I went to the place of worship, William Baird came on in great distress, informing me that his son had absconded from his master on Thursday last and had not been since heard of. When I got to Chapel I could see nothing of my son William. Mr Popplewell looked much about, in my idea as if looking for him. My fears were much alarmed, fearing he had been near the water and had fallen in. How I got thro' the service I know not, but to myself it was with great confusion. At noon upon going to Mr Levett's I found him at home thro' a hurt he had received yesterday. Drawing up a great weight with the crane, he was overpowered and the handle [hit] him over the face and had bruised him much and swelled up his eye. According to his own representation, it was little short of a miracle that he was not instantly killed.

Wednesday, 23 March
My sight fails me very much, which renders preaching in the evening very difficult as I use notes and have never made use of glasses in the pulpit; but this evening I did better than for some time past.

Lord's Day, 10 April
I have this year entered upon the 23rd year of my ministry at Hull.

Monday, 9 May
On Saturday I set off for Burlington and got there about 6 in the evening fatigued beyond anything that I had ever experienced. ... Today after dinner returned to Hull, much wearied about half after 8.

Lord's Day, May 29

I rode to Swanland in the morning where I have been preaching today. . . . The horse I rode flew out of the road in passing a carriage, but mercifully I received no harm.

Lord's Day, 12 June

I feel as if I should not be able to go on long in the ministry thro' weakness but perhaps may be prevented from other causes. At present we enjoy peaceable times, but how long they may be continued God only knows. It was my opinion several years ago that if the Americans had been overcome, the Dissenters would soon be crushed in England. At present the Ministry (if not one higher) seems to be much against them; and the clergy are quite violent. At the Visitation last week at Beverley, a very inflammatory sermon was preached in opposition to the Dissenters at Beverley. It is not improbable that troublous times are coming.

Lord's Day, 19 June

The intention of my preaching upon [John, 3.14] was to introduce the boxes which were that day fixed to receive the weekly collections. One pound 16 shillings were found in the four boxes.

Monday, 18 July

We have been much alarmed today with the report from Birmingham of the riot raised and persecution of the Dissenters. They are burning down their meetings and destroying their houses and property.

Thursday, 21 July

The mob has done amazing damage at Birmingham.[165] The loss is estimated at 300 thousand pounds. Their depradations lasted four days, but the military have got there and the mob are now following the same work in the country. Where it will end God only knows.

Friday, 12 August

Wrote to Mrs S Robinson and paid a very unjust demand of her for teaching two of my children.

Lord's Day, 21 August

My brother Sommerville, living with us, was so kind as to preach for me. . . . I afterwards called the church together, laid the case of a member under suspension before them, and he was ordered to be reinstated in his place and privileges.

Lord's Day, 28 August

My poor daughter Maria has been very bad, and continues so; the Lord prepare her and us for whatever he has appointed.

Lord's Day, 4 September

My dear child Maria has been very ill since the 28th ult. On last Lord's day she was blistered, which did not act well. Since which times our minds have been exercised between hope and fear. Yesterday morning, after a very heavy night she seemed to revive and took much notice of us. Towards the evening convulsions came on, we thought her dying several times; but this morning about 10 minutes after 2 she expired. She was a very lovely and engaging babe, and discovered very strong marks of intelligence and affection.

Wednesday, 7 September

I have been called this day to follow my dear Maria to the silent grave, and deposited her with my aged father at Sculcoates.

Wednesday, 14 September

Yesterday and the day before I have been much engaged in preparing a vault in the chapel and removing John and Maria into it.

Lord's Day, 18 September

Mr Rhodes preached this day for Mr Beatson, and after sermon in the afternoon opened his case. Reflected upon the church in Fish Street for not receiving him into communion and asserted that the reason was that they looked upon him as an Arian, which was a very false representation; for it was his avowing that he was a Sabellian[166] and refusing to subscribe to the doctrine of the Trinity that he was refused. It has made a great noise in the Town; but I am well satisfied that he was not admitted into the Church, as I have reason to believe he would have been a very troublesome member in it.

Wednesday, 21 September

In the morning engaged with the joiner who was fixing some shelves in the study. Preached this evening. . . . There were many more people than usual, I apprehend expecting that I should take some notice of what Mr Rhodes had said on Sabbath day; but if so left them disappointed.

Wednesday, 28 September

After dinner we went as far as Newland Tofts to drink tea with Mr Puckering. We had a large party and a very agreeable excursion. Upon our return home we were informed that William had again put out the bone of his foot. This is the third time, and I fear he will be lame for life.

Thursday, 29 September

My son William has been obliged to go again to Nafferton to have the bone in his foot set. This is the third time it has been out and I cannot but fear the consequence may be bad. It will be a great mercy if he be not lame for life.

Saturday, 8 October

This forenoon my son Joseph was walking in the Butchery[167] when a coal porter pushed him down, just as a waggon loaded with furniture was going by; the hinder wheel went over his body and crushed him very much. Had it been both the wheels or had that gone over his head or breast, thighs or legs, it must either have broken his bones or killed him on the spot. He was brought home and bled directly and got to bed. He fainted twice or thrice; after which he seemed better, but upon being got up again fainted afresh. What will be the event we cannot say at present.

Lord's Day, 9 October

Mr Leggatt and I have changed pulpits. I went to Cottingham this morning. Preached to a very small congregation. . . . I had very little liberty in the work and a strong impression on my mind that I should never preach more in that place. It might probably arise from the idea that Mr Leggatt was about to leave them; and a fear that they would not get the Gospel after his removal. . . . Joseph is much better.

Monday, 10 October

Joseph was got up this morning and desired that we would put on his clothes. I did so. When I had dressed him the track of the wheel that had gone over him was very visible. The waggon that passed over his body weighed 16 hundredweight without any thing in it. It appears nothing short of a miracle in Providence. . . . I this day went to see the place, to notice if I could trace out any natural means of the preservation but, the more attentively I viewed it, the more evidently it appeared to be all of God.

Lord's Day, 6 November

The collections of the day for the poor at the table and in the boxes amounted to £7.1.6¾.

Thursday, 10 November

I have been out at dinner and either to tea or supper all this week which has left me empty as a sieve; without affording any means for a fresh supply.

Friday, 25 November

My dear son Samuel left Hull about 3 this afternoon in his way for London. I have been favoured with his company above a month. But the parting hour came as it must with all that I stand connected with in this world. I accompanied him to the boats, but he would not suffer me to go over the Humber. I have been very uneasy about his travelling in the night as there is no benefit from the moon.

Wednesday, 30 November

This morning about ten Mr Riddell accompanied me to Newland Clough[168] to converse with I Breeding [?] who, tho' a member of the church and under rebuke, never attends, but he was not at home. It was very pleasant when we set out, but rain came on as we got to the house and we were obliged to return in it.

Lord's Day, 4 December
Early this morning I had a singular dream about my dear Maria. I thought that she was brought home in her coffin. Upon it being opened, she was alive – eat, drank, walked and appeared uncommonly lively with her eyes. I thought that I said she should not be buried again. Then awoke, and found it to be about the same time in which this day three months I saw her expire. For a time it affected me very much, lest she should have been buried alive, but upon recollecting the time she was kept and the evident marks there were of her being in a putrid state, that idea was soon removed. Sweet babe, I loved her much.

1792

Thursday, 5 January
I have been very much engaged this week about a dispute which has risen about the ground which should have been secured to the Chapel by Samuel Wright Esq. Monday a meeting of the Trustees was called when an attorney was desired to speak to Mr Wright. Tuesday afternoon he sent for me. Wednesday morning Mr Gilder and I again waited on him proposing to give him up 5 feet in breadth. This morning a meeting was called to confirm it and this evening he proposed 8 feet, when it was ordered that the Trustees would treat no further and that if he would not comply their lawyer should proceed.

Lord's Day, 15 January
[Preached an old sermon, from Isaiah 50.10 'Who is amongst you that feareth the Lord?']. I could but notice something particular in my being led to this subject. A person was present who seldom attends under my ministry, who had lately been in this very condition to such a degree as to be deranged in his reason, but was got better. He sat directly facing me; and I was quite uneasy lest he should think there was anything pointed or intended for to single him out. Perhaps my not being able to study as usual and led to fix upon that text was of God.

Friday, 27 January
I have been much indisposed today and yesterday thro' William. On Wednesday he fell down a ladder and hurt his knee, but did not mention it till Wednesday [sic] morning when he could not set his foot to the ground. Yesterday a person went over to Mr Carter, who this day came over about it. I was sent for and found him walking as usual. This is the 5th time he has been under Mr Carter's hands, once with his thumb, thrice with his foot and now with his knee.

Lord's Day, 5 February

William's knee was set a second time.

Wednesday, 8 February

Truly a minister's life is a series of trials. Could they see beforehand what they have to pass thro', how few would dare to enter upon the work. ... There has of late been a dispute between Samuel Wright Esq and the Trustees of the meeting about some ground adjoining the Chapel which was not to be built upon. As a Trustee I was forced to sign a writing claiming the right of the place. Hitherto he had always paid two guineas a quarter to the minister but he is so offended that he refuses to pay above half. ... Several of the members, I hear, are going to join the Baptists and have given up their seats, tho' they have never spoken to me upon the subject. A schoolmistress is also wanting for the poor girls and three of the poor members put up for the place so that some must be offended. But in that business I intend to have no hand. The more I consider the sentiments or the conduct of the Baptists, the more confirmed I am that they are like the Judaising teachers who opposed the Apostle Paul in the churches of Galatia.

Saturday, 11 February

I have this day closed up the 50th year of my life. ... I have this day been to Beverley with my son William. For several days I have been fearful that his knee was not right, and today my fears were confirmed. Mr Carter set it the third time today.

Lord's Day, 26 February

I have been very uneasy of late on account of the great people in the congregation. S Wright Esq has left the place because the Trustees stood up for the rights of the place respecting some ground and I hear Mr J Egginton is much offended because Mr Wright's pew was given to Hugh Ker Esq,[169] who had applied for it before: on this account he has not been at the place this afternoon. Sorry I am to see that my ministry has had so little effect.

Lord's Day, 20 May

The place was not so well attended as usual, I suppose on account of the New Church.[170]

Lord's Day, 29 July

This morning my son William got home safe from his Lincolnshire journey, but with much pain in his face thro' cold.

Lord's Day, 16 September

Was awoke this morning soon after 3 by the fire bell. Got up and from the back window saw that it raged violently but was at some considerable distance. It proved to be at a boat builder's in the

Groves[171] and has consumed most of the property. Tho' I went to bed again, did not get any refreshing sleep.

Lord's Day, 7 October

Poor Mr Beatson, the Baptist minister, tho' younger than myself in years and has been fewer years at Hull, was so troubled with his nervous complaint that he could not go forward with his work but dismissed the congregation about eleven.

Lord's Day, 21 October

The unusually wet weather that we have had thro' the summer and which still continues had introduced many disorders. The number of the sick is so much increased that I can neither visit them as I ought or make the provision that I could wish for the pulpit.

Wednesday, 7 November

I have this day had a very unfavourable report about my son William. Thoughtless youth, he has wounded my peace greatly and laid a foundation I fear for much future distress.

Lord's Day, 2 December

Yesterday instead of studying, I was obliged to go to visit Mrs Smith at the last mill on the Holderness Turnpike.

Lord's Day, 23 December

Agreeable to appointment, I went this day to Cottingham. It was the most severe day that I was ever out in. The wind was so remarkably high and directly in my face that I could with difficulty keep on the horse and it froze very hard. I did not set out till nine o'clock and when I got to Cottingham Mr Kidd[172] was not set out so that the congregation at Hull had left the meeting before he got to it. ... Returned in the evening and, tho' very severe, the wind, being in my back, it was very bearable to what it was in the morning. My mind has been very much hurt by Mr Kidd not keeping his appointment. Had he not received my letter there would have been some excuse, but he had both received and answered it. I should not have wished for a change at this season of the year but have been so much engaged both yesterday and the day before about the meeting at the Guildhall respecting the Declaration of our approval of the Constitution of England.[173]

1793

Tuesday, 1 January

At present, if I may judge from the sign of the times, the prospect is not very encouraging. As a nation we have long enjoyed liberty and peace in the way of our profession but certainly the Dissenters do not seem to have the favour of Government as used to be the case.

Last year the cry of Church and King raised the riots at Birmingham, and this year begins with the same spirit, while the cry is 'King and Constitution'. Yea, secretly tho' I apprehended unjustly, we are looked upon as inimical to both. The Nation and a great deal of Europe seem in commotion.

Lord's Day, 27 January

Being much perplexed and distressed in my mind with some business I had to attend to on Friday respecting my son William with some persons from Knottingley, I yesterday proposed a change with Mr Kidd. This morning I rode to Cottingham where I preached. ... I had much liberty in preaching and peculiar enlargement in prayer. I trust several of the people were refreshed as I am sure I was in my own soul. Having slept very little for several nights before, I rather think the ride was useful to me, as it proved a very pleasant day for the time of the year.

Lord's Day, 10 February

I received a letter from the Revd Mr Bennett signifying his indisposition, his thoughts of retiring and proposing my going to London to succeed him. Nothing but the idea of my not being useful at Hull could induce me to think of it.

Lord's Day, 10 March

The town has been in a state of great confusion this last week thro' the stopping of two of the banks. On which account I preached this morning from Matt 6.19, 20: 'Lay not up for yourselves treasures upon earth.'

Tuesday, 9 April

I have this day entered upon the five and twentieth year of my ministry at Hull. Of late have been much discouraged with the apparent want of success.

Friday, 19 April

This being the day appointed for a general fast. ... The meeting house was not very full. In the afternoon I heard Mr Dykes at the New Church. ... It was a very violent declamation against the French in which they were violently abused under the repeated epithet of wretches and the whole delivered not with the spirit of meekness but of wrath; not addressed to the judgement but to the passions. In my opinion it was calculated to do no real good.

Lord's Day, 21 April

The sick require my time and it appears my duty to endeavour to render them all the assistance that I can, but the healthy complain that they are not visited also. ... My sermon on Friday offended some because I could not prophesy smooth things. And I have heard of one of the members being in a very declining state.

Thursday, 16 May
Looking over my family expenses this morning and observing the great addition compared with last year, I felt my mind rather depressed and discouraged.

Lord's Day, 16 June
In the morning we had 200 of the 42nd Regiment of the Highlanders sent to the meeting.

Thursday, 11 July
My daughter Phebe had Miss Wright and Miss Rust to tea with her and in order to entertain them in the evening walked with them in the field before the house. Morris, the tenant of the field, ordered them out, struck Phebe on the side of the head and pushed her from the top of the bank into the ditch. Whether her foot be out or violently strained we know not, but it is much swelled and turned exceedingly black, accompanied with much pain.

Lord's Day, 14 July
Phebe has had a very bad night, crying out of pain like a woman in labour. I have been at Cottingham all day. . . . Upon returning this evening I found my poor child rather easier.

Lord's Day, 25 August
The meeting house having been under repair, last Lord's Day we had no service and the Sabbath before I was at Burlington. Since I got home I have had much trouble about some that have been dissatisfied about a window at the chapel, one wanting it down in hot weather and another insisting upon it being up. Also a person in the higher station in life who wished to join the church yet retain the fashionable amusement of cards, plays etc. Each of them have taken such offence as to threaten no more to come to the place. My spirits have been much cast down upon these accounts and the effects were such as to bring on a kind of ague both last night and this morning. Hindrances of this kind prevented my studying much yesterday, but after a restless night I got up about five this morning and added a little to what I had done yesterday. In the work of the day have been assisted beyond expectation.

Lord's Day, 13 October
About half after 9 Elizabeth set off for Shields on board the *Frances*, Captain Curry.

Lord's Day, 10 November
The tidings today are very alarming *viz* that the plague is broke out in America and rages dreadfully.

Lord's Day, 17 November

The Yellow Fever[174] having broke out in Philadelphia and orders have been issued to order ships from thence being ordered to perform quarantine.

Lord's Day, 24 November

Yesterday my son Samuel called on us upon his return from the North with the purpose to stay with us a few days.

Thursday, 28 November

This day I have been called to part with my two eldest children, Samuel, who has been with us since last Saturday went for York in his way for London and William [out of his apprenticeship from 31 December 1793] about noon went over the Humber on his way to the great city to look out for a place.

1794

Wednesday, 1 January

O what a year has the last been to many of my fellow creatures! What awful devastations have there been in the earth. Both the King and the Queen of France have not only been tumbled from their thrones, but finished their checkered lives upon the scaffold. An hundred thousand of the inhabitants of that country have been cut off this year by war, besides what have fallen of the Austrians, Prussians, Dutch etc. What scenes are to open this year, who can conceive? Truly it may be said the nations are mad. Despotism or anarchy seem as if they must prevail for a season. I may live to see sad or suffering times.

Lord's Day, 5 January

I this day received a letter from my dear daughter Elizabeth informing me of a very narrow escape on the first instant as they were crossing of the River Wear. The current being very rapid, the boat in which they were was near being overset and the ships coming down had like to have run them down, but by a sudden turn of the boatman they were mercifully got out of the way and were delivered.

Friday, 28 February

Today being appointed for the general fast, I preached in the forenoon from Jer 8.6; *What have I done?* A pleasing solemnity sat upon the face of the assembly. My endeavour was to keep politics out of the pulpit and to treat the subject in as close a manner as I could in an address to the consciences of men.

Tuesday, 18 March

It is a gloomy and dark day at present and a bad spirit hath gone forth. Men mistake and greatly misrepresent one another. For a man to be a Dissenter is in the idea of many the same as being a republican; nay, he is often secretly calumniated as such, and thus has his reputation stabbed in the dark. Now I can appeal to the great searcher of hearts that having since read over De Lolme on the English Constitution and Blackstone's Commentaries,[175] I not only approve but venerate the Constitution of this country; and wish that not only the form but the spirit of it may be preserved. But I know not how to account for it, of late I have had strange forebodings of mind that some heavy storm is about to break forth upon the Dissenters, and that I may suffer thereby. I have, I hope in faith, committed myself, my family and the people I have been connected with to God. Much of the last night has been spent in fear, and I hope in faith also.

Wednesday, 19 March [? GL writes 18 March, though a separate entry from the preceding one]

I heard … of Mrs Crawford in Chapel Lane being under great concern of soul thro' the sermon I preached last Lord's day afternoon. And this afternoon Andrew Postill came on in great distress of soul: he said that he had hardly had a dry cheek or a closed eye since last Sabbath morning: that as soon as the text was given out he was struck in such a manner as he had never been before.

Thursday, 10 April

I have had a very narrow escape from having a broken leg. This morning as I was going up a ladder in the garden my foot slipped and my leg getting entangled between the spells, I fell and the ladder twisted round. Providentially I fell against a wall which supported me for a season till I could get disentangled. My leg is much bruised, but hope in a little time it will be no worse.

Lord's Day, 15 June

It is this day five and twenty years since I was married. What reason have I to be thankful that God gave me so good a woman and so good a wife. She has been a helper indeed. How grateful should I also be that He that gave her has spared us together so long. That he has given us so many children, all of them well formed, and that he has been pleased to give us a supply – an ample supply for them hitherto. … The times look very dark and the Dissenters are a suspected and despised people. What is behind the cloud it is impossible to conjecture. I sometimes fear that Popery will again prevail and that we may be called to seal our testimony with our blood.

Lord's Day, 22 June

My eldest son coming to Hull yesterday, I changed with Mr Kidd today that I might have more of Samuel's company. Preached two old sermons at Cottingham and in the evening walked home as soon as I got out of the pulpit.

Lord's Day, 3 August

On Tuesday last Mr William Bowden[176] was married to Miss Burn. I was present upon the occasion and the day was spent in a very Christian like manner. Friday and yesterday the Assize was held at Hull and Judge Lawrence was upon the Bench.

Lord's Day, 24 August

Yesterday was a day of exercise. Tidings came from Bastia in Corsica that Dr Egginton was dead. His mother and aunt being at Buxton I was sent for and desired to break it out to them by letter. Mr James Smith also called upon the same business. As the painful task fell upon me I discharged it by letter as well as I was able.

Wednesday, 1 October

I have been all the day taken up with Mr Bottomley. He with Mr N Levett breakfasted with me. In the forenoon he read over at the vestry the letters etc that had passed relative to the dispute between himself, Mr Brownfield, Mr Mackley etc. Upon the whole Mr Bottomley appeared to have been very much misrepresented and injured. Dined at Mr Norrisson Levett's. After dinner called with him at 15 places. Drank tea at Mr Rust's and in the evening Mr Bottomley preached.

Tuesday, 21 October

I this day received a very pressing invitation from the Committee appointed to establish the new Yorkshire Academy to take on me the office of the first Tutor. But age, situation and principally want of abilities I believe will lead me to decline it.

Lord's Day, 26 October

I answered the letter of the Committee relative to the office of Tutor on Friday and in the negative. My son Samuel got to Hull on Thursday night and in good health.

Wednesday, 5 November

Tidings have arrived that Mr Hardy, Secretary of a Society for procuring reform in Parliament and who was indicted for High Treason, was acquitted on this day to the honour of an English jury. It has been a most important trial; and hope that it will be productive of some great events. Perhaps the thing that was intended to be frustrated may hereby be promoted.

Saturday, 29 November

A bad fever prevails in the town, some call it the Scarlet Fever, others represent it as the Yellow Fever. Several have died. They are seized with a complaint in the throat and hurried out of time into eternity in a very short space. I heard of one man who died the night he was seized with it.

Lord's Day, 7 December

Truly I am weary of myself. . . . I wonder the people are not as tired of me as I am of myself.

Notes to Vol 6

[164] *4 January 1791.* Her husband, Rev John Sommerville (otherwise Somerville) of Sunderland, prayed and read from the bible at GL's ordination, 14 March 1770 (Darwent 3).

[165] *21 July 1791.* Birmingham Riots. Joseph Priestley welcomed the French Revolution but was wrongly accused of being a Revolutionist himself. This erroneous belief led to the Birmingham Riots of 14-16 July 1791, the immediate excuse being a dinner to celebrate Bastille Day. Violence, condoned by the authorities, resulted in extensive damage to Priestley's home and property.

[166] *18 September 1791.* Arian: a denier of the divinity of Christ. Sabellian: a sect founded by Savellus, of whom little is known, criticised for failing to do justice to the Son in its theology of the Godhead.

[167] *8 October 1791.* Butchery: the narrow road from the Market Place to the Humber, later incorporated in Queen Street.

[168] *30 November 1791.* Newland Clough. A clough (often written and pronounced locally as 'clow') was a sluice. The low-lying Hull area suffered severe flooding and this was an outlet for such surplus water. Newland Clough Road developed into the present Clough Road.

[169] *26 February 1792.* Hugh Ker was a merchant of Fish Street.

[170] *20 May 1792.* Rev Thomas Dikes (also Dykes) (1761-1847) used money left by an aunt to build St John the Evangelist's church as a chapel of ease to Holy Trinity church. Opened in 1792, it was the first to be built outside the Old Town (on a site where the Ferens Art Gallery now stands) and was a great centre of Evangelical influence. Though Dikes was friendly with Dissenters in religious matters, he preferred not to cooperate with anyone who objected to the Establishment of the church.

[171] *16 September 1792.* Groves: An industrial area of flax and cotton mills in Drypool which also developed into a squalid ghetto of sub-standard housing largely occupied by Irish immigrants. Groves is possibly a corruption of Growths: land which grew (ie was reclaimed) between the natural river bank and an artificial bank erected to prevent flooding.

[172] *23 December 1792.* Rev Anthony Kidd, brother of Rev Thornhill Kidd of Cleckheaton, was appointed minister at Cottingham in 1792. In 1817 he removed to Hull, where he kept a school. The Kidds were an important family in the Congregational ministry. See Darwent 76-81.

[173] *23 December 1792.* GL was a Constitutionalist, devoted to the British Constitution, as established by the Glorious Revolution.

[174] *17 November 1793.* Yellow Fever: Scarlet Fever

[175] *18 March 1794.* J L de Lolme, An essay, containing a few strictures on the union of Scotland with England and on the present situation of Ireland . . . (1786) and W Blackstone, Commentaries on the Laws of England (1765-9).

[176] *3 August 1794.* William Bowden was elected a deacon at Fish Street in 1801. elected at the same time was James Shrapnell Bowden. Both were on the fund-raising committee to pay off the mortgage 1799. Both were signatories to the 1803 petition asking for Dissenters to be excused from training in arms on the Sabbath. William Bowden was a Russian merchant resident in West Parade, Anlaby Road, co-partner with J Bowden and W Lowthrop in Wright, Bowden & Co, and shareholder in the whaler, *Cumbria*. J S Bowden, a merchant, also lived at West Parade with a counting house at 18 High Street, and was an investor in whaling ships.

Vol 7 1795-1798

1795

Lord's Day, 11 January
After service I was obliged to stop the Church;[177] and Dinah Chapman for uncleanness was excluded.

Lord's Day, 18 January
Yesterday evening died Master James Thornhill, an uncommon child for learning. He was at school on Friday and died the next day. This morning died Mrs Mason, mother to Mr Rust, after a very short confinement.

Wednesday, 18 February
Just as we were going to bed we were alarmed with the appearance of a dreadful fire. Upon opening the window found it to be very near us. It burnt with great violence. Upon going out I found the malt kiln belonging to Reaves[178] to be in flames and without any prospect of saving any part of it. Had the wind set towards us, humanly speaking, I should not at this hour had a house to call my own. But as the wind was full east, the wind drove the flames to a quarter with which no building was connected with it.

Wednesday, 25 February
I found much pleasure both in preparing and in publishing the sermon [for a public day of fast]. But having the hymns and everything to give out was much wearied. The deacons afterwards wished for it to be printed but I have no inclination to revisit the press, nor am I able to think that much profit would follow from any thing of mine.

Lord's Day, 12 April
On Thursday died suddenly of the gout in the stomach Hugh Ker Esq. He was a member of the Church and a great and good man. Rich, yet humble, wise, yet meek. A diligent attender, a serious hearer and a man that had deep insight into divine truth. It is a great loss to the family, to the church and to the town at large. By it I have been much affected.

Lord's Day, 19 April
Last Monday we had an account of my brother-in-law Mr Ansley being dangerously ill. Many letters have passed between Samuel and myself upon the subject since; I expected a further account today, but, not hearing, fear he is worse. He will be a man much missed in the family and in the business. Preached today a funeral sermon on occasion of the death of Hugh Ker. . . . In the afternoon [preached] upon the subject of educating young men for the ministry and sending missionaries to the heathen.

Lord's Day, 26 April
On Wednesday Joseph was taken ill of the scarlet fever and sore throat.

Lord's Day, 3 May
In the course of the last week Joseph is much recovered of the fever etc. But Phebe and the servant are very poorly and this day Hannah has begun in it.

Tuesday, 26 May
We were much alarmed with George today. About 2 this afternoon he was taken ill with a kind of shivering fit as if dying. The physician said that matter was forming in the throat and ordered a blister to be laid on directly.

Wednesday, 27 May
This being the day for the Association of Ministers rode to Cottingham. The forenoon and afternoon spent together. In the evening two very useful sermons were delivered by Mr Tapp[179] of Cave. . . . Got home about ten and found George much the same as I left him in the morning, but John seized with the same complaint and confined to the bed.

Lord's Day, 31 May
This evening died John Ansley Esq, my wife's brother. He had been ill of a dropsy and a complication of complaints for some time. May I be as true and as diligent a disciple to Jesus Christ as he was to this world.

Thursday, 4 June
John continues very ill and so much afflicted with pain in his ankles that he cannot bear his feet to hang down. This being the day for celebrating the King's birthday it has been spent in a diet of noisy joy.

Lord's Day, 21 June
I am ashamed and blush at my ignorance. Clearly I have neither gifts nor ability for the ministry. How to go on I know not; nor yet dare I retire.

Lord's Day, 19 July
Thro' the great quantity of corn exported to the armies and the scarce supply of the last harvest flour is no[w] 4s per stone, starch 1s 4d the pound and every article in proportion; and it is much feared that there will not be a sufficiency to the next harvest. For as the summer is advanced we have had but 3 warm days and the sun has hardly ever made its appearance. The alarming state of things and

the still more alarming prospects led me to preach this afternoon from Hosea 7.14.

Tuesday, 28 July

Flour is now got to 4s 3d per stone and with all but the husk in it. But this day we have been much alarmed with the accounts in reference to the future harvest. Hitherto the prospects were said to be very promising but today it is said to be greatly injured by the fly, and, if it does not entirely fail, it will be a very small supply. We have attempted to starve the French and now it looks as if God would give us to know the want of bread in all our quarters.

Lord's Day, 2 August

By previous agreement I this day changed with Mr Williams.[180] Rode to Swanland in the morning. Repeated two sermons that I had delivered lately.... In the interval of the worship I was called to visit and pray with Robert Levett, brother to my servant. Yesterday he was leading hay. A boy who was frightening the birds from the Carr[181] rattled every time he passed by. He desired him not to do it again, but upon his return he made a greater noise than before. Upon this the horses took fright, threw him and the waggon went over him. He was very sensible but died in about an hour after I left him. I have not yet broke it out altogether to his sister and am almost afraid to do it.

Lord's Day, 9 August

On Tuesday there was a riot in the town on account of the dearness of provision, but it happily ended only in breaking a few windows. ... In the forenoon I had much pleasure in the work and so also in the afternoon, but being very hot several of the people were very sleepy.

Lord's Day, 30 August

I have been much indisposed all last week. Believe it to have been brought on thro' an unhappy dispute about the opening one of the windows at the meeting and the pride and passion discovered between the contending parties.

Wednesday, 16 September

Left Hull to attend the meeting[182] in London on the business of sending missionaries to the heathen. Got to London on the 17th. Preached at Tooting on the Sabbath, attended at the Castle and Falcon in the evening, when it was resolved to form a missionary society. [Many sermons preached in succeeding days.] ... Left London on the 6 October but did not get home till 8 o'clock on Saturday evening.[183]

Lord's Day, 1 November

No sooner had I concluded the service than one of the deacons informed me that on Thursday the King going to the House of

Parliament had been insulted, shot at, and his state coach broken to pieces. Where things will end it is impossible to conjecture.

Thursday, 5 November
I have been very uncomfortable in the anticipation of the return of this day as of late years I have not had in my power to speak of the nature of civil liberty and the blessings resulting from the Revolution[184] when William mounted the throne as I used to do.

Tuesday, 10 November
I have this day received some very ill treatment from one who was a mean in my first coming to Hull.

Wednesday, 11 November
This day my son William got from London to spend about a week with us.

Lord's Day, 22 November
There has been and still is likely to be much confusion about the chief seats in our synagogue. What things will come to in the event it is impossible to conjecture.

Friday, 25 December
Just before I went to preach my eldest son arrived from the north. Having seen him in good health I went and preached with much pleasure.

1796

Friday, 1 January
A new period of time, big with events to the world, nations, families, churches, individuals and perhaps myself is now opened before me. The wilderness is before me, the path is not to be traced, so full of turnings and windings is it that I know not where it may end or when it may end.

Lord's Day, 10 January
Just as I was going out to the meeting Mr Sherson of Arran in Scotland called upon me upon a begging errand for their meeting. A more inconvenient season could not have been fixed on upon various accounts. . . . In the afternoon Mr Sherson preached. . . . He spoke in such broad Scotch that I fear many of the people would not understand him.

Lord's Day, 24 January

Disappointed in the coach, I walked to Cottingham in the morning. ... Returned in the evening in the coach.

Thursday, 11 February

I have this day finished the 54 period of my life and a very painful day it has been to me. Several of the Church being offended at my daughters putting feathers in their hats which in this day have become very common have reproved me and my wife with some degree of severity. Concerned I am that ever there could be in me or mine any occasion of offence, tho' I had expressed my disapprobation with them before. However, some expressions I could not help discovering a degree of resentment against, and this has caused much altercation. The effect has been very painful to myself and family and probably others also. It also made me very low and brought on the bile on my stomach which has confined me to the bed most of the day.

Wednesday, 9 March

This was the day appointed for a general fast and humiliation. In a season when no man is at liberty to speak what he thinks, if he differs from those in power, and when to mention our national sins would be a crime, I had no pleasure in the prospect and found as little liberty in the work. ... To me it appears that this nation is verging fast towards destruction, and much I feel for my family and country. Happy shall I be to find that such forebodings are without foundation. I do love my country and sincerely wish it true prosperity. This day has proved one of the most dark and gloomy that I ever saw. It has been as if Providence had hung both heaven and earth with mourning.

Wednesday, 16 March

The ordination of two young men in Lady Huntingdon's connection[185] at Mr Barnard's.[186] I attended. Mr Frost of Beverley read portions of Scriptures, prayed and proved the propriety of ordination from Christ ordaining the 12 Apostles. It was a most superficial production. The two young men in succession then gave an account of their experience, their call to the Ministry, the doctrines they intended to preach and the reasons which induced them to prefer that connection. The former was either a very weak man in his intellects or much confused, the latter delivered himself with great confidence and energy. More like a champion in a contest than a confessor of the faith as it is in Jesus. A Mr Borrowby then prayed, and in my opinion with much seriousness and heartfelt devotion. After which Messrs Frost, Borrowby and Barnard laid hands on them, the latter, as well as I could hear, pronouncing words to this effect: 'Having received authority for the dispensation of the Gospel, receive thou also authority for that ministry and the Lord help you.' Immediately after which he went up into the pulpit and delivered a discourse. ... I must confess that I was not satisfied either in their authority or their manner of communicating it. There was not that seriousness and solemnity about the business that I could have wished. Nor were they ordained to any particular church, but to go forth like Apostles and preach the Gospel to the world.

Lord's Day, 3 April
Yesterday a man rode 50 miles to Howden and back if possible to have procured a supply.[187]

Lord's Day, 1 May
I was much hindered yesterday in visiting Mr and Mrs Penrose[188] on the Holderness Turnpike who had a child killed by a stroke from the sails of the mill.

Wednesday, 1 June
I have been a journey to London to preach before the Missionary Society. Left Hull May 4, got to Broad Street on the 6. [Preached on a number of occasions in various places.] Left London on Monday and got to Hull this evening about 5. Have been much hurried while about and on Friday so ill that I thought I should never return. . . . The church in Fetter Lane have made some overtures for my removing from Hull to London; but I came at the call of God and should not wish to remain without the same director and guide.

Lord's Day, 12 June
Samuel has been at Hull today but it affects me to see that instructions to children will do nothing unless God accompany them with his grace and blessing.

Thursday, 30 June
I have experienced a very wonderful interposition this evening. After changing my shoes and putting on my slippers, as it was near bed time, I did not tie the strings, and in coming down from my study on[e] of them got under the slipper by which mean my foot slid from under me and I fell down several of the stairs. My hip and right elbow were bruised but happily life was spared and no bones were broken.

Tuesday, 20 September
I have had a concern of very great importance upon my mind this morning. My son William wishing to fix in business, I had written to him about a house that was vacant and, having received his answer approving of it, I thought it best to apply to Mr Riddell to desire him to examine if the shop could be enlarged.

Thursday, 22 September
My wife has been extremely ill and confined to her bed all day. The physician ordered a blister and other means. I have also been about

197

the shop for William and purchasing part of the ship *Vine*.[189] It has been a day of great concern and much anxiety with me.

Lord's Day, 27 November
Dr Alderson[190] ordered a blister yesterday to be laid upon the right side which caused me a very restless night.

Lord's Day, 4 December
On Tuesday I had to attend the funeral of Mr Spyvee at Drypool.

Lord's Day, 25 December
Today, tho' a particular festival with many, I have had little to do directly with the subject of the day. . . . After shewing the grounds of this joy [Luke 24.52] I concluded by wishing all my hearers a merry Christmas from such a joy founded upon such proper views of the person, work and doctrine of Christ as these disciples had. The afternoon sermon was upon the improper manner of commemorating the birth of Christ.

1797

Lord's Day, 8 January
The Providence of God has remarkably appeared on behalf of my son William's property. As his first stock was coming by sea, a ship full of men came up with the two ships in which were his goods, but upon their firing a few guns they sheared off. Today a fire broke out in a house near to his shop. It injured Mr William Bowden but was mercifully got under. What is singular in both cases and from both elements he uninsured. . . . The hearing of the fire just as I was going up into the pulpit fluttered me much and has affected me thro' the whole service of the day.

Lord's Day, 15 January
On Tuesday last my son William opened his shop in the Market.

Lord's Day, 5 March
Having obtained a supply upon the recommendation of Dr Williams, viz Mr Spencer, he preached today but his voice was weak, his manner ungraceful and totally confined to his notes. I fear the people will be dissatisfied, altho' the matter be good.

Wednesday, 8 March
Mr Spencer preached. . . . It was a good sermon but the people do not like him.

Monday, 3 April
The Apostle exhorts to lay aside the sin that more easily besets us:[191] on the contrary I have of late been exceedingly tempted and

horrified in that way. Mentally, tho' not actually, I have been in all manner of evil.

Lord's Day, 9 April
28 years this day since I first stood up in Hull as a stated minister.

Lord's Day, 14 May
I preached a sermon for the benefit of the Hull General Infirmary... after which there was collected at the door £19.2.7¾. On Thursday I paid into the bank of Messrs Smith and Thompson[192] £20.18.1¾.

Lord's Day, 28 May
We were much alarmed last Thursday by my wife crying out fire. Going into the cellar she caught the cap on fire which communicated to her hair and had not Phebe run to her assistance she had probably been much burnt.

Lord's Day, 4 June
The nation is in a state of confusion and the Navy in a state of anarchy: report was that a conflict had commenced and that blood was shed.[193] I fear we are upon the precipice of destruction.

Monday, 5 June
George while helping to get in a chest of soap which weighed about 300 weight it fell upon him and crushed his leg and ankle much. But hope no bone is dislocated or out of joint.

Lord's Day, 9 July
One of my hearers has this day left the place because I do not represent good works as a ground of acceptance. I am thankful not for his departure, but for the testimony that he has given to the doctrine in turning his back upon it. It is the truth that offends, and there is nothing like error and sin to drive men from under the Gospel.

Lord's Day, 30 July
On Tuesday the 25 died the Revd Thomas Clarke, DD, vicar of Trinity Church in this town.[194] He is the 6th minister that has been removed since I settled in this town. I have seen Messrs King, Burnett, Harris, Jones, Robinson and now Clarke. There was something amiable in him – hopeful – and he was removed very suddenly.

Wednesday, 16 August
This evening Mr Thornhill Kidd,[195] a young man and a member of the church who I was first instrumental of inducing to think of the ministry and got under the care of Dr Williams, preached the

lecture. .... It was a sermon which indicated judgment, experience and a promising hope of future usefulness.

Lord's Day, 27 August

Friday was sennight I went to Bridlington. Preached there twice on the Lord's day. Tuesday went to Scarbro' to meet Dr Williams. Returned on Wednesday. Preached on Thursday evening at Bridlington. Got to Hull on Friday, and this day preached in the afternoon at Cottingham. In the evening walked home.

Wednesday, 15 November

This morning at 7 o'clock died the Revd Joseph Milner, lately appointed vicar of the Holy Trinity in this town. He was born at Leeds, afterwards eminent at Cambridge for Classical learning. Appointed curate and afterwards vicar of Ferriby. He was Master of the Grammar School at Hull, Lecturer, and upon the death of Dr Clarke, appointed vicar. He was a man of great learning and piety, a sound faithful Gospel minister, and much owned of God in the conversion and building up of souls. He was a lover of good men of every denomination, but as a churchman high in his sentiments. I have been intimate with him for many years, and conversed with him for a few minutes last Wednesday when he spoke very affectionately and observed that 'nothing but the doctrine he had preached would support a soul in such a season as he had experienced'. And upon my observing that I believed many were pleading for him with God not only in the Established Church but out of it, and that I hoped God would spare him for greater usefulness, he replied, 'God's people may differ in lesser things but there is one Spirit in which they are all united,' and that is the strongest bond. But as to usefulness at our time of life, we are not to expect great things, we have to be thankful for what God has wrought and it will be well for us to see that the work stands firm.' [Reprints obituary from *Hull Advertiser*, Wednesday, 15 November 1797]

Tuesday, 19 December

This being the day appointed for a general thanksgiving for the successes of our navy, tho' the prospect is so dark and an accumulating weight of taxes pending over the nation.

Lord's Day, 24 December

We have lately had some uncomfortable discovery of proud and petulant tempers in some of the members of the church.

Lord's Day, 31 December

In the course of this year death has removed that great and good man, the Revd Joseph Milner. His places both as Lecturer[196] and vicar[197] filled with those who know not the Gospel.

1798

Lord's Day, 18 February
The Revd Joseph Booker of Heckmondwike is at present at my house collecting for the support of his family, after he has been confined in York Castle for a false debt.

Lord's Day, 11 March
I have lately been overpowered with study, visiting the sick and the disorder of some of the members. Three of whom have lately withdrawn without assigning any reason. Upon inquiry into the cause, one informed me that several thought I was proud and sought only the favour of the great. The testimony of my conscience supports me that this is falsehood.

Lord's Day, 18 March
The Revd T Carter,[198] formerly of Preston in Lancashire, but lately in this town and preaching in the new chapel Dagger Lane,[199] was removed by death. . . . He was a good man, full of faith, love and zeal for God.

Tuesday, 20 March
I was this evening called to speak over the grave of the Revd T Carter. The assembly was large and very attentive. It was a solemn occasion and I had much assistance and ease in addressing the audience.

Lord's Day, 25 March
I have looked forward with some degree of anxiety to this day, especially to the evening when I had to preach upon a solemn subject, by night, in a strange place, under great disadvantages from my sight, and to a large assembly. . . . This afternoon Mr Nelson of Swalwall preached for me. . . . His discourse consisted of 6 heads, but such a multiplicity of divisions and subdivisions (not the most natural), and all delivered in such a Scotch tone that I was very glad when he had done. In the evening I preached a funeral sermon in Ebenezer Chapel to a large and attentive multitude.

Lord's Day, 1 April
Mr Nelson, who had been at Hull collecting for the case at Swalwall, is found to be a man of a very bad character and has left Hull under great reproach.

Wednesday, 4 April
We have too many meetings for speaking to the flock but no opportunity is found to get acquainted with their state. . . . It occurred to me that, if instead of a church meeting every fortnight, there could be one alternately for conversation of Christian experience it might be profitable. I intend to speak to some of the

deacons upon it; and if that does not seem agreeable, with God's aid I will endeavour to visit the church individually in the course of this summer.

Thursday, 26 April

This day died the Revd John Beatson, formerly pastor of the Baptist Church in Hull. We set out in the ministry much about the same time. . . . He was younger than myself, a wise and judicious minister, but as riches rolled in upon him his health declined and he retired from the work of the Ministry.

Saturday, 28 April

I had to attend the remains of the Revd J Beatson to his funeral. He was buried at Preston in Holderness and at the back of the church by his own desire.

Thursday, 10 May

This day my son William Lambert[200] was married to Miss Fearne. . . . We accompanied them to Welton and returned in the evening.

Monday, 16 July

Today was the meeting of the ministers at Cave. I had not been ten minutes in Mr Tapp's house before a person came running to inform us that Mr Earnshaw had fallen in the lane. We hastened to the place where we found him laid upon the ground and seized with a paralytic stroke on his right side. With difficulty we got him into a chair and carried him home. The event gave me such a shock that I could not recover my spirits thro' the day.

Lord's Day, 26 August

Since I wrote last in this book [Lord's Day, 5 August] I have been upon the ramble. Spent one week at Hornsea where I preached four times, I hope not without success. Since that I have been at Harrogate where I preached once and at Knaresbro' once. Have been at home today where I delivered two discourses.

Wednesday, 12 September

This day I heard of a very awful event. A person who has lived a very dissolute life and embraced Deistical principles;[201] and by whose company and conversation Lewis Baldwin, who formerly stood a member of our church, had been much hurt in his morals, died last Saturday in the greatest agonies of distress. His cries were so dreadful as to claim the attention of the whole neighbourhood, and he expired exclaiming that there was no mercy for him.

Thursday, 20 September

I have this day experienced a very wonderful deliverance. Going to speak to the vicar, the Revd Mr Bromby,[202] upon the profanation of the Sabbath by the military and requesting his interposition on the occasion, as I came out of the house either my foot slipped or the heel of the shoe caught upon the first step, which made me stagger down two other steps and after struggling some seconds to save myself I fell upon my right hand and knee. Have bruised the latter very much and so strained the tendons of the hand that the pain is very acute and I am able to use it very little. But my head also being much affected with pain, the physician ordered me this evening to be bled.

Lord's Day, 18 November
In the course of the last week Joseph Egginton Esq, the Mayor of Hull, having buried his wife, I gave a discourse.... Himself and the whole family attended, and I hope something might be rendered useful.

Lord's Day, 9 December
This has been a silent Sabbath. In going out to the lecture on Wednesday evening I caught cold. It was so thick a mist that little was drawn into the lungs but water. The cold lays so heavy on my head and upon my voice that I am unable to do anything to any purpose, even in the family. Mr Crackroad[203] seized the opportunity as several of my people were there to preach upon baptism, which was hardly generous as he himself had been speaking at the monthly prayer meeting upon the necessity of union amongst professors of different denominations. But we live in days when men seek their own and in which preaching and practice are different. The intemperate zeal of Baptists, was there nothing else, is to me a presumptive proof that they are wrong. They represent it as the *only way*.

1799

Thursday, 31 January
Last night I have been most grievously harrassed with temptation, and, tho' not harried to the extent, was in the course of the night pressed almost to despair that such vile thoughts and strong workings of iniquity should be found in me.

Thursday, 7 February
A Lutheran minister[204] who is come to this town to preach to the Germans employed at the two Sugar Houses[205] in this town was this day introduced to me by Mr J Carlill. He is a man of great intelligence and in the course of conversation remarked that all the revolutions now taking place in the earth are conducted by the Jesuits and intended for the future advance and establishment of Popery. [Continues at length on this theme.] ... If I did not misapprehend the sound the gentleman's name is Trevor [in fact Triebner].

Monday, 11 February

This is a memorable day [his 57th birthday, an occasion for a religious meditation]. . . . In the course of the last year of my life, my son John has been threatened by a severe illness but is now upon the recovery. My son William married and has a near prospect of an increase and my wife's health has been greatly established.

Lord's Day, 24 February

It is truly astonishing; but it proves the truth of that declaration that the silver and gold are the Lord's and that the hearts of all are in his hand. More money is subscribed than is sufficient to pay the debt of £400. There should have been a general collection today to gather in the gleanings but there was no room for it, unless the object be enlarged beyond the debt.

Friday, 22 March

This day being Good Friday my sons George and John had borrowed guns to go a shooting. I felt a great reluctance but could not absolutely refuse them. In family prayer I recommended them to the divine protection. John having an old gun, Joseph loaded it, and in firing the barrel burnt and bent like a sickle. The shock whirled him round but mercifully he received no real injury.

Wednesday, 1 May

On this day I set out on a journey to London in company with Mr Rust, Mr Sedgwick and my daughter Elizabeth. We travelled in chaises that night to Lincoln, the next day to the Hardwick Arms at Harrington, and arrived in London half past two. . . . Attended a meeting of the Directors of the Missionary Society on the 7th. . . . The next day was upon a committee for the promoting religious knowledge by little pamphlets at Paul's Coffee house at 7 in the morning; at half past two attended the ballot and choice of Directors. . . . [Account of his preaching and attendance at services] . . . Left London on the 22[206] about half after 7 in company with Mr and Mrs Ralph Turner,[207] got to Stilton that evening, the next night to Brigg. To Barton Friday morning between 8 and 9 and arrived safe at home after a troublesome passage near noon, May 23.

Notes to Vol 7

[177] *11 January 1795.* stopped the Church: detained the congregation.
[178] *18 February 1795.* Timothy Reeves [*sic*], brewer of Carr Lane. His son, also Timothy, was baptised by GL 1793.
[179] *27 May 1795.* Rev William Tapp, appointed minister at South Cave 1791. Died 1819.
[180] *2 August 1795.* Rev David Williams came from Skipton to be minister at Swanland in 1786. Built a new chapel and increased the congregation during a 40-year ministry.
[181] *2 August 1795.* Carr: the marsh lands to the west of Hull (from the Old Norse, *kjarr*). Hull's Carr Lane led to these carr lands.

[182] *16 September 1795.* London Missionary Society was founded in 1795 by a body of Congregationalists, Anglicans, Presbyterians and Wesleyans to promote Christian missions to the heathens. GL was a member of the first board of directors. The first 19 missionaries under its auspices were sent to Tahiti in 1796.

[183] *16 September 1795.* An apparent error here. If he left London on Tuesday, 6 October, and did not divert from his journey, he would have arrived in Hull before Saturday, 10 October.

[184] *5 November 1795.* Glorious Revolution. GL would have approved of the Glorious Revolution of 1688 which ended the reign of the Catholic James II and ensured a Protestant constitutional monarchy, but he was concerned about the attacks made on Dissenters as a subversive element in a period when the example of the French Revolution raised fears of similar events in Britain.

[185] *16 March 1796.* Selina, Countess of Huntingdon (1717-91) established chapels, known as The Countess of Huntingdon's Connexion, which aimed to restore what she believed to be the simplicity of the Apostolic Church. Her wealthy and influential friends included William Wilberforce. GL writes 'Huntington'.

[186] *16 March 1796.* In 1747 Rev Samuel Barnard left Ebenezer Chapel, Dagger Lane, where he had been an Independent Calvinistic minister, to found Providence Chapel, Hope Street, an important branch of local Congregationalism. He was engaged in controversies over baptism.

[187] *3 April 1796.* supply - of provisions at the time of food shortages.

[188] *1 May 1796.* The 1791 Hull directory includes Penrose & Co, miller, Humber Bank. GL baptised Hannah, daughter of John and Sarah Penrose (Sutton), 1780, and a sister, Sarah, of the same parents but with the address Drypool, 1784.

[189] *22 September 1796.* The *Vine* was probably the brigantine built at Thorne 1797. She was engaged in the Hamburg trade. See 19 December 1799.

[190] *27 November 1796.* John Alderson (1758-1829) was Hull's most eminent physician, who took a leading part in the town's cultural life. See Bickford 3-4, ODNB.

[191] *3 April 1797.* See Hebrews 12.1.

[192] *14 May 1797.* [Abel] Smith and [Thomas] Thompson's Bank originated in 1784 at 25 High Street (Wilberforce House). After Thompson's death in 1828, the bank was renamed Samuel Smith, Brothers & Co, moving c 1830 to grand purpose-built premises in Whitefriargate.

[193] *4 June 1797.* The Spithead Mutiny provoked by a demand for better conditions, was on 15 April 1797.

[194] *30 July 1797.* Revd Thomas Clarke was William Wilberforce's brother-in-law.

[195] *16 August 1797.* Thornhill Kidd: see 23 December 1792.

[196] *31 December 1797.* See 27 June 1801 for reference to the Lecturer, Rev Josiah Rodwell.

[197] *31 December 1797.* See 20 September 1798.

[198] *18 March 1798.* The *Hull Advertiser*, 24 March 1798, states that the Rev Thomas Carter, who died aged 38, was minister of the Ebenezer Chapel, Dagger Lane.

[199] *18 March 1798.* Ebenezer Chapel, also known as the New Dagger Lane Chapel, taken over from the Baptists by the Countess of Huntingdon's Connexion 1781, later passing to the Mariners' Church Society.

[200] *10 May 1798.* GL's son, William, grocer, married Miss Betsey Fearne, also of Hull, at Holy Trinity Church. GL was a witness. *Baines Directory* (1822-3) includes William Lambert, grocer and tea dealer, 56 Market Place.

[201] *12 September 1798.* A Deist was a believer in a supreme being with no specific denominational allegiance. See Appendix A.

[202] *20 September 1798.* Rev John Healey Bromby (1770-1868) served a record period as vicar of Holy Trinity Church 1797-1867. He was criticised in his early days for being merely a moral and philosophical teacher: this liberalism and lack of theological precision clearly incurred GL's displeasure. See 31 December 1797.

[203] *9 December 1798.* Darwent spells the name of the Baptist minister as 'Crakerode'. Later GL varies the spelling to 'Crackeroad'. See 5 November 1799.

[204] *7 February 1799.* He was the Rev Christopher Frederick (or Christoph Friedrich Triebner (1740-1815), who served as a minister in Georgia and suffered badly from both sides during the War of American Independence. He moved to England and settled in Hull, 'requested by some local business men to preach the word of God to the Germans employed in their sugar-houses' and others. While in Hull he produced a number of religious publications. He later moved to Leeds. See Barbara M Robinson, 'Pastor's Legacy to Hull', *East Yorkshire Historian*, Vol 4, 2003, 75-80. See 14 February 1808.

[205] *7 February 1799.* The sugar house was built by 1732 by Godfrey and William Thornton in the Groves (ie 'growths' - reclaimed land near the river in Drypool).

[206] *1 May 1799.* An obvious error here, either of departure or arrival. The journey London - Hull took up to 48 hours and GL could not have left London on 22 May and, after two overnight stops, arrived in Hull on 23 May.

[207] *1 May 1799.* Ralph Turner, merchant.

Vol 8 1799-1802

1799

Lord's Day, 7 July

Just before going into the pulpit one of the deacons remarked that, a report being in circulation against a brother, it was necessary that a note should be sent desiring him not to attend at the Table. This being so irregular as to order and time fluttered me to such a degree that I knew not how to get on in the service. Never do I recollect a more confused or uncomfortable season since I have been in the ministry.

Lord's Day, 14 July

Though I have had a great deal of uneasiness thro' the week on account of the occurrence of last Lord's day and fear the matter will end in a breach, as the manner of communicating the reproof was so ill taken as to frustrate the design; yet I have got thro' the business of the day with much pleasure and enlargement.

Monday, 5 August

Received the affecting account of the capture of the ship *Duff*[208] by a French privateer. It has greatly depressed my spirits . . . . Attended the Missionary meeting for prayer this evening, where I read the wonderful account of Dr Vanderkemp's[209] passage to the Cape of Good Hope and the narrative of the loss of the ship *Duff*.

Lord's Day, 15 September

Yesterday I received a letter from my daughter Elizabeth informing me she was to set out from London as yesterday in company with Mr and Mrs Brown and expected, all being well, to be at Barton on Monday. I do not like Sabbath day travelling, but as I could not foresee it, nor she prevent, I hope God will conduct her home in safety. This morning I received copies of 3 letters from Captain Robson upon his loss of the ship *Duff*.

Friday, 4 October

I have been hearing a sermon preached by Mr Fuller of Kettering this evening at George Street meeting. It was full of ideas, the good man's soul expanded thro'the whole – in short, it was full of God. It made me ashamed of every sermon that I ever preached or published. I sunk into my own nothingness.

Tuesday, 8 October

The Revd Mr Middleton, now or lately of Lewes in Sussex, drank tea with me. There was something agreeable in him and he related many striking anecdotes. Among others, that he once heard Dr Gifford[210] relate a very wonderful account of his grandfather. In persecuting times, after being imprisoned, on the expiration of his confinement it was agreed between him and his friends that they should meet in a wood, where he was to preach to them. Information being received of it, two officers were dispatched to seize him again. It was a clear frosty night when, upon their repairing to the place, they were found collected together. One, touched with some degree of compassion, said, 'Let us not rush in upon them poor creatures. We have him safe and as he is so old that, if he is once committed to gaol again, he will never come out. Let them hear him out for the last time.' Accordingly they sat down upon a bank and one of them seemed much struck with the honest simplicity, fervent zeal and serious earnestness of the old man. But, upon the conclusion of the service, they found that the heat of their bodies had so thawed the snow that the wet running behind them had so frozen the tops of their boots to the ground that they could not get up. The struggle they made so alarmed the congregation that Dr Gifford's ancestor was enabled to escape. Mr Middleton afterwards preached in Salthouse Lane.[211]

Lord's Day, 13 October

I was called to pray with a poor woman who had been in the pain of child bearing several days and had been under the hands of four surgeons; but could not be delivered. She expired about noon.

Lord's Day, 3 November

Of late several instances have turned up in the church of a very discouraging nature. Several given to drunkenness, one has been living in fornication with another woman's husband, another abuses his wife, and several do not fill their place in the church with regularity.

Tuesday, 5 November

Yesterday evening the Missionary meeting for prayer was held at my place. Mr Clarke of Brigg prayed. Mr Richards spoke from Isaiah 40.34. He was trifling and tedious to an extreme and detained near an hour and a half of the time to himself. Mr Crackeroad concluded with prayer, but there was so much compliments paid to the pride or folly of some ministers, particularly the zeal of Mr Richards and the abilities and usefulness of myself as was to me quite fulsome and disagreeable. . . . When I came into the pulpit [this evening] I found the spirit I used to experience on a 5th of November was extinguished by the temper of the times. My recollection failed me and my sight was so much impaired that when I turned to a quotation of Scripture I could not read it. In addition to all, the congregation were so small (probably in some degree owing to the preceding evening) that the collection for the poor which used to be from £3 to £5 was only £1.7.3½. I feel greatly depressed and discouraged; fearing I shall live to be useless or to see a reputable congregation dwindle away to nothing.

Thursday, 19 December

I met with a trial yesterday thro' the concern I have in the ship *Vine*. A bill was received yesterday for £230 as part of her freight to Hamburg. The money was readily advanced at the bank and received. But upon the bill being presented both acceptance and payment was refused. This obliged me to return £28.15 which [was] almost the whole that I had in the house for running expenses and Christmas notes.

Tuesday, 31 December

It has been a year of unusual expenses owing to the advance of almost every article, a journey to London at the Missionary meeting and the oppressive income tax.[212]

1800

Lord's Day, 19 January

I preached at the Charity Hall on Thursday.

Lord's Day, 2 March

Last Monday I received a donation of five guineas by the order of the late Mrs Robinson of Albion Street. This is the first bequest I ever received from any of my deceased hearers during the course of 31 years. She was only a hearer with us, and of late years was able to attend but seldom. I have visited her in former and in her last illness. She was a person of an amiable temper, well informed in her judgment and of a rich spiritual taste.

Wednesday, 12 March

Today being appointed for a general fast, as provision was so dear and the late harvest had failed in so considerable a degree, I seized the opportunity to preach from Ezek 14.13.

Tuesday, 18 March

My son John Lambert having for some time complained of a pain in his left side and having a deep and troublesome cough, I applied to Dr Alderson who ordered him to have a blister on his side and to take a medicine which he prescribed.

Saturday, 22 March

John Lambert alarmed me much with the complaint of a weakness at his breast: as he described it, as if all had fallen in.

Lord's Day, 30 March

I was ... informed that there had been a plan in the Cabinet to suppress the Dissenters as much as possible but that the first attempt had met with an opposition and that afterwards a more moderate scheme, but yet very limited, was brought forward and approved by all and that the proposal of Michael Angelo Taylor Esq[213] was intended to preoccupy the House of Commons as more lenient than either.... Since writing the above I have seen the outlines of the Bill proposed by Mr Taylor. It will totally set aside itinerary and village preaching and place the regular Dissenters under the power of the magistrate and lay their places of worship open to be suppressed by the slightest information from wicked and designing men.

Monday, 5 May
The Missionary monthly meeting was held this evening at Mr Lyon's place in George Street.

Lord's Day, 15 June
After the trial of one and thirty years I have reason to set my seal to the truth of that declaration [of Proverbs 18.12]. It is so long this day since I entered into the married state. O what a favour was it that I was directed to a person so suitable, that we have enjoyed so long peace and happiness together and that we have been spared to bring up so large a family and hitherto have had so much outward comfort in them (O to see the grace of God in them before we die). Hitherto we have wanted nothing that was really necessary and, tho' provision is now more than three times the price that it was when we began housekeeping and our family three times as large, yet blessed be God our bread is given and our water is sure. To his name be all the glory.

Lord's Day, 20 July
This morning I received a letter from my son Samuel informing me of his being taken ill upon the road 18 miles from Ingleton and confined at a village.... I got thro' the public services better than I expected.

Lord's Day, 27 July
All the former part of the week was a season of great anxiety. Wednesday I received a letter informing me that Samuel had not got to Newcastle, which increased my uneasiness greatly and I resolved the next day if I heard not of him to set out in search of him, but Thursday brought a letter saying he had got to Newcastle and was better; for which I wish to be thankful. What with anxiety and the heat of the weather (for we have had no rain but perpetual sunshine now for 7 weeks) I have been unfit for the study in private and public labour.

Lord's Day, 3 August
A hotter day I never experienced. When I took off my linen after the service it was as wet as tho' it had been taken from the washing tub and I was for some time as if I should have fainted. We have now been about 8 weeks without rain, and under a burning sun. The pastures are almost burnt up and the earth like heated sand.

Lord's Day, 10 August
Dr Alderson called and ordered me to take an emetic in the afternoon so that I have been fully exercised thro' the whole of the day with the poor frail dying body.

Tuesday, 12 August
I have been called this morning to part with my dear son George. He is gone to London to seek for a situation.

Lord's Day, 21 September
The first tidings of the day was that Mr Harrison Evison was dead, aged only 39. He has left a widow who does not expect an hour but she may be in childbirth and 4 children. I visited her this evening and after conversation prayed with her. She is the daughter of one of our former deacons. I was much affected indeed with the occasion of the visit.

Lord's Day, 7 December
In the afternoon, wishing to improve the event of the Emperor of Russia: a seizing all the British ships (an event of great consequence to this town)[214] [preached] from Matthew 6.19 and 20. . . . I was much confused by not being able to see my notes, and not recollecting the ideas I had upon the subject. To others it might not be so discernible but to myself it was very uncomfortable.

Lord's Day, 14 December
At noon an account came of the loss of the ship *Vine*, a vessel in which I had an 8th part. She was captured off Flambro' Head. It will be a considerable loss, not only in the ship but as the cargo was purchased for the owners.

1801

Lord's Day, 1 February
This day I delivered two discourses with as much pleasure as I had previously found in composing them. . . . From the attention of the people and the liberty of speech and thought I found in the work. I hope some good may follow. After the public services of the day I went on to see my son William, who has been all the last week confined by a fever. Though very low, I flatter myself there are some favourable symptoms of a turn in his favour.

Wednesday, 11 February
[Meditation on his 59th birthday]. Thro' the deficiency of the last two harvests and the speculation and avarice of men, we are reduced to eat bread which men would once have turned from with disgust.

Thursday, 5 March

This morning about 2 o'clock departed this life my much esteemed friend Mrs Rust. She died as she lived in peace, and an ornament to the profession she had made. And this evening about 8 died my honoured friend and brother-in-law, the Revd J Sommerville of Sunderland. He had been out that day, was then conversing with a friend, rose up to stir the fire, and sitting down in his chair died. I feel for his children lest they should not be comfortably provided for.

Lord's Day, 15 March

In the afternoon there was a funeral sermon for Mrs Rust from Paul 63.7. . . . A large congregation and very attentive.

Tuesday, 10 April

My son William's wife was this day brought to bed of a fine girl.[215]

Lord's Day, 7 June

Before I got home I was sent for by Mrs N Levett. Him I found in dying circumstances and after prayer returned to take some refreshment. Soon after he died. He was an intimate friend, once a useful member and officer in the church. But thro' a lapse he has not been in communion with us for some time.

Wednesday, 24 June

Today there has been an Episcopal confirmation[216] held at Hull and numbers have been confirmed in ignorance, error and iniquity. Many have been asked no question, others have been confirmed twice in the day, some have offered their tickets to another, many young men who came out of the country I saw in conversation with common prostitutes before their resort. One person I heard went home drunk, and all of them have solemnly vowed what they can never perform. I read over the service and, if I had not been a Dissenter in the morning, I should have thought it my duty to be one tonight.

Saturday, 27 June

This morning died the Revd Mr Rodwell,[217] Lecturer of the High Church, Master of the Grammar School and vicar of North Ferriby. He was seized on Wednesday morning after breakfasting with some friends as he was preparing to attend the confirmation of his flock. He was a young man, apparently healthy, but complained of a pain in his head and fell on the floor in a kind of apoplectic fit.

Lord's Day, 2 August

On Wednesday last I was at the opening of a new meeting house at Skipsea when I preached from Luke 7.5 . . . in the afternoon, Brother Williams of Swanland in the evening . . . and Brother Blake of

Bridlington. . . . After which I went to Gransmoor and returned the next day.

Lord's Day, 9 August
As I went into the country with my two daughters, H[annah] and E[lizabeth] to Waudby on Wednesday and saw the people in the height of haymaking, I preached this morning from Proverbs 27.25. *The hay appeareth and the tender grass.*

Wednesday, 19 August
Spoke at the Charity Hall . . . afterwards heard Mr Bowden[218] at Salthouse Lane. . . . The weather is intensely hot, and not a cloud has veiled the skies for several days. A merciful harvest time, but very trying to a feeble frame.

Lord's Day, 13 September
I read the copy of a letter from Dr Vanderkemp giving an account of an abundance of rain in Caffrerie[219] in answer to prayer. After tea I was under the painful necessity to break out to tell Mrs Hessey the account of her son George having lost his life in an engagement with the French. What a world of suffering and of sorrow!

Lord's Day, 4 October
This morning brought us the news of the preliminaries of peace between England and France being signed.[220] The horses were taken from the Mail Coach and men dragged it about the town. Blessed be God I had better tidings to announce if the people were but prepared to receive them viz Peace with God. However, as there had been great confusion at Hope chapel[221] on account of Mr Barnard, and the Riot Act was obliged to be read to disperse them, and severe reflections thrown upon the Dissenters as a turbulent set, I preached from 1 John 4.1.

Saturday, 24 October
The Revd William Small of Grimsby drank tea with me this afternoon. Speaking of the Popish bishops who were called upon by His Holiness to resign their dioceses in France, he said I suppose you know that the present Pope is an Englishman and a native of Yorkshire. This led to the following narrative: 'His parents were members of the Independent Church at North Owram. When he was a lad they sent him to school at Halifax. From thence he run away from them and got to London. In London he got to attend a stable at an inn. For his good behaviour he got to serve in the house, from thence he went to wait upon a gentleman and afterwards lived in a nobleman's family, from whom he was recommended to the Spanish Ambassador. With the latter he returned to Spain and was afterwards in Italy. All the while his thirst and pursuit was after knowledge. In Italy he was so highly esteemed as to have any situation proposed to him in Church or State. The former he preferred, and was gradually advanced till he was made a Cardinal.

Upon this advancement for the first time he wrote to his parents, exhorting them to renounce the heretics with whom they associated, and come over to the Mother Church. Upon their doing so they should be amply supplied; but if otherwise, they would die in their sins. That this letter was shewn to the Revd Mr Walker, then tutor of the Dissenting Academy at North Owram, who said he had never seen Popery so ably defended as in that letter. And finally that he was in such favour with all the Cardinals that they had chosen him Pope.' I enquired what was the name of his parents? the assumed name under which he had gone? or the person from whom he had received the account? In neither of these I obtained satisfaction. But it was remarked by writing to the Revd Joseph Cockin of Halifax I might obtain information respecting the two first; and as to the last he could not at that season recollect.[222]

1802

Lord's Day, 24 January
Last Wednesday being a most severe storm of wind, which has done considerable damage to the town and especially to the chapel in Hope Street, I spoke this afternoon from Psalm 107.29. *He maketh the storm a calm.*

Lord's Day, 7 February
Dr Alderson ordered me to be bled yesterday; but on pricking one vein they could not get above a spoon full of blood, and in the other arm they could find no vein.

Wednesday, 5 May
Left Hull for London, which I entered on Friday at 6 in the morning without accident or alarm. The next day walked to Chelsea, the place of my birth; and had many pleasing reflections while viewing the house in which I was born. ... Monday 10th attended with the Directors of the Missionary Society from 4 to 9. The public services of that society commenced on Wednesday 12th [List of preachers at various services]. ... Left London on Tuesday 25 at 5 o'clock and got home on Thursday about 4.

Tuesday, 2 June
This day being appointed a day of general thanksgiving for the restoration of peace.

Lord's Day, 20 June
This morning Mr John Coulson, son to the late Alderman and brother to the present Mayor,[223] dropped dead in St John's Church.

Lord's Day, 4 July
Tomorrow the general election for members to serve in Parliament commencing, and a strong contest being expected, I spoke from 1 Kings 18.12. *How long halt ye between two opinions, if the Lord be God follow him, but if Baal follow him.*[224]

Lord's Day, 18 July
The chapel in Fish Street being enlarging, we are accommodated by the Methodists with their meeting house in George Yard.[225]

Wednesday, 18 August
This evening I was requested to speak to the sailors at their evening school.

Lord's Day, 31 October
This day the chapel in Fish Street was reopened after the enlargement, and a very numerous assembly attended. … When I first began to preach in Hull I could not be certain of 20 hearers; and this day there cannot have been much less than 1,000.

Monday, 22 November
I this day received a letter from my son Samuel informing me that a Mrs Stead who formerly lived next door to my wife's father at Leeds was dead and had left to my family £200, whether in the stocks or no is not said. She was no relation, no acquaintance has been kept up with her, consequently no expectations entertained. Nay, one did not know that such a person was yet living and, though I have frequently been in London, I never thought of enquiring for or seeking after her.

12 Fish St Chapel interior, pre-1869 restoration (Darwent)

Friday, 24 December
A very bad spirit has lately manifested itself amongst several of the people, who, because they could not be indulged with pews to their mind, have withdrawn their subscriptions from the Rotherham Academy and the school. I cannot say but it concerns me much to see that Satan has got such power amongst us.

Friday, 31 December
I this day received a very kind and affectionate letter from several of my people, including £11 as a present for a new gown and cassock. The manner of doing it was more than the gift itself.

1803

Lord's Day, 9 January
My eldest son left us this afternoon for York. It concerned me much, but to argue or remonstrate against it I knew would be in vain. His connection with a family not friendly to religion – bad example – pleasure – and worldly if not irreligious companions – I fear have done him more hurt than all the worldly prosperity he may acquire will do him good.

Wednesday, 19 January
In the morning of the day, I was so oppressed with a particular temptation that resistance seemed to be in vain, but I have to record the truth of the Spirit being with the word: for the portions of Scripture that came in course to be read, both in private and in the family, were so directly to the point that the tempter was repelled and I was delivered. Spent the forenoon in writing for the *Evangelical Magazine*, and in the afternoon visited some of the sick.

Friday, 11 February
I have just heard that yesterday the Revd Robert Green,[226] who has preached for several years in the old meeting house in Dagger Lane, finished his course. Poor man, he had some strange and I fear dangerous ideas; having embraced the sentiments of Swedenborg,[227] he spoke very reproachfully of the Trinity, the Righteousness of Christ, and various other scriptural doctrines.

Lord's Day, 3 July
The house adjoining to the chapel, being taken for the officers' mess, we have been much disturbed both today and last Lord's day by the drums in the afternoon.

Lord's Day, 31 July
Through the act passing for arming the country and to teach them the use of arms on the Lord's day, I have much been engaged thro' the past week. Meetings were formed to prevent it, a petition drawn up to Parliament against it and deputies sent to York to converse with others about it. But every effort being too late, as the bill was hurried so precipitately thro' the House it was resolved to address the people expressing gratitude for the clause exempting scrupulous consciences, urging them to accept of it, and recommending a day of public prayer etc.

Wednesday, 24 August

This day being set apart for prayer and fasting, it was conducted with great seriousness [List of services in the various chapels].

Notes to Vol 8

[208] *5 August 1799.* The *Duff*, captained by Captain Robson, was captured on 19 February 1799 by the French privateer, *Le Grand Buonaparte*, on a missionary voyage to the Pacific.

[209] *5 August 1799.* Dr Joannes Theodosius Vanderkemp was a missionary sent by the London Missionary Society to South Africa.

[210] *8 October 1799.* Andrew Gifford, Baptist minister and numismatist (1700-1784), grandson of another Andrew Gifford, also a Baptist minister.

[211] *8 October 1799.* Salthouse Lane Baptist chapel, built 1757, replacing Manor Alley. Enlarged 1790, moved to South Street 1866 and later demolished.

[212] *31 December 1799.* Chapel funds were taxed.

[213] *30 March 1800.* Michael Angelo Taylor (1756/7-1834), a somewhat eccentric Whig MP.

[214] *7 December 1800.* The embargo on British shipping by the Tsar Paul I and the subsequent capture and marching inland of British seamen is described in Rosalin Barker's *Prisoners of the Tsar* (Beverley, 1992).

[215] *10 April 1801.* Hannah Lambert, daughter of William and Betsey, born 10 April 1801, baptised 13 May 1801.

[216] *24 June 1801.* The confirmation was conducted by Archbishop William Markham.

[217] *27 June 1801.* The *Hull Advertiser*, 4 July 1801, records that the Revd Josiah Rodwell, MA, aged 28 was 'held in high distinction' by those 'who knew how to appreciate his character': a somewhat cryptic obituary. See 31 December 1797.

[218] *19 August 1801.* Rev Edward Bowden was the son of James Shrapnell Bowden. See 3 August 1794 and Darwent 87.

[219] *13 September 1801.* Caffrerie: probably Kaffraria, 700 miles north-east of Cape Town, where there was later a missionary station. Vanderkemp (see 5 August 1799) worked in Kafirland, his diary referring to 'a kraal of Caffrees'.

[220] *4 October 1801.* Peace negotiations which began on 1 October 1801 were concluded by the Treat of Amiens on 27 March 1802. Britain was weary of war but 'the terms were some of the most shameful in British history'. According to William Windam, former Secretary of War, Britain gave up all she had taken and France kept all she had acquired.

[221] *4 October 1801.* Providence Chapel, Hope Street, was a Congregationalist chapel founded in 1797. Closed 1903. Destroyed by bombing 1941.

[222] *24 October 1801.* This story appears to be without any foundation. The Pope 1800-20 was Pius VII, born Luigi Barnabà Chiaramonte, of noble parentage.

[223] *20 June 1802.* Edward F Coulson, High Street merchant, was mayor 1801-2.

[224] *4 July 1802.* Samuel Thornton was re-elected along with John Staniforth, a new MP.

[225] *18 July 1802.* The Methodist chapel in George Yard was built c 1785. In 1905 it was replaced by Queen's Hall on an adjoining site.

[226] *11 February 1803.* Rev Robert Green was minister at Old Dagger Lane Chapel (formerly Independent), taken over by the Swedenborgians (see 15 November 1807) and used until 1840. The *Hull Advertiser*, 12 February 1803, records his age as 70, and states that 'upwards of twenty years' he had been minister of a dissenting congregation in Hull.

[227] *15 November 1807.* Emanuel Swedenborg (1689-1722) claimed that his soul had been permitted to travel into hell, purgatory and heaven, his writings becoming the scriptures of the Swedenborgian sect.

Vol 9 1803-1807

1803

Lord's Day, 4 September
Dr Milner,[228] Dean of Carlisle, being to preach this morning at St John's Church, I expected to see our chapel very thinly attended; but to my great surprise it was much the same as usual.

Wednesday, 19 October [mistakenly dated 12 October]
This day being appointed for a general fast, in the morning at 7 o'clock there was a meeting for prayer which was well attended. At half after ten the public service began. . . . The place was well filled. The congregation very attentive and on the whole a *general* fast I have not seen entered into with so much seriousness before.

Lord's Day, 30 October
A report had been circulated last week that the French had landed at Sligo in Ireland, which proved to be false.

1804

Lord's Day, 8 January
Last week a young man called upon [sic] who is an apprentice to one of my hearers who seems to be under deep concern about his soul. He informed he was born of Roman Catholic parents and brought up in that religion but has been under serious impressions ever since he first attended under my ministry, which has been for about two years. He seems to have clear views of his state as a sinner, and of the only method of acceptance thro' Christ alone.

Friday, 13 January
My time has been very much taken up today by a man under great distress of soul. He informed me that about 15 years ago he returned from Russia in very low circumstances. His father told him he would spare him some of his furniture for his rooms, for which he might pay him in future. The father, being a very profane man, with horrid oaths and curses frequently demanded the money. However, one day he addressed his father thus, 'You cursed old rogue, why are you always teasing me?' The father died in peace with him. But reading in the Scriptures that he that curseth father or mother shall die the death, it fastened upon his conscience, but of late it had troubled him. For more than a week he could get no rest night or day. I endeavoured to hold out encouragement to him upon that subject but to foster conviction on his mind, on account of his sins against God, and recommended to his attention several portions of Scripture. What will be the result I know not. But he called on me again in the evening and looked very wild under a settled gloom. I cannot but fear it may issue unfavourably.

Lord's Day, 6 May
Thro' the abounding iniquity which prevails in the town I spoke this morning from Isaiah 9.18.

Friday, 25 May [general fast]
In the afternoon I heard Mr Shirley at St John's from Nehemiah 4.14. It was a very martial sermon. But I fear upon the whole that the people have not entered into the spirit of the service today as on the last fast day. The awful impression they then felt is in great measure obliterated and more pains has [sic] been taken by some to depict the misconduct of the French than to strike at the vices of the English. There is danger that we should be left to fast for strife and debate and to smite with the fist of wickedness.

Lord's Day, 10 June
Just as I was going to the place of worship this morning I found my mind much fluttered on being informed that the place where we keep our provision for coolness had been robbed of all the meat and butter. Only the Thursday night in the preceding week the safe had been robbed of 3lb of butter etc that at breakfast we had nothing but dry bread. Certain it is that it must be done by somebody who is well acquainted with the house and where we put our provision. However, it is a mercy that they did not break into the house.

Friday, 13 July
After a heavy and dragging day I have just finished a sermon. The whole forenoon was a continual running up and down stairs, and receiving and dismissing triflers. This so discomposed my thoughts, deranged my ideas and depressed my spirits that I have been very unfit for the labours of the study.

Tuesday, 17 July
Mr Thomas Riddell, whose father was one of the first instruments of bringing me to Hull, this forenoon wrote me a very long letter, the purpose of which was that, as he had not been indulged in having two pews thrown into one, he could not attend under my ministry with either pleasure or profit and withdrew with his family. To this I returned an answer couched in as tender language as I could consistent with conscience and wished him and his much soul prosperity under whatever minister and in whatever place he attended. This was followed in the afternoon by a second letter in which he attributes the conduct of the deacons in their refusal to me. However, knowing that this was not the case and that, had they indulged him, two other families would probably been driven from under my ministry, I returned no answer.

Thursday, 13 September
Lottery. I trust it is neither from covetousness on the one hand, nor a distrust of a divine Providence on the other; but, both from age and

growing infirmities. I am led to conclude that, should I be spared a little longer, if my sight should be continued, which I often fear, I think I shall not be able to go thro' the work to which I am now called, and then I must either see the congregation decline, be compelled to relinquish the work of the ministry, or must have an assistant. In either case the yearly produce of what I have would not be equal to the supply of my family. I therefore feel a strong inclination to cast the lot into the Lord's lap, by purchasing the share of a ticket in the lottery, leaving the disposal of it to unerring wisdom. Should such a supply be added He can easily send it, and if not the loss can be no considerable injury to my family.

Thursday, 26 September

I have reason this day to set up a fresh Ebenezer of praise to the God of all my mercies who has spared me to see my youngest child (Joseph) complete the 21st year of his age. His deliverances have been great, particularly when a waggon passed over his body and a gun burst in his hands: the barrel of which I still preserve as a memorial of his escape from death.

Tuesday, 2 October

This has been an evening of severe trial. My poor dear son John Lambert left us without saying I am going to leave you. The packet he sent to his brother William broke open the business and included three others, one for myself, another for Mr Woodhouse and a third for Blaydes, Loft, Gee & Co.[229] His affairs are clearly stated, his moral character has been irreproachable. He mentions going into the country for a few months, and that we are not to expect to hear of him for three weeks or a month. But when, how, or why gone, not the most distant hint. It is a most profound mystery: for the greatest affection and cordiality have subsisted in the family. I am greatly oppressed. Lord undertake for me and keep him under thy care and conduct. I have not a doubt but that he is gone out of the nation, tho' he has not taken one thing with him but the clothes upon his back. The trial is severe, but I deserve this and infinitely more for my undutifulness and want of affection towards my heavenly father.

Wednesday, 3 October

After a most anxious day spent in the sympathy of friends, contrivance and inquiry, in the evening as I was going to the chapel praying to that God who had all hearts in his hand and individuals under his eye, that he would favour and regard my dear lost sheep, I met my dear child returning home. What I felt was inexpressible to describe. Lord thou knowest what is the heart of a father.

1805

Lord's Day, 13 January

I visited Mrs Carlill senior who is very ill.

Lord's Day, 10 March
On Friday, as the supply of water for the family is to be taken off till the conveyance is cleansed, I was forced to assist in emptying the bath, which was more than my strength was equal to and left me greatly exhausted.

Thursday, 9 April
It is thirty-six years this day since I began my stated ministry at Hull. So long the Lord has supplied and maintained me; truly I may say with the Apostles I have lacked nothing for the support of the body, the supply of the mind, the comfort of a large family or the edification of the church. From a very small beginning I have seen a very gradual increase till there is now a large congregation and a respectable Christian church.

Lord's Day, 25 August
The galleries in the Chapel being altered and a collection to be made towards paying the expenses, I was requested to preach there on this occasion of re-opening the place this day. As it has rained most of the day, I went in the stage this morning, and walked home this evening, much fatigued. I preached from subjects on which I had spoken before and found freedom of speech, but particularly in the afternoon. The collection was but small, but nearly double to what they had expected. On my return home I found the room full of company, one of whom stayed supper.

Thursday, 5 September
This evening I got home about 8 from my journey to Whitby where I have been to the opening of a new chapel. I left Hull on Tuesday 6 in the morning for Scarbro' where I arrived about 3 in the afternoon. After calling upon several friends I preached a lecture in the evening to a large and attentive audience. Took the carriage at 8 in the morning and reached Whitby about 2 in the afternoon. Preached on the Thursday forenoon on the opening the place. . . . The following Sabbath I preached twice [and] on Tuesday evening. Each time with much liberty of speech and great attention on the part of the people. Left Whitby on Wednesday at two, and after a most fatiguing journey thro' the high hills and bad roads so that I was obliged to walk much of the way from Whitby to Driffield. I arrived safe and found all well at home. Blessed be God.

What reason have I for gratitude and, more especially from the following circumstance, which has affected my mind greatly. Upon leaving Scarbro' for Whitby one the passengers in the carriage was the eldest son of Colonel Tindall, a young man of 22, going to Whitby to see a young lady to whom he was shortly to be married. On the Monday following he with another young man went out in one of the houses to bath. The sea was rather rough but they both would swim. However, poor fellow he was drowned and the body not found till the next morning about three. But what was peculiarly affecting we had to follow the corpse most of the way to Scarbro';

and, not being able to pass the procession from the narrowness and badness of the road, had actually to join in the procession.

Lord's Day, 3 November

The rapid progress of the arms of the French against the Austries [sic], our national allies, who appear from report to have lost about 40,000 men, led me to seek the improvement of so solemn and awful an event[230] in the forenoon from Isai 26.9.

Thursday, 5 December

Today being the day appointed for a general thanksgiving for our fleet under Nelson and Collingwood, I preached from Psalm 96.8. A cold laid upon my voice, which made me fearful of a confirmed hoarseness, but thro' mercy I got above it and preached with great vigour and hope not without feeling the subject myself with others. A collection being requested after the service by the Patriotic Fund for the relief of the maimed and the widows and children of the slain, the sum of £26.11.10 was put into the boxes at the doors.

Monday, 30 December

I have a singular Providence to record this day in the preservation of my son John Lambert. As he was skipping from a vessel in which he had been doing business on the Garrison side his foot slipped and he fell into the old harbour between the ship and the wharf. He sank above the middle in water, but, help being at hand, a rope was let down and he was drawn up.

Tuesday, 31 December

Today in visiting a person in English Town,[231] the road being exceeding bad, and places dug to receive the water, my foot slipped and it was with great difficulty that I recovered as nobody was nigh. Had I got in, it is very probable I should have been drowned.

1806

Lord's Day, 5 January

I fear much trouble is coming upon me in the church in virtue of two young men members of it going to the Rotherham Academy.[232] The deacons seem inclined to recommend one but not the other. Consequently no recommendation has been given to either and both stand suspended till the Committee receive it, tho' they are informed of the painful circumstances in which I am placed. Their conduct is cruel to an extreme after all my exertion in behalf of that seminary. I fear the consequences but dare not in conscience set my hand for the admission of the one to the exclusion of the other.

Saturday, 1 March

This morning at 4 o'clock died Mr Josiah Jones, a deacon of the church to which I minister. He was instrumental of bringing me first to Hull and has always manifested the most sincere respect towards myself and my family. In the early part of my ministry he subscribed very handsomely towards my support when we were few in number. There was an uncommon sharpness of expression about him and of all the persons I ever knew I never found one so deeply depressed or elevated in his spirits. Often has he appeared as in the deeps of despair, and in a few months elevated to a degree of levity, but I believe it was owing to a bodily disorder, which he called the gout on his spirits, and at some seasons his disorder bordered upon insanity. With all his foibles I have no doubt but he was a good man and finished his course with composure, in peace and safety, aged 70.

Lord's Day, 27 April

The reason of my preaching last Lord's day afternoon upon 1 Peter 2.11 was in consequence of two letters received from a person signing himself a member of the church and intimating his distress as a parent on account of his child or children living in fornication adultery. A third letter received this week intimated that the persons he wished to hear it were not present, but as they would be there this afternoon, requested me to renew the subject. Now, though I was not altogether satisfied with the manner of the application, yet remembering that if the watchman does not warn the sinner and he perish in his iniquity, his blood will rest upon the watchman's head, I complied.

Lord's Day, 11 May

Mr Offley of Wolverhampton (who came to beg for a chapel there, but found us pre-engaged to Driffield), preached in the after[noon] from Paul 40.2.3. He delivered many scriptural truths in a very unconnected manner, but which had nothing to do with his text. I felt uneasy that I had asked him, but did it lest a good man and a minister of Christ should be offended and being a stranger to him or his abilities.

Thursday, 29 May

On Tuesday the 20th we began to uncover the house in which I live in order to raise the rooms in the upper storey. So long we have been open and exposed but during all that time there has been no rain, except one shower, which would hardly have wet a cambric handkerchief. Just as the last tile was put in its place it began to rain and seems likely to continue. Thanks be to that God who has thus caused this work to prosper.

Lord's Day, 1 June

The alteration, in raising the house, has placed me quite out of my element, so that I can neither get to my books or engage in study as I could wish.

Wednesday, 18 June

My wife, and, in her, myself and family, have experienced a wonderful deliverance this day, which, as in duty bound, I here record. As she was taking an iron from the heater-stove, a large lump of sugar which had for some time hung up in the kitchen fell; providentally as she had been in a stooping posture and was rising, it struck her only on the back, near the right shoulder; had it been upon the head it would probably have proved instant death, and, even as it was, it is wonderful that a fracture or at least a dislocation of the bones did not follow. Probably unseen angels had a charge to ward off everything fatal.

Lord's Day, 13 July

We had a most awful day on Friday of thunder and lightning which continued most of the day and was very dreadful. One man killed in a boat on the Humber and 7 others rendered speechless. A mill much injured on Holderness Turnpike road, another man [sic] torn to pieces near Grimsby and many houses injured.

Lord's Day, 10 August

As Master Betty[233] is expected to perform at the Hull theatre this week and is accounted a young Roscius,[234] I preached this forenoon from 1 Peter 1.13. *Followers of that which is good.*

Lord's Day, 14 September

The tax gatherers being at this season collecting for the Property Tax, I spoke this morning from Matthew 22.21 and in the afternoon from Luke 13.34.

Friday, 10 October

A very wonderful deliverance has been this day effected for my grandchild Sarah.[235] She and her brother were at nurse and, the latter being sleepy, the nurse left her while she went up stairs to lay the boy upon the bed. No sooner had she turned her back than Sarah got on the fender to reach the rack on which they roast their meat. Her frock caught fire and she ran out of the house. Her screams brought down the nurse who wrapped her apron round her and extinguished the flame; but not before her right arm and chin were so burnt as to produce several large blisters.

Lord's Day, 26 October

As errors of a Socinian cast are creeping into the town, I preached this forenoon from Mark 18.5 and this afternoon from Mark 6.5.

Lord's Day, 14 December

Having lately heard with much concern of some of my hearers being addicted to too much liquor, I preached this forenoon from Luke 21.34.35.

Lord's Day, 21 December

I am much concerned to find the standard of error is erected in this town, tho' I have not seen it. A Mr Severn[236] who is come to the chapel in Bowalley Lane has published what he calls a vindication of Unitarianism and Socinianism. I have no fear for truth. It will stand but is dangerous and may pervert some.

1807

Monday, 23 February

This afternoon about 3 my dear son John Lambert left us to go to Manchester. As he was never from home before, has not been used to travelling, but especially as he has been such an orderly and respectable a young man and not acquainted with a single individual in the place where he is gone, I felt very anxious and was much affected.

Friday, 22 May

This morning died Mrs Elizabeth Body, who has been in fellowship with our church about 20 years and prior to that had been united to the church in Dagger Lane under the Revd J Burnett. From a young woman she has been disposed to the best things and used to attend with her venerable father David Belphrage at Swanland Chapel. She was regular in her attendance, spiritual in her conversation and found a pleasure when she could find an opportunity to do good. In her husband's time (who behaved but very ill to her) when they kept cows, after delivering her milk, of an evening in winter, she used to leave her kit at the chapel door and regularly attend the lectures and church meetings. I have lost much in her prayers, example and conversation; for she was a Christian indeed. She desired there might be no funeral discourse for her.

Lord's Day, 7 June

The election for the County of York concluded on Friday at 3 o'clock when the numbers were for W Wilberforce Esq 11,808, Lord Milton 11,177, and [Viscount] Lascelles 10,990. To allay the party spirits and passions of many I preach an Electioneering Sermon in the forenoon from Isaiah 4.2 and, as many had fixed upon the season as a day of thanksgiving for the stop put to the slave trade, in the afternoon I spoke from Gen 45.4,5,7.

Wednesday, 8 July

This morning at 6 o'clock I set out for Driffield to attend the ordination of Mr Hobson. The service began at half after 10. [Lists speakers, including himself]. It was a happy honoured day.

Thursday, 9 July

Left Driffield at 10 and got to Skipsea about 12. At two a Congregational church was formed there. Mr G Foster gave out the hymns, Mr Hawksley prayed. I spoke from Acts 13.1, after which the persons forming the church stood up in a circle with their hands joined to each other, while the Covenant was read and Mr W Foster being one of them prayed. Mr Earl then closed the service with prayer. May the Lord establish this part of his Zion. Returned in the evening and arrived at Hull a little after nine.

Lord's Day, 26 July
The aspects of public affairs assuming a very gloomy appearance. The Russians beat and peace said to be made between them, France and Prussia.[237]

Saturday, 1 August
The Revd Samuel Christian Frederick Frey,[238] son of a learned Jewish rabbi, a convert to Christianity, travelling in company of the Revd G Collison[239] in seeking aid for the London Missionary Society, this evening addressed his brethren of Abraham's race at my chapel. The place was full, tho' few Jews I fear were present being prohibited by order of their chief rabbi by an awful curse. ... The greatest sincerity appeared in the man, and a peculiar savour accompanied what he advanced. I trust he is a Christian indeed and without guile. He was 2 hours and half in the service but I think no one could say he was too long.

Saturday, 15 August
I was much encouraged this evening while reading Isaiah 37.18.19 in reference to the state of the nation. The menaces of Bonaparte against this nation after his victories in Holland, Switzerland, Germany, Prussia and against the Russians, seemed to ensure him success;[240] but from the above passage, comparing those nations with our own (bad as it is) leads me to hope that God will yet interfere for our safety.

Lord's Day, 30 August
Mr John Wray, who is going abroad soon as a missionary, preached in the afternoon from Matt 8.11. But it was delivered in such a lullaby tone, the language so poetical and the plan so diffuse that I was not comfortable under the sermon. He is a good young man, aims at doing good, and I hope will be succeeded [sic], but I wish more care had been paid by his Tutor to the forming him for a preacher.

Lord's Day, 4 October
On Saturday night died Mrs Job, a member of the church, and yesterday Mrs Rebecca Carlill senior, a member also, and just as I was entering the pulpit I was informed that Mrs Egginton had this day been seized with a paralytic stroke which affected me so much that I was doubtful whether I could go on in the service.

Lord's Day, 18 October
Dr Milner, Dean of Carlisle, preach [sic] at St John's Church in the forenoon; and the Mayor was sworn into office which made the place rather thinner than usual in the forenoon; but upon the whole there was a respectable number of people.

Friday, 10 November
After a week's absence upon a visit to J Boyes Esq of Anlaby I this day returned home with peculiar pleasure to finding family all well. Late as the season of the year is, to see nature even in its annual decay appears beautiful. The discoloured leaves of some shrubs intermixed with those which retain their verdure all the winter forms a pleasing variety. The situation is delightful and the order of living superior to mine; and everything was done to render my stay agreeable; but, after all, home has its peculiar advantages and delights. I changed pulpits with Brother Williams on Lord's Day and hope the change may be profitable to some.

Lord's Day, 15 November
After the morning service I was much affected, being informed that Mr James Burnett had shot himself about 2 hours before. He was the son of a minister, had a large family and supposed to be in a good way of business as a woollen draper in the Market Place. In profession he was a great advocate and supporter of the doctrines of the renowned Swedenborg.

Saturday, 28 November
On Monday last seized with a pain in the side which was followed with a very trying night. Applied to Dr Alderson on Tuesday. Medicines seemed to succeed till Friday when I was affected the same as last year. Bled, blistered and took an opening draught. Succeeded by a sleepless night. The palpitation at the heart continued to a great degree, and then stopped as if life was at the close.

Lord's Day, 29 November
Dr Alderson gave me 90 drops of opium which gradually overpowered the pain. . . . The Apothecary ordered me a sup of Madeira and water as he apprehend [sic] me sinking fast.

Saturday, 6 December
Many friends of my own as well as other connections have been very kind in their inquiries and calls; particularly the Revd T Dikes and Revd Mr Clarke, whose conversation was truly fraternal. My kind brother Hobson came from Driffield to officiate for me in the Sanctuary today, when a collection was made for the school. Much good I hope will issue out of this apparent evil. Thanks be to God for an all sufficient servant and an affectionate people, especially in a time when the Church and the world, the town and the nation, are in such a state of confusion. Mr Lyon[241] and his people have disagreed, and I am told he preached his last sermon to them this

afternoon. He is a man of great mental abilities and capable of great exertions, if only he be rested and grounded in the truth as it is in Jesus. But I would judge myself but not another man.

Wednesday, 9 December
Lyon has thrown off the mask and avowed himself an anti-Trinitarian, an anti-Satisfactionist. I might almost say an anti-Veritas, an opposer of all saving, sanctifying and supporting truth.

Lord's Day, 13 December
In the afternoon ha[d] some pleasing and encouraging conversation with my dear daughter Eliza. I trust God has begun his good work in her. She is diffident but I have no doubt of her sincerity.

Lord's Day, 20 December
Yesterday was highly gratified by a visit from the Revd Mr Marsden[242] from Botany Bay. His conversation was truly interesting and informing; among other things he related a visit they had from Tippai, the King of New Zealand, who abode with them four months. In person a fine well made man and of a mind attentive to every occurrence and reflecting upon all he heard or saw. Having obtained a potato from a ship that called at his island he planted it, increased the produce for himself, and when considerably enlarged he distributed part amongst his people and taught them how to cultivate them. Upon being presented with a peach at Port Jackson, he tasted it, went and examined the tree on which it grew very minutely, and preserved the stone to plant in his own country. He was also very attentive to the making of a cordage and the building of vessels and discovered some knowledge of the nations of the earth and the unity of the Godhead.

Notes to Vol 9

[228] *4 September 1803.* Dr Isaac Milner was the younger brother of Rev Joseph Milner, headmaster of Hull Grammar School, lecturer at Holy Trinity church, and an influential Evangelical leader. Isaac, also President of Queen's College, Cambridge, always regarded Hull as his home.

[229] *2 October 1804.* Blaydes, Loft, Gee & Co were shipowners and general merchants of Trippett, Dock Bridge. The *Bethia*, later renamed *Bounty* (of the Mutiny fame), was built in the dry dock alongside Blaydes House, 6 High Street, now the University of Hull's Centre for Maritime Historical Studies. The Blaydes were prominent merchants and shipowners for over 200 years and through seven generations, also taking a leading part in Hull's civic life.

[230] *3 November 1805.* On 17 October Napoleon forced a 30,000-strong army at Ulm to surrender. On 21 October Nelson secured his great victory at Trafalgar.

[231] *31 December 1805.* English Town. In the early 19th century Thomas English, a shipbuilder, developed a number of streets (the principal one English Street) near the Humber on the west side of Hull, known popularly as English Town.

[232] *5 January 1806.* The Rotherham Academy (1783-1794), based at Northowram, had removed from Heckmondwike. After its closure in 1794 it was re-formed and remained there until 1888 when it joined with Airedale College to form the Yorkshire United Independent College at Bradford, which existed until 1958. It is now represented in the Northern College at Manchester. Its first tutor was the Rev Edward Williams.

[233] *10 August 1806.* William Henry West (1791-1874), known as Master Betty, a juvenile actor who lead a brilliant, though short-lived, career. See ODNB.

[234] *10 August 1806.* Quintus Roscius, a renowned Roman orator and actor, died 62 BC.

[235] *10 October 1806.* Sarah Lambert, daughter of William and Betsey, born 22 April 1802, baptised 8 June 1802.

[236] *21 December 1806.* Rev William Severn, formerly a Wesleyan, became Unitarian minister at Bowlalley Lane.

[237] *26 July 1807.* The French defeated the Russians in the Battle of Friedland, 14 June.

[238] *1 August 1807.* Joseph Samuel Christian Frederic Frey, a German Jew from Berlin, was baptised in 1798.

[239] *1 August 1807.* Probably the Rev G Collison of the London Missionary Society. See 15 October 1809.

[240] *15 August 1807.* By the Treaty of Tilsit, 7 July 1807, Napoleon was to have all German lands between the Rhine and the Elbe and accepted the Tsar's mediation in concluding a peace with Britain.

[241] *9 December 1807.* James Lyon, Baptist minister at George Street chapel, signed the 1803 petition pleading for Dissenters to be excused from training in arms on the Sabbath. GL sometimes misspells his name as 'Lyons'.

[242] *20 December 1807.* Rev Samuel Marsden, government chaplain in Sydney, afterward the 'Apostle of New Zealand', and did all in his power to aid the Tahiti mission.

Vol 10 1808-1810

1808

Lord's Day, 7 February

In my returning home [from Fish Street] I got an ugly fall as I turned off from the walls on to the narrow flag stones which the Dock Company have laid for our new road.[243] I feel some pain in my right arm and knee on which I fell, but have reason to be very thankful that there is no broken or displaced bone.

Lord's Day, 14 February

Mr Triebner, the German minister, who is about to leave Hull, was present [at the chapel] and expressed much pleasure in being there. I feel much pity towards him and he has been much persecuted during the war in America, has been greatly discouraged while here, and is now in his old age forced to seek for a congregation in London.

Lord's Day, 28 February

Finding myself so unequal to the work of the whole Sabbath, on Thursday I addressed a letter to the deacons and church signifying the propriety and necessity of obtaining a regular assistant. . . . In the afternoon the Mayor, having requested a collection for the British prisoners now detained in France, I preached from Gen 14.14, *'Abram heard that his brother was taken captive'*. I found pleasure in the work but much fatigued after it. The collection amounted to £20.12.1d.

Lord's Day, 17 April

Today being what is commonly called Easter Sunday.

Lord's Day, 24 April

A motion was determined by the church on a proposal the preceding Sabbath respecting persons sitting down at the Lord's table as occasional communicants who had scruples or conscience about signing any creed or confession of faith. It was determined in the negative. Blessed be God who has thus far helped me. The motion originated with a person who has been a great troubler of our Israel, and fear it will still be the case as long as he belongs to the congregation, or is continued in the body. He is peculiarly ingenious in the invention of mischief.

Monday, 25 April

Received a letter from the person referred to above which I answered.

Tuesday, 26 April

Called upon the above person with whom I had conversation, but fear to little purpose.

Thursday, 28 April
Received another letter from the above intimating his displeasure with the determination of the church; requesting a copy of the case proposed to them and concluding that he might think it his duty in vindication of his character to address a circular letter to the members of the church. I hear also that two other letters were sent to two of the members.

Friday, 29 April
Prepared a letter by way of reply but do not intend to send it till after the Sabbath. I fear he will excite much trouble, for his is of Ishmael's disposition. His hand against every man.

Lord's Day, 8 May
I have had renewed trouble from the person referred to before. Intended to have sent him a letter last night but was prevented by the following article inserted in the weekly paper, the *Rockingham*. 'We hear that a few gentlemen of this place, friends to religious liberty, who consider the imposition of any human creed (by whomsoever selected, or however orthodox) as a sacramental test, to be an intolerable burden and contrary to scripture and reason, intend forming themselves into a society which will admit a mixed communion of Christians.'

Saturday, 28 May
Mr Payne[244] has been supplying for two Sabbaths with a view to inviting him as a stated assistant. It was proposed to raise him a salary by subscription, and I had concluded that the deficiency must be made up out of what I received from the pewage. Two of the deacons called on me today saying they had seen several of the people, who all appeared satisfied in Mr Payne and would be ready to come forward with subscriptions, but wished to know what Mr Lambert proposed to do towards it. I expected that it would not have been required for me to lead in the business, but if necessary to fill up deficiencies. I cannot say but I felt my mind hurt, as I have now been with the people over 40 years. Have received little from most of them but the pewage and for many years had not more than 70 or 80 pounds a year. It is only since the enlargement of the place that I have been able to square with the expenditure of the year after paying £35 interest on the debt of £700 and the income tax at ten per cent. It does not discover the greatest generosity in the people, but former strength is not to be recovered, and past services are often forgotten. However, it is all more than I deserve. All as to this world with me will soon be over, and if I cannot by any means proportion expenditure to income, I must remove myself and family to a more retired situation. That God who has cared for me so long deserves my confidence for the future. I mentioned forty or fifty pounds, which they appeared to think sufficient if not more than sufficient. But what grieved me was this, that heretofore it had always been

intimated that in having a supply there was no thought of taking anything from me; and now it was expected that I should be the first to specify what I would do towards it as a stimulus to others. The same was the case when the former debt on the place was paid off, and about three years back when the running expenses exceeded the quarterly collections. And it is not usual for the servant of the family to pay out of his wages a proportion towards building or renting the house in which he serves. In many of the people I have found a want of generosity, in a few the greatest kindness.

Lord's Day, 29 May

In the morning found some pain in my head and depression on my spirits in virtue of one of the Methodist preachers, who had been 40 years in their connection, committing suicide.[245] He was taken some months ago with a paralytic stroke in the pulpit, which has ever since disordered his senses. He perpetrated the rash act yesterday, and this with what happened yesterday greatly affected me and leads me to plead, Hold thou me up and I shall be safe.

Thursday, 2 June

My wife was taken with a shivering fit at tea time which alarmed us very much. Dr Alderson was sent for, who ordered a saline julep.[246]

Lord's Day, 5 June

Today being Whitsunday. . . . After [the afternoon service, when Mr Payne preached] the church was stopped, and I addressed them something to this purpose. My dear Christian brothers and friends, the kind and very liberal manner in which you have come forward with your generous subscriptions to procure an assistant under my declining years and increasing infirmities calls not only for my grateful acknowledgements but I trust will never be erased from my mind, and as Mr Payne, who has now been ministering to us for about four weeks, is obliged to return to Leeds, I wish to be informed of these two things: 1st whither so far as you can judge at present his ministry be acceptable and likely to be profitable to you? And 2nd whether it may not be proper to request him to return as soon as possible, that after a few weeks' further knowledge of each other a more full and specific application may be made to him to settle with us. These questions were put separately and decided in the affirmative with the greatest unanimity.

Thursday, 9 June

This morning at six o'clock my sons George and John left us, the former for London and the other for Manchester. My family are now scattered and probably will never again be all collected together again in one place, or should that be the case it is hardly probable till I am removed out of the world. I thought it likely that it was the last parting upon earth, but what a mercy is it to have to leave them with

God and to commit them to his parental care, and what an additional comfort to see them so steady, so affectionate one to another, so dutiful to us their parents and so much respected by others. … I accompanied them to the coach and left them in good spirits.

Lord's Day, 12 June
This morning I had a letter from my son John informing me of his safe return to Manchester and that he had left his brother George at Huddersfield well.

Thursday, 23 June
After preaching the lecture last night and visiting, soon after 4 this morning I went to Hornsea to the opening of a new place of worship. [He preached in the morning, Brother Arundel in the afternoon and Brother Hobson in the evening.] But as I had to return in the evening to Hull I did not stay the last service. It is a peculiar pleasure and has a promising aspect to see so many tents set up for God as is the case at present and it gives me peculiar satisfaction to have seen it at Hornsea.[247] Several years back, I went there to spend a few days and bath. There were then a few Methodists but, tho' they had a room fitted up, they had none to speak to them but a vain, foolish old woman, who assumed greater state tho' not actuated with a similar spirit with Deborah. Some wished for me to have leave to preach there, but it was refused; upon which I spoke, both parts of the day in the rooms I had taken for a lodging, and was well attended. The people discovered an ardent desire to have some one to help them; and hence began the missionary exertions of some of my brethren. But taking a house and getting connected with a person whose conduct proved bad, all was for a time overturned here and the gospel was carried to Skipsea, Beeford etc. However, good had been done at Hornsea, and I trust one Dixon was converted, who afterwards removed to Green Hammerton and is joined to the church there under the charge of Mr Jackson. The chapel at Hornsea is a plain, neat, light place and will seat about 300 people.

Lord's Day, 26 June
Yesterday and today have been much hurried [?] by letter from my sons SAL and GL respecting the settlement of the latter at Leeds. This morning a letter was received from Mr Hirst signifying that all was agreed upon, which appears very hasty.

Lord's Day, 3 July
On Tuesday my brethren Bowden and Rust called on me to go forward to Rotherham, where we arrived in the evening. The next day was the annual meeting of the subscribers to the academy. Some disagreeables had occurred which required examination and detained me on a committee till 12 o'clock. The next day proved the quarterly of ministers there when Mr Hammond and Mr Bowden

preached. I had been requested to be one of the preachers but I have been so exercised with the toothache that I could hardly summon attention to him. On Friday we set out on our return, but, being hindered thro' the want of carriages, we did not get to North Cave till past 10 o'clock in the morning; set out again at 6 and found all well. Many disagreeables and disappointments on the journey, but blessed be God, no appearance of an accident.

Lord's Day, 10 July

If spared till tomorrow I am going to Harrogate with my wife, for the benefit of her health. May God render it profitable for I have little prospect of pleasure from the excursion.

Thursday, 28 July

This morning about half after one we got safe back from Harrogate after a very merciful preservation thro' the whole journey. Got to private lodgings at High Harrogate on the 11th inst. The Sunday following heard at the church in the morning a sermon without a foundation. Attended the Methodist chapel in the afternoon and preached in the latter on the evening. The Saturday following left Harrogate at half after 6 and soon after 9 got to Leeds. My son George with Mr Hirst who is come to settle with him in the grocery business got there a few minutes before us. Heard Mr Barnes of Wakefield at Salem in the morning, Mr Eccles at the White Chapel in the afternoon, and a long preacher in the evening at the rude [?] Methodist meeting. On Wednesday afternoon half past 2 we left Leeds, and got home this morning where we found all in health and peace. Called on Messrs Egginton's and got completely drowned with rain. Wrote a letter to George including him the needful to prosecute his undertaking.

Lord's Day, 31 July

I have again been privileged to preach to my people. . . . Mr Payne spoke in the afternoon. . . . When I compare the morning with the afternoon sermon and the age of him who made the former with the author of the latter, I am ashamed of myself and humbled in the dust of self abasement. But the success depends not on man's abilities, but on God's blessing.

Lord's Day, 7 August

I have gone thro' one of the most busy and perplexing weeks that I can remember. A perpetual succession of company and to very little profit. No time for reading, study or retirement. Even private and family duties hurried over in a slovenly manner. On Thursday morning my son George came home ill from Leeds, where he had only a week before opened a shop at Leeds, in consequence of his having some time past laid in a damp bed at Manchester. The same day Mr Neal, a student under Mr Vint[?], who called on me at Harrogate with his wife, a daughter of Mr Cocking of Halifax, came soon after dinner and have quartered themselves on us at every meal and almost every hour except breakfast and bed, the latter of which we could not afford them. Thus has my time been engrossed by strangers who have intruded themselves upon me without previous knowledge or invitation. In short, at this time of the year and especially during the vacation, my house is like an inn, open to all comers. . . . Lord, pardon the fretfulness of my mind under such hindrances and give me patience and grace to profit even by these hindrances.

Friday, 12 August
I have to record a wonderful escape and deliverance of my son Joseph: as he was gathering some pears from the tree in the garden this morning, the large branch on which he stood suddenly broke, gave way with him, and he fell on the wall, but the branch not only broke the force of the fall but mercifully prevented him from dashing upon the stones in the back yard. . . . I myself also had a very narrow escape as I was passing by Casson's[248] mill in my way to see a sick person. A man going out of the gates with a cart left the gates open, when a mastiff dog, chained but very fierce, rushed out and was within a few inches of seizing me; but being at the extremity of his chain it prevented the injury. Another man came instantly to my aid and made an apology for the omission of his fellow labourer. . . . I have been every day quite overdone with company of late, which leaves no time for thought, retirement or study. . . . To preach without studying I cannot; and find no time for it.

Lord's Day, 21 August
George continues very weak, but the complaint we hope is removed from his chest. . . . After the service the church were requested to stop, and Mr Payne being proposed as a stated assistant was chosen and the deacons requested to inform him of the resolution of the church.

Lord's Day, 28 August
My son George left us on Tuesday for Leeds better in health in some respects, though far from recovered. The last week has been a continual succession of hurry from company. I could hardly get to the study but the bell rang for me to leave it.

Wednesday, 7 September
I was very much alarmed this morning by a letter received by my son William from Mr Gee at Bridlington, saying that he was sorry to hear that his sister Eliza had been so very ill at Leeds that, when the apothecary was called in, he found her alive and that was all. Another person from Leeds said she had been ill of the cramp at her stomach but was better. About half an hour after, I received a letter from her in which she takes no notice of it. From the whole I trust she is better and wishes to keep us unacquainted with it. However, I wrote to her at Leeds and have desired an answer by return of post. . . . This evening all of a sudden Miss Sommerville left us to go by sea to Newcastle. Poor woman I pity her much. No parents, no home,

and what is worst of all, her own fretful temper is her continual tormenter.

Lord's Day, 11 September

I received two letters on Friday, one from George, the other from Elizabeth, informing me that, though she had been ill of the cramp in her stomach and bowels, she was recovered and purposed on Friday going to Cleckheaton upon a visit to our friend Mr Kidd.

Thursday, 22 September

A very melancholy occurrence happened in our neighbourhood last night. Mr Hare, who had been for near forty years in the family of Mrs Smith, having the gout in his brain, got from them in the evening and we were searching for him till 12 o'clock; he had been in a low spirited way for about a week and he was found drowned this morning in the Humber. This is the second person that I have seen brought to that house who had been drowned. . . . [Footnote added later by GL.] I have heard since of another man who inhabited a back part of the same house being drowned and I recollect it.

Lord's Day, 25 September

In the course of the last week died the Revd Mr Thompson, Chaplain to the Trinity House.[249] He was in Hull when I came to live in it and is the last minister but one (Mr Beverley) but is removed by death when I came to it. [Lists clergymen who have died.]

Thursday, 20 October

I have experienced a very narrow escape today. In visiting a sick person in Lower Union Street, as I was coming away, the stairs being remarkably steep and narrow, I slipped from one and fell down about four stairs and sprained my left foot and find that I have shook my whole frame. Blessed be God no bone is broken, nor I hope dislocated but I have a good deal of pain.

Thursday, 27 October

I got up this morning before 5 o'clock, having a journey before me. At a little before 7 set off for Market Weighton[250] to the opening of a new chapel in which I preached in the forenoon from Exod 25.8. The attention of the people was uncommonly fixed and serious, and the place crowded, for it will not hold above 250 according to appearance. Mr Eccles of Leeds preached in the afternoon from John 4.24 and Mr Hobson of Driffield was to speak in the evening, but, as I had to return to Hull, I did not stay. It is a great pleasure to see the spread of the gospel in dark and different places and to notice the zeal of the people I minister to. . . . In consequence, 2 places for worship have been built and both of them afterwards enlarged at Hull, and one at each of the following places, Swanland, Skipsea,

Hornsea, Patrington, Pocklington and Weighton, besides several others in different places hired or fitted up for public worship.

Tuesday, 1 November
I was prevailed on by a friend this afternoon to go to see Mr Daniel Lambert,[251] who exhibits himself in this town as a prodigy for bulk and indeed such he is, weighing upwards of 700 lb. His body, legs and arms are of an enormous size, but his head, hands and feet small in proportion. He appeared unwieldy and a burden to himself, sitting against the wall upon two chairs, and continually shifting from side to side. He appeared an intelligent man, but could give but little account of his ancestors. What a mercy it is to be proportionable, able to move about and, if a wonder to many, to be such from what God has wrought in us, rather from an excess of corpulency or other peculiarity.

Thursday, 3 November
My daughters Hannah and Phebe this day experienced a merciful interposition of divine Providence, and a very narrow escape; as they were turning out of Trinity House Lane into Silver Street the frontispiece of a garret window fell from the roof of a house within a very small distance from the spot on which they were. Two steps further would have placed them directly under, which might have been of fatal consequence. As it was, their face and eyes were only affected for the present by the mortar and dust.

Tuesday, 8 November
Mr Lyon … is become a Socinian and going to preach in Mr Matthew Henry's pulpit at Chester, called this evening to take leave of me. I behaved to him I hope with the civility but yet with the sincere [sic] of a Christian. In parting told him that I wished the spirit of Matthew Henry's doctrine might haunt him every time he went into the pulpit and that he might be found on the sure foundation, that we might meet at last in Heaven; but to remember there was but one way to it.

Wednesday, 16 November
A letter received this day from my daughter Eliza at Leeds affected me with pleasure and pain, the former to hear that her brother George's health is so happily established, the latter to hear that Mr Joshua Whitehead and his wife, who formerly lived servants with my wife's father, after hard labour and being much prospered in the world were almost stripped of all by the failure of a nephew.

Wednesday, 23 November
I have been overpowered today with friendship. A succession of calls has detained me (or rather chained me down to my chair) till 8 o'clock this evening; our parlour was kept full and five stayed tea, tho' unexpected. The consequence is I find my spirits and bodily strength exhausted; and to be kept continually talking is no probable

method to cure a hoarseness. I have lost the day. Lord pardon the trifles which have murdered so many hours of life.

Lord's Day, 4 December
A collection for the support of the children at school. The amount was £9.13.10½.

Lord's Day, 11 December
One person having sent one pound in addition to the collection for the school; two others became annual subscribers to the support of it; and an unknown friend having sent 30 Bibles to be distributed amongst the children.

Lord's Day, 18 December
[Reports Mr Payne's sermon that afternoon]. It was a close discourse, and I hope will be made useful to myself and others. But, when I consider his youth, his short standing in the ministry and the composition and weight of his sermons, I am ashamed and blush to preach to the same people or before him. Surely I am more brutish than any and have not the understanding I ought to have. The good Lord pardon my weaknesses and succeed my poor (tho' I trust sincere) desires to serve him and his cause.

1809

Lord's Day, 8 January
Ebenezer Bettison was drowned on Wednesday with two others in a dreadful storm as they were going in a boat to secure a lighter in the Humber which appeared to be in danger.

Lord's Day, 29 January
The victory accompanied by a retreat of our brave troops in Spain in which Sir John Moore was killed[252], the spread of desolation amongst the nations and the shades of Providence that spread over our own country led me this forenoon to point out the propriety of waiting on and looking for God to appear from Isai 8.17. . . . After the public services of the day I went on to my son William to see his youngest child Phebe, who appeared in a convulsed state from the measles falling on her lungs. I felt much from the affecting scene and was deeply troubled under a sense of original depravity. Why should an infant suffer so much, which has never offended, if there were no depravity, why a holy and gracious God punish innocence if there were no corruption or why the express looks and extended arms of a babe only a few months old seem to cry for help?

Thursday, 31 January

Though my son William's child appeared upon the whole better yesterday than before this morning at 7 o'clock it closed its eyes without a sigh or groan. The parents are much affected.

Friday, 3 February

Attended the funeral of my son William's child to Sculcoates, where he has procured a vault in connection with the graves [sic] of my own father who now lays in it, and where probably in a short time I may be laid by him.

Friday, 24 February

My daughter Phebe going to visit her sister and brother at Leeds, I got up soon after four; and a little before six attended her to the coach. Soon after my return I was taken very ill and either fainted or was very near it. Soon after I turned very cold and have continued very unwell all day.

Tuesday, 4 April

I have been to Cottingham today expecting, according to appointment, to meet the ministers as usual. But thro' the severity of the season, being severe frost and snow, only Mr Tapp and myself got to Mr Kidd's. The business of the meeting was of course postponed; but we had some conversation with Mr Tapp respecting Mr Gray's will and the trial in which he has been concerned, in consequence of it. I do not envy his enjoyments, tho' large, as I fear it will stain his character and prevent his usefulness. It was a most unfavourable event, his being in the room when the will was made and the person in so weak a state of body and mind. On my return home I found a letter from Mr Thomas Riddell relinquishing the two pews which, to oblige him, had been thrown into one. I may say he has been a great disturber of my peace and injured me much in my temporal support. By his accommodation with two pews, I lost £1.4s. in the removal of others; and now £6 more as, I apprehend, nobody will incline to take it in its present state. But tho' he is the agent only, and a divine permission in the deduction, I find no envy or ill will to him in my mind. It has all originated from not suffering him to overturn the order of the church that he might become Lord of it. But I had rather submit to beg my bread than to have him rule with as high hand over me.

Lord's Day, 14 May

A young man related to one of the members of the church fell with a ladder 30 feet high by a truck than ran against it as he was painting. He was much bruised and cut but no bones broken, and Mr C Newbald,[253] as [he was] walking in his staith, a trap door fell, which grazed his leg but might have killed him.

Lord's Day, 4 June

Yesterday died Mrs Gilson, who has been long confined to her bed and who has long stood in union with the church, an early convert to Christ under my ministry and in her infancy brought up a Roman Catholic.

Tuesday, 6 June

I went this evening with great expectations to St John's Church to hear a young man whom I had heard highly spoken of as evangelical in his views but was greatly disappointed [gives a critical analysis of his sermon]. ... I was greatly dissatisfied and really distressed to think that a leader of souls should be so ignorant of the way in which he should guide them; and did not leave the church without praying that God would open his understanding and lead him into the way of truth. His voice was very disagreeable in itself and gave a most uncertain sound indeed. The name of Jesus Christ was only once mentioned, and even then he was kept quite in the background.

Tuesday, 13 June

The East Riding Association being appointed this year for Hull, several of the ministers assembled today to be in readiness for tomorrow. [Service] The place of worship was well filled, the preacher earnest and the people attentive. It was a well studied discourse.

Wednesday, 14 June

The ministers, 12 in number, breakfasted at my house. About ten we adjourned to Mr J S Bowden's back parlour. Prayer was offered by Mr Bottomley, after which the resolutions of the Association were read when each minister gave an account of the state of religion in his own church. Dinner succeeded. After fixing things for the succeeding year the letter addressed to the church was read. Several cases were attended to. After tea the meeting concluded with prayer and in the evening Mr Bottomley preached. ... It has proved a pleasant and I trust will have been found a profitable meeting: to myself the most agreeable and I may say the most consistent that I have ever attended in any association of ministers.

Friday, 30 June

Today our Humber dock was opened; but not with that splendour with which I saw the former,[254] when my two eldest sons were children. I have seen what was formerly land and afforded pasture for cattle turned into water, and ships sailing adorned with all the colours of different nations where cattle quietly grazed, or lambs wantonly sported. ... This afternoon I applied to Dr Alderson who ordered me 4 grains of Calomel and to take 2 spoons full of Epsom Salts tomorrow morning.

13 Pages of Lambert's journal

Monday, 10 July

[Ministers' quarterly meeting at Swanland] On my return this evening how great was my surprise to find that death had entered my next door neighbour's house and removed Mrs Walker. She was formerly a woman who made a fair profession of religion and united with the church under my charge, afterwards left us with her husband (a man of no appearance of religion) to join the Anabaptists, but soon either left, or were excluded from that connection and attended at no place of worship but seemed to be decidedly of the world and in it. She has been troubled with an asthmatic complaint for some time, but died quite suddenly.

Saturday, 15 July

Dr Alderson was sent for last night on account of the complaints I have long found in my chest and sides.

Lord's Day, 30 July

Last Tuesday the Archbishop[255] confirmed, held a visitation and delivered a charge. The vicar Bromby preached the sermon from 1 Cor 12.25. Said much in favour of the national establishment but expressed a wish that those things were done away which tended to keep Dissenters out of it, in particular the 39 articles, and discovered great liberality towards them, but whether from a love to good men or a laxness towards divine truth I cannot say. The charge delivered all related to temporalities, the residence of the clergy, the advance of all livings under £150 a year and the repairs or building of parsonage houses. The whole might have suited an heathen temple as well as a Christian church.

Thursday, 10 August

One of my hearers, a very rich man whom I have known from a youth, influenced by the person who wished to open a door for all to enter the church without attending to the usual order, had discovered his displeasure in withholding all his subscriptions to the Missionary Society, the Academy and the assistant (tho' he was the first to propose and urge the latter). Last night a ship loaded with currants in Grimsby Dock was set on fire by lightning and entirely consumed, and, what was more affecting, a boy on board was consumed with it.

Tuesday, 22 August

Today after dinner my son John Lambert having received orders from his employers Messrs Philips and Lee to proceed to Heligoland went on board the vessel and fell down to Grimsby roads to await for convoy. I feel very anxious for him as I hear the Island not more than ¾ths of a mile long and crowded with buyers and sellers, their provisions and accommodations very bad and from accounts little preferable to [a] set of smugglers.

Lord's Day, 3 September

Yesterday we had a letter from John Lambert informing us of his safe arrival at Heligoland and of the wretched state in which he found things there. I wish him well and safe back, though it may render England and its comforts more prizable.

Wednesday, 13 September

This day sennight I set out for Leeds with my daughter Eliza. Had very agreeable company all the way especially from York where we took in the Revd Mr Robinson of Leicester, we got to Leeds about 4 where I found my son George in good health. [Lists Sunday preachers] . . . On Monday my son drove me in a gig to Cleckheaton, where I first began my public ministry. Mr Kidd being out, I walked in the chapel yard among the tombs of many of my former hearers with the Revd James Dawson in the midst of them, who succeeded me in that place. Dined with Mr Kidd, called upon the only three persons in the place who remembered my being there; afterwards walked to Gomersal and got tea with my old friend Mr William Burnby. On our return, the horse tired so that we did not get to Leeds till after dark. In getting out of the carriage my foot missed the step, but as I was falling my son caught hold of me or I must have been dashed upon the stones with my back against the curb stone. . . . I left Leeds at 6 and after a safe and comfortable journey reached home about 8 in the evening, where I found all well.

Friday, 15 September

This evening we were pleasingly surprised by the return of my son John from Heligoland. He gives a dreadful description of the place which consists of a rock which might be walked around in an hour with ease. The beach is covered with warehouses formed in caves or out of old ships. From this you have to go up 190 steps to the top of the rock, which is the residence of soldiers, tradesmen, foreigners and English. Beef is two shillings a pound and a lodging in a sledge roofed garret four shillings a night. O the privileges and blessings of our native country, may we both enjoy and improve them to the glory of that God who has thus dealt bountifully with us.

Thursday, 21 September

The supporting teeth which sustained some artificial ones which have greatly assisted me in speaking for several years failing, I have been all day yesterday and part of the two preceding under the hands of the dentist. But what he has done I fear will not answer. In that case I should be unable to preach; this, together with a view of future support for myself and family, has rather oppressed my spirits.

Lord's Day, 24 September

I have not enjoyed one comfortable meal since the alteration in my mouth, have had my rest broken and experienced considerable pain. But after baptising a child last Friday I attempted to preach this forenoon from Ezek 34.15 and got thro' better than I expected but not without considerable pain. If they continue fixed they will help in speaking, but not I fear in eating.

Tuesday, 10 October

I have been spending a fortnight at Anlaby with Mr Boyes, where I have received every mark of attention and kindness. Preached last Sabbath at Cottingham and the preceding at Swanland. This day was the quarterly meeting of ministers at my home.

Saturday, 14 October

I have been brought into great perplexity this afternoon by the wire getting loose and at last coming entirely out of the artificial teeth which I lately got to assisting me to speak. The consequence is that I can neither eat with them nor speak without them. So that I am not unable to deliver tomorrow the sermon I had prepared but have been under the necessity of applying to Mr Payne. After being absent from my place two Sabbaths and preaching to other congregations just on my return, and the very evening before I expected to engage, to appear idle (without being able to tell the cause) must appear singular to my people and is very painful to myself. I fear I must be under the necessity of going to York to have something done.

Lord's Day, 15 October

In the afternoon I found myself so unwell that I did not go out. Read in the family this evening Collison's Religion[256] exemplified in the death of Elijah, but found some trouble in my mouth.

Tuesday, 17 October [He writes 15]

After several fruitless trials to fasten the artificial helps I had obtained for speaking, after writing to York, receiving an answer and applying to Mr Rust for help to drill the hole deeper, I have been under the necessity of going to York to the dentist. Set off at 6 in the morning and got back to Hull soon after 8 in the evening. Thanks be to God for a safe and pleasant journey, and may it be crowned with success.

Lord's Day, 22 October

Preached this forenoon from John 2.19.21. But felt some uneasiness from the fear that my late journey to York had not altogether answered. At times the teeth intended to help in speaking seemed to give way. However, I got thro' but not with that composure and comfort that I could have wished.

Wednesday, 25 October

This day being appointed as a royal Jubilee of the King's 50 accession to the throne, I spoke in the forenoon from Prov 8.15. But there being a grand cavalcade to the Church, our place was but thinly attended. However, the collection for the poor amounted to £19 within a few halfpence. I got thro' the work better than I expected.

1810

Lord's Day, 14 January
On Tuesday last I went to Cottingham where the ministers' quarterly meeting was held. Mr Tapp being present took up the greater part of the afternoon in the vindication of himself respecting the will of the late Mr Gray of Elloughton concerning which there have been two trials at York and finally determined against him, but he refers the full decision to the greatest of all judges. This rendered the meeting less agreeable and profitable than it might have been.

Wednesday, 17 January
I have been this day called upon to sign a petition to Parliament for a repeal of those sanguinary laws which exist against sentiments and the repealing the Test Act[257] so far as it respects marine or military concerns. I confess I have no hope of its success, nor do I think it a proper time of making the application, but, as all investigation has a tendency to bring truth to light and as every man's conscience ought to be left free, I could not see it right to withhold my approbation.

Lord's Day, 4 February
A separation among the Baptists in George Street have open[ed] a place today which has been shut up for some time in Dagger Lane. This is the fourth separation among the Baptists that has taken place in this town since I have lived in it. What a disgrace and injury to religion are such strifes and divisions.

Lord's Day, 11 February
Sixty-eight years have been rolled over this day, since I came out of my mother's womb, a sinful conception into a world of trial and temptation. How little would it be conceived that, when it was declared to her that a man child was born, that I should be where I am and the parent of so large a family. I have reason to adore sparing mercy and multiplied mercies connected with it.

Thursday, 15 February
This day my son William hearing that Mr Adam intended declining the linen drapery business had applied for my son Joseph, and this evening it was agreed to sign articles tomorrow morning. May God smile upon the undertaking and cause it to prosper. It is a great concern and almost makes me to tremble, but nothing is too hard for the Lord. O Lord, I beseech thee, now send prosperity.

Monday, 19 February

This has been a day of hurry, accompanied with pain and pleasure. I got up soon after 4 in the morning and after getting things ready for my son Joseph's journey for Leeds and Manchester, a little before 6 I accompanied him to the coach. Soon after 7 John and George Lambert arrived by the Mail. The former had gone from Manchester to Leeds to see his sister Eliza, and finding she had come to Hull, he, accompanied by his brother George, came forward to Hull, and returned by the same conveyance soon after 3. Much snow has fallen in the course of the day, which I fear will render the roads bad. Eliza has been very ill most of the day.

Lord's Day, 25 February

Joseph is not yet returned from Manchester but John has informed me by letter that he left George well at Leeds and set forward for Manchester, where he arrived safe. Eliza has been very ill all the week. She has taken besides other medicines James's Powders[258] 6 times and has had a blister, but the fever is not removed yet, though I would hope rather better.

Wednesday, 28 February

This day was observed as a fast day by royal command. In anticipating the work of the day, I felt a great reluctance to engage in public, and had requested Mr Payne to preach, which he did from James 4.10. It proved a very favourable circumstance for this morning I accidentally dropped the artificial teeth which I have to assist me in speaking on the carpet and broke the wire which supports them and was obliged to send them to York (at an uncertainty whether the dentist be at home) to see if he can supply the defect. . . . Another fast day is now concluded, and I wish it may not be an increase to our national crimes. There is danger from the false views of those who applied the day in fasting for strife and debate.

Lord's Day, 4 March

Eliza continues very weak and ill. The fever is not removed. Bark has been prescribed but doth not agree with her; the family are almost worn out, and Hannah is to leave us this week to keep Joseph's house.

Monday, 12 March

This day my son Joseph opened his shop and began business in the Market Place. It proved a most uncomfortable day, incessantly raining from morning to night. However, several friends have been with him to give him a token of their respect and good wishes.

Lord's Day, 1 April

The increasing expense of the place of worship greatly exceeding the quarterly collections, I was this day desired by the deacons to renew the proposal of depositing in the boxes weekly contributions as the place was now £60 deficient. . . . I went to Drypool and baptised a child. Before I had finished there two friends came, and one of them talked so much and so long that, having taken very little food, I found myself quite exhausted.

Wednesday, 18 April

As I was shaving myself this morning I was seized as sudden as if I had been shot, with convulsive affection on the valve of the windpipe. My breath was stopped, succeeded by a violent effort to breathe and afterwards strong coughing. I was alone and could not stir from the chair on which I had thrown myself for some time. Afterwards I rang the bell, but nobody except myself heard it. Afterwards I knocked with my foot, and my wife came, but I was then able to speak. Tho' I was before in all appearance in good health, and it did not last more that a quarter of an hour, it shook my whole frame and left me so debilitated that I could hardly stir. What it was I know not, but I thought myself dying and was enabled in faith to resign myself up to God. It has his voice in it. Be ye ready.

Saturday, 6 May

Mr Eccles preached this forenoon. Mr Payne in the afternoon. Two of the members came on after the service and complained much of the latter, that his sermon had been a continual quotation from different parts of the Scripture and that they could not profit under him. I am concerned to hear such repeated complaints as I am confident it is his wish and desire to be useful. There may appear some want of animation, but I apprehend it arises from bodily weakness.

Lord's Day, 20 May

Just before I went out to preach I received an anonymous letter by the post which I did not read till after the service. The substance of it was complaining of not profiting under Mr Payne's ministry and of their resolution to call a church meeting if things were not remedied. He preached this afternoon from John 6.37, after which I baptised Mr Hyde's child, but I was in a state of the greatest confusion all the time I was engaged and happy when I had to conclude. My voice seemed no way equal to the engagement.

Tuesday, 29 May

Mr Payne having had some hints that some were not happy under his ministry came on to converse with me upon the subject. I felt very much for him but held back nothing from him that I did know. Shewed him the letter but that we had never been able to find out the author and being without a name fully believed that things were not as bad as there represented. He is a man of a most amiable disposition and has always acted towards me with the greatest kindness. I am very uneasy and fear the consequences, but would refer it with all my concerns to God.

Thursday, 14 June

Mr Payne called upon me early this morning to inform me of the death of Mr Thomas Riddell[259] and to request me to accompany him in breaking it out to his father. But the latter not being up, it was agreed for Mr Payne to stay and breakfast with the old gentleman and that I should go on afterwards. It is an affecting Providence as he was from home under the care of a physician at Ripon, Yorkshire, and his wife had come over to Hull to take the children from school at this vacation. He has been long out of health of a dropsical complaint and went off in a fainting fit. Poor man, he has been a great troubler of my peace, but probably he did not mean it. However, there was a divine permission in it, and I hope that I was enabled to look beyond the instrument to the hand that held it. I have felt no enmity against him, and it would have been a high gratification could I have served him in any way for the good of himself or family. But I still think that the church did right; and, had his proposals been acceded to, it had been all in confusion if not in ruins before this.

Lord's Day, [24 June]

Mr Thomas Riddell, who was buried last Wednesday morning, I hear retained his bad spirit towards myself and the church till very near the close of life, and had written a very strong letter to his father upon the subject, which the family prevented being sent. I am much concerned to have heard it but forgive and pity – yea more attribute it to the effect of the palsy upon his spirits.

Lord's Day, 8 July

The monthly meeting for prayer for the spread of the Gospel at home and abroad was held at our chapel last Monday evening. . . . On Tuesday morning I went to Scarbro', it being our association [Lists preachers including himself]. . . . Returned on Thursday. Dined at Driffield and arrived in safety at my own house about 7 in the evening. . . . [Went to hear Mr Payne preach] . . . well handled but he has some impediment of speech which renders it in some manner unintelligible at times.

Lord's Day, 22 July

Last Monday morning at 7 o'clock my wife and self went for Elloughton upon a visit to Mr Robinson, where after spending four days we returned on Thursday evening and got home soon after 9. The country is delightful in that part, the hills commanding a very extensive prospect. Most of the time was spent in walking about, except on Wednesday evening when upon very short notice I preached in the school room to a very attentive audience which filled the place.

Lord's Day, 12 August

On Tuesday Mr I[saac] Burnett died which affected me very much. He was the son of the Revd J Burnett, late of Hull. Had been in business and might have done well, but thro' imprudence failed several times. He once was a member of our church but thro' love of liquor was reproved, suspended, and finally excluded. For a long time he has been a near vagabond, traversing the streets, often in a state of intoxication. … Last night had also a very sleepless night and much perplexed in mind about the expenses necessary for repairing the dry rot which is again making ravages in the chapel. Having some conversation with a friend in the evening about the manner of providing a fund for the expense. … A letter from my good old friend and brother Bottomley of Scarbro', containing the account of the derangement of his eldest son and the necessity of sending him to York.[260]

Lord's Day, 26 August

In the evening one the members of the church who had been for some time in a backsliding state came to have some conversation. I trust there is a time of revival and refreshing in his soul. … I was much refreshed by what he said.

Thursday, 30 August

On Thursday evening half after 11 died Mr William Sleight, a young man only 22 years of age who had been in business for himself as a glover for about half a year. He had not been well for a day or two, but had attended his shop that day till 7 in the evening. About two years back he had a severe illness, upon his recovery he joined our church and has been uncommonly diligent in attending upon the means of grace whenever and wherever he could.

Lord's Day, 9 September

Tuesday afternoon my wife and I went to Tranby upon a visit to Samuel Cooper Esq where we spent two days and three nights and got back to Hull on Friday 11 o'clock forenoon.

Thursday, 13 September

I have been informed that another anonymous letter was sent to Mr Payne last Lord's day morning similar to and breathing the same spirit of discontent with his ministry with that which I received some time back. I am much concerned on his account, on my own, and lest the peace of the church should be disturbed. I fear we were rather too precipitate in fixing. He is a valuable man, of a most amiable temper, and think it must arise from his manner of delivery rather than what is delivered by him.

Wednesday, 3 October

On Friday sennight went to Anlaby on a visit to J Boyes Esq. Preached on the Sunday following at Cottingham from 2 Tim 3.15 when a collection of 3 guineas was made for the British and Foreign

Bible Society, and last Sunday preached at Swanland from Rev 1.7 and returned home last night. . . . I have been much among the great and have received every civility and indulgence from them, but I have returned to my little cot with pleasure, and I trust with a good sentiment respecting poverty and riches, content with a happy mediocrity. Times never were more alarming than the present. Failures, bankruptcies[261] and suicide are taking place every day, and public credit shaken to its very foundation. No man knows today what will be his circumstances tomorrow. Sir Francis Baring[262] dead. The renowned Sir Abraham Goldsmid[263] shot himself (said to be the 2 pillars of the City of London), Selby, Pontefract, Bradford and Leeds Bank said to be stopped.

Wednesday, 17 October
This day my son Joseph was married at Elloughton to Miss Elizabeth Robinson. They have long kept company together, but at last formed their union in a very private manner and with great reserve towards the branches of my family. However, I hope he has made a very prudent choice and the desire and prayer of my heart is that the blessings both of the upper and the nether springs may attend them. I did not hear of its having taken place till tonight, Saturday [sic] evening, as he is on a journey to Manchester.

Lord's Day, 21 October
The Chapel having been repaired and painted, it was resolved after the particular subscription to have a public collection.

Wednesday, 24 October
Received a note this forenoon from Mr Payne wishing me to bring his case before the church as to their approbation of his ministry, as some had intimated that they were not fully satisfied, and wishing me to speak at the church meeting this evening as he found himself much exhausted. Though from a cold and sore throat I could not comply with the latter, I waited on him personally and being caught in the rain as I went I got very wet. I fear we shall have great uneasiness for, though some are dissatisfied, others are much attached to him, and, should the latter be the majority of the members, yet even a minority, should they not withdraw, would leave his mind as well as others very uncomfortable.

Lord's Day, 18 November
On Friday I had to devote the whole day to some very unpleasant business at Cottingham respecting Mr Kidd which required my meeting the church at 6 in the evening, after being engaged all the forenoon with a committee.

Lord's Day, 25 November
My eldest son arrived from London on Friday eveninig and appears in very good health.

Wednesday, 12 December
This afternoon two gentlemen from Cottingham waited upon me respecting the business referred to on the 18th ult. Like a spark upon tinder it not only caught hold, but, while I hoped it was extinguished, I find it has spread wider, and the power of prejudice is likely to blow it up into a flame. Fresh improprieties are brought to light, and, though everything criminal is acknowledged on all hands to have had no existence, the cause of God is likely to suffer in that place. The Methodists on the one hand stigmatize Gospel doctrines, and the Socinians on the other profess a great concern for the honour of the Dissenting interest. . . . I have omitted mentioning that my son John from Manchester arrived at Hull on Monday sennight and that his brother Samuel and sister Hannah left us for the North the next day (Tuesday) at half after 3 o'clock.

Lord's Day, 16 December
Yesterday my son John left us for Leeds and Manchester.

Thursday, 20 December
On Wednesday died Mrs Barbara Burn, a valuable Christian and an intimate and affectionate friend. It was to her house that I went on my first coming to Hull, and she and her husband were two of the eleven that formed themselves into the church. She has been a steady, exemplary and useful member, and all things taken into the account has hardly left her equal. One of the members drank tea with me this afternoon and intimated that several of the members were much hurt and offended by the last two sermons that I had preached on the Sabbath mornings, supposing that it was my intention to throw all the blame on them for not profiting under Mr Payne's ministry. This was far from my intention. I know that God only can teach ministers and make their sermons profitable to the people. . . . However, it is evident that many of the people are dissatisfied and that dissatisfaction engenders prejudice, and where that may terminate it is impossible to say.

Friday, 21 December
Today died Mrs Elanor Usher, her former name was Kerton, a daughter of John and Elanor Kerton, formerly poor but honourable members of our church. Her husband had when young been sent to sea, but not liking it went to husbandry work and afterwards came to work for a brewer in Hull, where he married. He earned a guinea a week. They had a house neatly furnished and three children when a person informing the press gang of him he was seized and taken on board the tender. Here he was detained for several weeks till by begging and borrowing she procured his release by finding two substitutes in his place. He returned to work with his former master,

soon after which he was seized with a brain fever and died, leaving her with 3 children and in a family way. When in labour two physicians and two surgeons attended her. The child taken away by force and she in about a week died, leaving three orphans without friend or support. It is one of the most perplexed and complicated dispensations of Providence that I have ever been conversant with. And yet no doubt there is equity and wisdom in the whole.

Saturday, 22 December
Though I have not been well in myself I was called this afternoon to attend the funeral of my good old friend Mrs Burn to Sculcoates. On getting into the coach on our return from the grave, my foot slipped from the step, which bruised my shin very much and at first I feared it was broken, but thanks be to God neither bone nor shin was much injured. . . . I received a letter from a Mr Walker of Broad Street, London, who, though unknown to me, expresses his mind having been richly regaled with the perusal of the 1st volume of my sermons, and wishing to have copies of any other that I have published; and though I cannot supply him I would render thanks to God that thereby I have been enabled to preach to many who I never saw, and that I have received so many evidences from various quarters that they have not been published in vain.

Tuesday, 25 December
My son William and his wife came to dinner, and Joseph and his wife to tea and supper.

Saturday, 29 December
My wife having been much troubled for more than a week with violent cramps in her feet and eyes and much affected on her right side, we this afternoon made application to Dr Alderson who has ordered 3 grains of Dr James's Powders to be given, and a blister put on the outside of the right thigh. As several of the family on her side have been troubled with the paralytic affections I thought it prudent to apply in time.

Lord's Day, 30 December
Mr Harness of Bridlington preached for Mr Payne in the afternoon from 1 Peter 1.8. But, though I sat almost under him, I could hear but little on account of his voice and even what I could make out was so very very confused that I was no better, but I fear worse for being present. I found an uneasy and fretful frame of mind, partly from a conviction that the people could not hear him, and from the idea of the closing service should prove an unprofitable season. . . . My wife has been confined at home all the day with the blister. It was taken off in the evening and appears to have done well, if it do but effect the desired end.

Monday, 31 December

[Reviews the year's events.] As a minister, though I have reason to be thankful for much help in my work, yet I have to mourn over the little apparent success that seems to have attended it. ... On the whole things appear greatly on the decline. ... My son Joseph has been settled for himself in business in the very shop in which he served his apprenticeship, and has since married. ... My son John has been over from Manchester to see us, and am glad to find he has given full satisfaction to his employers, by the handsome present they have made him and the way in which they expressed their satisfaction. ... In the course of this year Providence has removed by death a person who had been very troublesome, seemed to have an implacable enmity to me (I trust without cause) and did all that he could to prejudice others against me. I attribute it to a restless, irritable mind, rather than a bad heart; that his removal (may it have been to a better world) has had a wonderful effect in promoting peace, which I hope I studied, prayed for, and did all in my power consistent with truth to promote.

Notes to Vol 10

[243] *7 February 1808.* The Humber Dock was in course of construction. See 30 June 1809.

[244] *28 May 1808.* Rev George Payne, MA and later DD and LLD, assistant to GL 1808-12. A considerable scholar and man of great ability, he nevertheless had enough critics in Hull to lead to his resignation and his move to Albany church, Edinburgh (see Darwent 37-8). He later became tutor at a number of colleges and published some influential books.

[245] *29 May 1808.* 'On Saturday morning [28 May] at this place suddenly, aged 67, Mr Joseph Bradford, many years a respectable preacher in the Methodist connection. He had suffered considerable mental injury from paralytic strokes in the course of the years.' *Hull Advertiser*, 14 June 1808.

[246] *2 June 1808.* Saline draughts were recommended for vomiting, the unpleasant taste being disguised by mixing in a julep, a sweet-flavoured cold drink.

[247] *23 June 1808.* Missionary visits were made from Fish Street to Hornsea c 1800. A house was licensed for worship by the Independents 1807. Bethseda Chapel was built in Southgate and licensed 1808.

[248] *12 August 1808.* Casson and Stickney were makers of ships' biscuits. Later Casson and Penrose had Blockhouse Mill.

[249] *25 September 1808.* Rev George Thompson, vicar of Drypool, was chaplain of Trinity House 1763-1808.

[250] *27 October 1808.* John Wesley preached at Market Weighton, 23 June 1788, in the Methodist chapel built 1786.

[251] *1 November 1808.* Daniel Lambert (1770-1809), the most corpulent man of his time. At his death weighed 52¾ stone. (ODNB)

[252] *29 January 1809.* At the Battle of Corunna, 16 January, the French defeated the British under Sir John Moore.

[253] *14 May 1809.* Charles Newbald: see 11 July, 1 August 1811.

[254] *30 June 1809.* GL had witnessed the opening of Hull's first dock, originally called simply The Dock, later Queen's Dock, opened 22 September 1778.

[255] *30 July 1809.* Edward (formerly Venables-Vernon) Harcourt (1757-1847) was Archbishop of York from 1808 to his death, making a primary visitation of his archdiocese in 1809, the first for almost a century. This would be the occasion on which the Archbishop 'sat stern and unbending', listening to Bromby's sermon 'strongly tinged with liberalism'.

[256] *15 October* 1809. Collison's Religion refers to George Collison (1772-1847), President of Hackney Theological Academy, who preached a sermon, *Religion exemplified in the character of Abijah* (1809).

[257] *17 January 1810*. Test Act: see 1 February 1790.

[258] *25 February 1810*. Dr James's fever powders were originally a patent medicine invented and patented by Dr Robert James, 1747. They became extremely popular and were widely imitated. They consisted of antimony sulphate and powdered hartshorn and were used to reduce fever.

[259] *14 June 1810*. Thomas Riddell: see 1 January 1781.

[260] *12 August 1810*. Either Bootham Park Hospital (1777), a purpose-built lunatic asylum or The Retreat (1794-6), a pioneering Quaker establishment for the treatment of the insane.

[261] *3 October 1810*. Notices of the bankruptcy of a number of Hull businesses appeared in the local press in February 1810.

[262] *3 October 1810*. Sir Francis Baring (1740-1810), merchant and merchant banker, government adviser and director of the East India Company (ODNB).

[263] *3 October 1810*. Sir Abraham Goldsmid (1756-1810), merchant and financier, who enjoyed great success as a pioneering bill broker but who committed suicide on his inability to repay a loan to the East India Company (ODNB).

Vol 11 1811-1813

1811

Monday, 7 January
Another breach has this day been made in the church by the death of Mr Peter Gun; he has been in communion nearly thirty seven years. He was a poor, afflicted and, I hope, pious, man, but has been for several years reduced almost to childhood, and by working at the white lead mill had long been lame in his hands.

Wednesday, 9 January
I heard a sermon this evening from Rom 8.9 with which I was very much dissatisfied with [sic]. It was delivered in a most dry, dull and heavy manner, but that was not the worst [Criticises its doctrinal content.]

Friday, 11 January
The thaw came on today and in going down the yard my feet slipped from under me, and I got a very ugly fall which bruised my right arm below the elbow and shook me all over. Blessed be God that no bones were broken or dislocated. I afterwards dined and drank tea at Mrs Spyvee's, but walked with fear and trembling.

Monday, 14 January
My wife has for some time past been exercised with pain from her hip on the right side down to her toes. We have thought it was the cramp or rheumatism or both, but last night it was so severe that she could not forbear crying out. Before breakfast I went to Dr Alderson who ordered her Dover's Powder[264] and soon after came on himself. She has been confined to her bed all day with a view to bring on a perspiration which had not been effected at 5 this afternoon. The doctor thinks it to be the same complaint which was so troublesome about two years and a half back and for which she went to Scarbro, but it was then an eruption externally.

Tuesday, 15 January
My wife has been severely handled with pain today, especially in the afternoon and evening. About 6 we thought she would have died, and I went with all haste for Dr Alderson. The pain made her sick and the sickness for a time almost deprived her of sight. On administering a saline julep, it returned immediately and strained her to a violent degree. We are now ordered to rub her with equal parts of opium and spirit of turpentine.

Saturday, 19 January
My wife continues still much indisposed. I have met with a singular occurrence today which has rather surprised me. Mr Gulliver, one of my hearers and husband to one of the members, has been ill for a

long time of a liver complaint and I have visited and prayed with him once or twice a week ever since November 1809. His wife came to me this afternoon in great distress intimating that he wished to receive the sacrament of the Lord's supper and that Mr Morley should administer it. I told her that my practice was never to give it in private; and advised her to let him have his way, but should expect that he would request the minister of his choice to visit him in future. The last time I was with him I spoke as close to his conscience as I possibly could and I apprehend this has either alarmed him or offended him.

Lord's Day, 20 January

Last Monday Mr John Dunden, a member of our church, went down to Grimsby in order to see a son going on a voyage. In this he was disappointed. Going to see a friend near the lock between 7 and 8 in the evening (thro' the glimmering of the lamps on the water) he mistook his path and fell in. He called for help and it was soon obtained, but tho' so soon got out and had taken in little water, and exclaiming after he was taken into the house, 'Lord help me', he expired though every mean was used for his recovery.

Tuesday, 22 January

Thro' mercy my wife is much eased of her pain but still is very weak and confined to her room. . . . My annual and unknown friend has sent me a present of five guineas.

Lord's Day, 17 February

The times are very dark, trade dull, the nation in a lamentable state, the King deranged and his son, though appointed regent, shackled, and religion in a low condition, which led me to preach this forenoon from Isaiah 3.10 and I was much favoured with divine assistance.

Wednesday, 13 March

The day being fine and the sun warm, I walked out in the forenoon and went on the Humber bank A man was about two yards before me with a spade on his shoulder and a dog which was running came full force against his right knee. Whether the cap of the knee was displaced or the joint dislocated, but he could not set his foot to the ground. After staying with him some time, I found the wind affect me and walked on over half a mile, but on my return found him in the same situation and a person gone for help to carry him home. How easily might his condition have been my own.

Wednesday, 20 March

The collection [for the British prisoners detained in France] was £15.11.8. . . . In the afternoon I heard a sermon at St John's Church. . . . It was a discourse without any division. There was a large congregation to hear it.

Lord's Day, 24 March
A persecution has again lately lifted up its head in some parts of the kingdom.

Tuesday, 9 April
This is the anniversary of my first settlement in Hull which has closed up the 42nd year of my ministry.

Thursday, 23 May
Lord Sidmouth having brought forth his Bill[265] in the House of Lords on Tuesday, I received the copy of the Bill and forms of petitions to the two Houses of Parliament. In the evening Dissenting ministers of different denominations held a meeting and resolved on a public meeting at our chapel tonight. A vast concourse of people assembled, the greatest order was preserved, the speakers in seconding the resolutions were admirable, and the meeting continued from a quarter before 7 till near 10 at night. I was voted into the chair on this occasion and believe a more respectable and orderly meeting was never held on a similar occasion.

Friday, 24 May
This morning's post brought us the joyful news that Lord Sidmouth's Bill was thrown out of the House of Lords. Hundreds of addresses were presented against it. More than 100 by Lord Holland and more than double that number by Earl Erskine, in short, as the Archbishop of Canterbury remarked, *a flood of addresses*. To God be the praise for the success that has crowned the spirits and the exertions of the Dissenters.

Lord's Day, 26 May
After a week of extraordinary exertions and fatigue and after the success thereof by the rejection of Lord Sidmouth's Bill by the House of Lords against the Dissenters, I preached this forenoon from 1 Thess 2.15 with great enlargement. . . . We had a collection for the opposition to Lord Sidmouth's Bill £16.17.1.

Lord's Day, 2 June
Another public meeting was held at the chapel on Thursday last to pass some resolutions of thanks to the noblemen and others who had assisted in the rejection of Lord Sidmouth's Bill. On Friday I received a very singular letter either from a Swedenborger or a madman respecting his being appointed for the conversion of the Jews and signing himself Ruler over the house of God. This morning he knocked me up soon after 6 o'clock, as he had also done a neighbour thro' mistake of my house. On going down to him he began talking in a strange manner and requested me to lend him ten or 20 pounds, which upon my refusing he said he would now go to a Jew and would ask him. He had requested Mr Cambs [?] (at the next door) to come in with him, which I considered as a favour or I know not what might have followed.

Saturday, 22 June
During the last night I have had full proof of the defilement of the heart and of Satan's power on the mind during sleep. Images have been presented to my mind so unusual, so unnatural and so abhorrent even at the very season that could not originate from God, from my own mind and from what I ever heard or saw in others, but so unchaste and polluted as could only come from the author of all evil.

Monday, 3 July
Yesterday being the day appointed for the Eastern Association to be held at Swanland, I left Hull after dinner [Lists those present.] ... I afterwards slept at Anlaby. Today the forenoon was taken up in giving an account of the state of our several churches.

Thursday, 11 July
I had a letter to write and bills to procure for London to send upon the closing up the account of the receipts and expenditure on Lord Sidmouth's Bill, a box to pack and send off by the mail for Leeds, and to preach the lecture in the evening from Isaiah 54. 7.8. This morning Mr C Newbald[266] called to signify his intended marriage and the probability of his leaving his present connection with our church. At eleven went to spend the day with Mrs Egginton at Cottingham and preached there in the evening.

Tuesday, 16 July
This day my son Joseph's wife was safely delivered of a fine boy.[267]

Thursday, 1 August
This morning I heard the bells ringing on account of the marriage of one of our church members [Charles Newbald][268] to a lady of high church principles, and as a preliminary to which he was to conform to her mode of worship. This led me to review the reasons why I am a Dissenter. [Lists 7 arguments, beginning 1 Because I acknowledge no other head, king or lawgiver in the church but Christ 2 Because Dissenting churches in my view of things come the nearest to the plan of the Apostolic Church. 3 Because I am not obliged to call any man master or be under the authority of archbishops, bishops etc. 4 Because I am the subject of my people's free choice and also of their attendance and support.]

Lord's Day, 11 August
Not having to preach this forenoon as Dr Williams[269] was come to Hull to collect for Rotherham Academy. I attended the vestry prayer meeting in the morning at 7 o'clock and was much delighted. The Dr preached a very excellent discourse in the forenoon. ... The collection £21.5.6.

Monday, 12 August
After a very uncomfortable night.... Being engaged to dine with Dr Williams at Mr Rust's, I went but ate little. In the afternoon I felt better and heard the Dr this evening at our place of worship from 1 Pet 1.8.... He introduced an anecdote of Thomas Paine.[270] Being at an hotel in New York at an ordinary, after dinner he and a player, one of the company, agreed to go upstairs to converse on politics and religion. Being full of wine, in coming down stairs he fell and wounded himself much. They took him up and laid him on a bed, besmeared with blood. A person seeing him in this state said to a companion, 'Follow me and I will show you a strange sight.' This was done and then says he, 'Behold the author of the age of reason.' About two months since, Paine died. His horrors were indescribable, his shrieks heard thro' all the house. The physician attending on him heard him exclaiming, 'Lord [have] Mercy on me! Christ have mercy on me!' He was asked [if] he then believed that the Christ he called was God, and could save him. The physician receiving no answer said, 'I will qualify the question. Do you desire to know him as able to save you?' To which he replied, 'I do not know that I have any desire about it', and became stupid and died in that condition. The account was delivered with great pathos and was truly affecting. The Dr then proceeded to show the effect of faith viz love to Christ and joy in him.

Lord's Day, 1 September
I have had Dr Alderson and Mr Fielding[271] this evening.

Friday, 13 September
My eldest son left us today on his return to London. He is generous, affectionate to all the family and possesses a number of good qualities, but I have much concern about him, both for his soul and body. The former I fear he thinks little about and the latter he indulges too freely, which I fear may hasten his death – from evident fullness I cannot but apprehend some danger of a fit.

Saturday, 21 September
I have this afternoon followed the corpse of my old friend and fellow traveller, Mr Riddell,[272] to the tomb. He died on Wednesday morning at 2 o'clock after enjoying wonderful support upon a dying bed. He has been a useful and honoured instrument in his day in promoting the cause of Christ in Hull and other places. He was judicious, zealous and active. One of the first in the promotion of the church and the last survivor of the original number.

Tuesday, 1 October
This day week my wife and I went to spend a week at Anlaby with J Boyes Esq and returned this morning. It has been rain every day except Sunday, when I preached at Swanland in the forenoon from Zach 9.16. At which time excepted, I never got out once of the gates.

They have been very kind, but I felt very happy in returning to my own tents to find all my family in good health.

Lord's Day, 13 October
Last Thursday my son George and daughter Eliza left Hull for Leeds and I have since heard arrived there in safety.

Lord's Day, 20 October
On Thursday the Revd W Tapp of Cave broke his leg by leaping out of a gig after setting his daughter down at his own door. The horse took fright or proved unruly and run away with him in the chair. His son jumped out and received no hurt but he received this injury and is laid aside by it.

Friday, 1 November
This morning opened with a dark cloud over me and my family by a letter received from my eldest son to his brother informing us that by his speculations in underwriting he was completely ruined. This was an engagement I was always averse to. No young man could have a better prospect before him or had greater advantages to do well, being connected with one of the first houses in London and had done well till being determined to be rich he grasped the shadow and lost the substance, even all that he had. It is a blot on my family which I cannot but feel keenly.

Tuesday, 10 December
The days are very short and when candles are lighted, my sight has become so bad that I can read very little. This makes the time hang very heavy. It is only in the forenoon that I can see, and that is the only time in which I can get out to see the sick; for after dinner if I go out it raises my cough and greatly affects my breath.

Monday, 16 December
By a letter received from my son Samuel today we are informed of the death of Mr Tom Ansley, my wife's nephew. He has been in a deranged state for some time, and, though not 30 years of age, is cut down by the scythe of death. His father left him a large fortune, when young he was rather ungovernable, married not very agreeably to his family, had no children, no employment and probably not the most happy in his domestic connection. Well has the psalmist said men heap up riches but know not who shall gather them. This has been verified in his father, another of whose sons married, had one child, left it and his widow a large fortune, who is lately married again to a Colonel Turner.

1812

Tuesday, 7 January
Solomon describes the effects of age by 'the grinders being low', but mine have not only been low but (one excepted) they are gone and

to assist speech and chew food I have long been obliged to have artificial assistance. Last night, while at tea, the hook formed of gold wire broke, and I imperceptibly swallowed it. Being curved and sharp at each end, I thought it prudent to take an emetic last night and that not having brought it away I have this morning taken salts. Have also sent the artificial teeth to the dentist at York for fresh help; and should he be at home hope for their return tonight. But if this should fail I know not what I must do. Indeed if the piece of wire which I have swallowed should not come away, it is impossible to conceive the consequence. I have now the sentence of death in myself but leave that and every event in the hands of that God who performeth all things for me.

Wednesday, 8 January
Yesterday I took physic in order to pass the hook I had taken in with my food, but I fear without effect. But last night before I had been in bed 5 minutes there was a violent knocking at the door and an alarm that the house was on fire. I got up and found the kitchen chimney blazing out and roaring at a most tremendous rate. Two neighbours and another man were let into the house and the flames soon subsided. It is not above a month since we had it swept, nor had we any great fire to occasion it. It must have been from the neglect of the chimney sweeper.

Monday, 13 January
I have this day received a very long and affecting letter by the post signed a Member of the Church complaining of great declension in their own soul and in the church and attributing the low state of the church to the ministry of Mr P[ayne]. The letter is written in a good spirit by a person of no mean abilities, one who has known the church for 17 or 18 years and compares the state of the church then with things at present. I am much concerned, cannot but say there is too much truth in his remarks and, tho' I feel keenly for Mr P, something must be done.

Thursday, 16 January
Yesterday I had a meeting with the deacons and laid the letter mentioned above before them. As being without a name they thought it ought not to be noticed, but, as some facts alluded to in it were known, they ought to be mentioned to Mr P, and Mr Rust undertook the painful task. To me it is a matter of great concern. But trials come not alone. Today my son Samuel wrote his brother that thro' the badness of his underwriting business his partnership in the house was dissolved, would be gazetted, and that he must be made a bankrupt. In the church, the world and in my family it is a dark and gloomy day.

Lord's Day, 19 January

The stoppage of the bank at Leeds,[273] and the dissolution of the partnership of the house in London with which my eldest son was connected have so affected my spirits that I knew not how either to study or preach. However, with difficulty I put a few thoughts together and this day I delivered them with much confusion. . . . However, some intimated that it had been made a profitable subject to them.

Tuesday, 21 January

I this day received of Mr J S Bowden ten guineas being a legacy left me by my kind and highly esteemed friend Mr Edward Riddell, who was one of the first instruments under God of bringing me to Hull. It was what I had little expected for, though it had been in a former will, thro' the influence of his son it was left out in his last, but he had told me in his last illness that he had desired his daughter Bowden that it was his desire that it might be paid, the same as if it had been mentioned in the will.

Lord's Day, 26 January

The affecting strokes on my family have greatly affected my spirits. I scarce know how to appear in the pulpit or like to meet anybody in the streets, tho' I am not sensible of anything wrong respecting my own conduct, not do I know anything except imprudence in the case of my eldest son; and as to the other it demands pity.

Wednesday, 5 February

This day being appointed for a general national fast.

Saturday, 8 February

I have been in a constant succession of hurry and confusion for several days, thro' a proposal to forward a petition to Parliament for the abolition of the penal laws against the Dissenters, and that it must be done with all speed. But, as the notice was so sudden, the season allowed so short, the impracti[ca]bility of rendering it general, and the Catholic question being just rejected, as well as the restrictions on the Prince Regent ready to terminate, I thought with others it was best to postpone it, or at least to take more time in doing it. The late encroachments on the act of toleration render the aspect of things very discouraging.

Lord's Day, 16 February

Mr Payne has signified his intention of leaving us – altogether I have been very uneasy.

Lord's Day, 23 February

Mr Payne having sent a letter to be read to the church tomorrow evening respecting his withdrawing as an assistant, which may excite different feelings in the minds of different persons, I preached this forenoon from Paul 12.2 and found much pleasure in the work.

Monday, 24 February

A church meeting was called for this evening at 7 o'clock in consequence of a letter from the Revd G Payne respecting his determination to relinquish the office of assistant to the minister. After it was read to the church it was proposed to request him to stay (if he did not leave the town) till midsummer instead of leaving as he proposed, at the end of March. I felt very unfit for the business and uncomfortable in it; as I had attended Mrs Donaldson's funeral to Cottingham in the afternoon, I thought myself rather reflected on, if not unjustly charged.

Saturday, 29 February

None of the deacons have been with me, nor informed me of Mr Payne's answer. I have had my eldest son much on my thoughts today as it was the last time for his attending before his creditors.

Monday, 16 March

The deacons were with me this afternoon intimating that, since Mr Payne's letter had been read to the church expressive of his intention to resign, several of the people had intimated great concern, and that some thought the church should have opportunity to signify whether they accepted of his resignation or not. I told them it ought to have been mentioned at the time, that it would be difficult fully to get to the mind of the church, that the putting it to a vote might be attended with bad consequences and that even in that case a bare majority one way or other ought not to be decisive. But that really at my age I had not spirits equal to such a painful conflict and therefore must leave them to determine for themselves. The fact is the deacons are so attached to him that they are trying every method to retain him, whatever events may follow.

Saturday, 21 March

Last night Mr Reader called upon me upon the same subject with the deacons on Monday last and urged much the calling of a church meeting. But I see no object to be gained as I conclude Mr P would not be willing to *divide* the church nor to *stay,* provided the majority should be willing to retain him, or to have several if not the major part of those against him to retire and leave the place. Should this be the case — and I have heard it from some — I should not wish to continue with a divided church but be forced to resign the office of pastor. This morning my son John left us on his return to Manchester. . . . This evening Mr Bowden called upon the same subject with Mr Reader and his appearing to think that many wished for a meeting. After tea I wrote the following: Dear Sir, Though I could never think of calling a meeting of the church on my own account upon the unhappy business we conversed upon this afternoon, yet if it be thought necessary and expedient by others if they will in writing signify their desire — the subject on which it is called — and the season, I will give public notice of it and remain, Dear Sir, Yours sincerely GL. It is a most perplexing affair for it will be attended with disagreeable consequences. ... While the servant was gone with the above I received a note from Mr P signifying his intention of preaching his last sermon this afternoon as an assistant to me in the ministry.

Tuesday, 24 March

The idea of Mr Payne's removal has produced a wonderful commotion. It has so affected and unhinged the minds of the people as to afford me considerable uneasiness and I had almost come to the resolution of preaching next Lord's Day on Jer 17.16, and after doing it publicly to have resigned the pastoral charge and thrown myself upon Providence. But Mr Rust called upon me, and after opening my mind freely and fully to him, and what he urged in reply, has rather composed my mind. I wish to do nothing hastily, nor one thing wrong, but look to God for counsel and guidance in all things.

Lord's Day, 29 March

The morning was unusually dark; my sight bad and my spirits oppressed; but I got thro' the morning service, though not as I could have wished. ... Mr Spry of Dagger Lane preached in the afternoon. ... He has a strong commanding voice but apparently a weak mind.

Wednesday, 8 April

A very painful office has been assigned to me today by a letter received from B Wright Esq[274] on the sudden death of the late Revd J Bowden of Tooting. The unkind conduct of several in his church had led him to give in the resignation of his pastoral office. His son-in-law Mr Washburn being invited to fix at Hammersmith he rode there to preach and administer the Lord's Supper last Sabbath morning. But while preaching he was seized with a fit, fell down and soon after died. This I had to break out to his son, who soon after set off for London. He was an amiable, affectionate friend, a faithful and excellent preacher and a shining experimental Christian. His case (as bearing some similarity to my own) has affected me much.

Saturday, 18 April

I was this afternoon called to visit Simon Joseph, formerly a Jew, who was very ill. Before his illness he had regularly attended public worship at the chapel and professed his faith in Christ as the Messiah, and the only saviour from sin. He had repeatedly wished to be baptised, but fearing there might be some deception, I had waived it. Though I had visited formerly when he had been very ill and he had always professed that Christ was his only hope. Today I found him in bed, much swelled in his body by a dropsy, still professing his hope of pardon and being saved by Christ alone, and desiring to die as a Christian. Though 84 years of age, I baptised him, and hope in doing so I have discharged my duty. He had never learned to read, had been affected by two strokes of the palsy several years back, and therefore was very weak in his understanding, but I trust sincere.

Friday, 15 May
The death of Mr Perceval, the Prime Minister, being shot as he was going into the House of Commons, has rendered this week all anxiety and confusion. Such men stand in slippery places and like their inferiors are in jeopardy every hour. May it have a warning voice to all that the great who consider themselves as a kind of inferior gods may remember that they are but men. The times are awfully tremendous and portend something great either in a way of judgement or of mercy.

Lord's Day, 17 May
I have been so much troubled with a heaviness and pain in my head for several days as to be unable to study, and was driven to the painful necessity of preaching an old sermon this forenoon from Luke 8 22-24 which on account of the crowding on Monday last to see the *Anson*, a 74-gun ship, launched at Paull, on the very day, and probably the very hour if not the very minute when Mr Perceval, the pilot of the nation, was shot, was appropriate.

Lord's Day, 24 May
I received this morning before service a most pleasing letter from Dr Williams in reference to Mr Whitridge, intimating his supplying for us during part of the vacation and giving a most pleasing description of him as likely for a permanent assistant.

Wednesday, 27 May
This day was removed by death, after a long series of confinement and decay of corporal and mental powers the Revd John Beverley[275] aged 80. He had long ministered to the Dissenting Congregation in Bowlalley Lane, and was the last and only minister that remained when I first came to settle in Hull, whether in the Establishment or out of it. He was a man of an amiable and peaceable disposition; if decided, not very clear in his religious sentiments, far from being explicit in public, and in private intimating that all good men merit the same thing. Several of his hearers did not believe that he denied the divinity or atonement of Christ. If he disbelieved them he did not avow it openly, but his present successor is an open and a vowed Socinian.

Wednesday, 10 June
Today being the anniversary of the Hull Auxiliary Bible Society I attended the meeting. Many excellent speeches were made by Mr Scott, Swain, Payne, Birt and Dikes; and as they had fixed upon me to propose one of the resolutions (which I had no idea of before I went to the meeting) I was obliged to introduce it by a few words. However, I never was adapted to be an off-hand speaker and therefore should not have attempted it, could I with any decency

have avoided it. Indeed some of the speeches appeared too much studied with an intention to shine and were protracted to too great length.

Lord's Day, 14 June
Mr Payne intending to leave Hull tomorrow for Edinburgh preached another farewell sermon. ... I charitably hope he has no such intention, but it certainly has a tendency to keep alive animosities and promote divisions. But I still hope things will subside and that the God of love and peace will be with us, and prosper his endeavours amongst the people he is going to minister to.

Lord's Day, 21 June
I was standing in the parlour yesterday when a most vivid flash of lightning was followed by a tremendous clap of thunder. A man of the name of Witty who lives in Mytongate was struck dead upon the road as he was coming from Anlaby.

Tuesday, 30 June
The complaint, I am confident, is the *Angina Pectoris*. I consulted Dr Alderson this morning who ordered me to be bled and to take some pills, which has been attended to. The application was rather to please my family and friends than from any hope of a final cure.

Wednesday, 8 July
I left Hull yesterday soon after 6 to attend the Eastern Association held this day at Driffield. ... The forenoon of the day was devoted to the ordination of Bro Earle to the United Churches of Skipsea and Leven.

Monday, 3 August
This evening being the Monday monthly missionary meeting Mr Collison had intimated his intention to return and speak upon the occasion, and a public collection was to have been made for the benefit of the parent society. It was my province to give public notice of his intention at the last meeting and to speak if he was not present at this. Being disappointed, I entered the pulpit with considerable embarrassment, intending to speak from Zach 3.8-10, but my sight is now so much gone that I could neither read nor exactly repeat the words.

Friday, 7 August
Last night I went to bed rather uncomfortable in not being able to fix upon a text or subject. While sleeping it occupied my thoughts, but about 1 o'clock this morning I awoke with a text which opened and expanded to the view of my mind: I rose up and took the candle but the instant I turned round the lamp went out. I returned to bed but could not sleep for fear of forgetting the ideas, which kept increasing in my mind. At last I got up, struck a light and went to my study

where I wrote out the plan, which, thank God, with some degree of pleasure I have been filling up today.

Lord's Day, 23 August
On Wednesday evening my son George arrived from Leeds to spend a few days with us. Thanks be to God for his health continued and the success which has attended his endeavours.

Lord's Day, 30 August
My son George left us on Monday afternoon by the mail coach on account of the repeat of some riots taking place at Leeds.

Monday, 28 September
This being the day appointed for the formation of the Hull Juvenile Auxiliary Society to the London Missionary Society, after a very rainy day we assembled in the Girls Subscription schoolroom in Salthouse Lane at 7 o'clock. It had then cleared up. I was called to the chair which I filled as well as I could but not as I would have wished to have done. Several of my young friends acquitted themselves well in the speeches they delivered prior to the rules laid down. Mr James Bowden Jnr, Mr Shipham, Mr Wright,[276] two of the Revd Mr Dikes' sons and particularly Mr William Briggs,[277] who delivered a most excellent and animating speech and with great composure. I trust it will be followed with great usefulness and, tho' much ashamed of my poor attempts to serve so good a cause, I esteemed it a high gratification to be encircled by so many young friends who I trust will be useful and ornamental members in the Church of Christ.

Monday, 5 October
This day the election in this borough for Members of Parliament came on and the confusion has been great.[278] Though I have no vote, have espoused no party, not spoken a word for or against either of the candidates and have not even been a looker on, I had six panes of glass broken in my chamber window. Several others in the neighbourhood have been treated in the same way, but not equally in degree. It was unprovoked and I hope undeserved injury.

1813

Friday, 1 January
The year has been ushered in with a morning like the smile of spring. . . . The church is yet in an unsettled state in reference to an assisting minister. A person who had been recommended to us fairly is expected to visit us after two Sabbaths.

Thursday, 11 February
Seventy-one years have now been rolled up like a scroll since it was first said to my mother that a man child was born of her, and in the review of life's journey what a winding path presents itself to view! I

first drew my breath at Chelsea, where infancy and childhood passed by; after that, near Hampstead; then Tewkesbury in Gloucestershire; afterwards London, and finally Yorkshire. What interpositions of divine Providence have I seen! What abounding goodness and mercy have followed me, day after day, thro' a much longer life than has been allotted to many. A large family given, provided for, grown up and some of them comfortably settled. Now 44 years I have been settled as the teacher and pastor of an increasing flock. Have seen children's children and peace in Israel. And now, Lord when I am old and grey-headed, forsake me not, but my life which thou last made thy care, Lord, I devote to thee.

Lord's Day, 21 February

In the evening I went in a coach to Summergangs to see my friend Mr Gilder probably for the last time, as I found him hardly sensible, or like a person who being roused out of a deep sleep instantly returned to the same stupor.

Wednesday, 24 February

Death has this day deprived me of a true and a great friend in the removal of Mr John Gilder. A more upright man perhaps never lived. He had been a member of the church near 43 years, 41 of which he sustained the office of deacon. More than the last 2 years he has been confined to the house by a very tying and unusual complaint, supposed to be caused by the blood flowing to the head but being obstructed in its actions to the heart produced a continual giddiness that he could neither stand or walk and of late has been reduced almost to childhood. He was about 73 years of age.

Thursday, 11 March

This morning I received a letter from Jonathan Walker Esq informing me of the unexpected death of my kind friend Dr Williams on Tuesday night at 10 o'clock. It will be a great loss indeed to his widow, the family, the Church, the Academy and indeed to the Church in general. For piety, learning, knowledge of the truth or ability to explain or vindicate it, where shall we find such a man as he was, a man in whom the spirit of God so eminently abode.

Wednesday, 24 March

This day week I set out in company with Mr Bowden and his elder sons for Rotherham, upon the death of Dr Williams.[279] We got to Mr Walker's of Clifton about 7 in the evening. Thursday forenoon attended the funeral of my highly respected friend. Mr Boden of Sheffield spoke on the occasion and I concluded in prayer. It was a large funeral and conducted with great solemnity. Friday we went to Sheffield and called upon several friends. Saturday visited [more friends] and dined with Jonathan Walker Esq. . . . In the afternoon I preached the funeral sermon from 2 Kings 2.5. The place was crowded, pews doubly filled and many were obliged to depart because they could not get in. Monday we received the final answer from Mr Cooper[280] in the negative and in the afternoon attended a meeting of the committee for considering who was likely to succeed as Divinity Tutor. Yesterday we left Clifton about 8 o'clock and arrived safe in Hull about 9. Much fatigued but I hope thankful for mercies received.

Lord's Day, 2 May
Mr Browne,[281] who got from Rotherham last night, preached in the afternoon.

Friday, 7 May
I was this day called to a very affecting scene in visiting a daughter of the late Revd Robert Green in the workhouse. She had deviated from the paths of virtue and had a bastard child which was in the house with her. I found her sitting up in bed reduced to a mere skeleton. She had been despairing of mercy and was now insensible and speechless. She kept fingering the bed cloths and once or twice shook her head when I spoke to her, and when I prayed she appeared for a short time to attend, but soon tossed about as before. Truly the way of transgressors is hard as it leads both to despair and destruction. May my family be preserved from the paths of that destroyer.

Lord's Day, 11 July
St John's Church being under repair was shut up today, so that we had a fuller place than usual in the forenoon.

Lord's Day, 8 August
As very unfavourable tidings have been received from the Greenland fishery and some of the ships have arrived clean, I wished to improve that event this forenoon by preaching from Psalm 107.23.24. A large congregation and very attentive to the subject.

Lord's Day, 12 September
Mr Browne was proposed and ordered to be invited as the assisting minister.

Lord's Day, 7 November
This being the Sabbath after the 5th November on which day the wonderful news of the defeat of the French army under Bonaparte arrived, I preached this forenoon from 1 Sam 12.24 and found freedom of speech while engaged in that work. . . . But was very much embarrassed and confused in my address during the administration [of the Lord's Supper]. I am ashamed and grieved at the imperfections that manifest themselves in all my attempts to serve my God and the souls of my fellow creatures.

Lord's Day, 28 November

My mind much disturbed by an anonymous letter sent to Mr Browne last night. It was found to be from a member of the church and, if the motive was good, the tendency was bad. I hope it will not prevent his settling with us.

Lord's Day, 19 December

Last Wednesday being the day appointed for rejoicing on the wonderful political changes which have lately taken place I joined in the procession and accompanied them to the church where a sermon was preached by the vicar. There were afterwards a dinner, and fireworks in the evening, but I attended neither.

Saturday, 25 December

My sons William and Joseph dined with us and I baptised Joseph's two boys, born at a birth.[282]

Notes to Vol 11

[264] *14 January 1811.* Dover's Powders were a popular patent remedy invented by Thomas Dover (1660-c1742). They consisted of opium, saltpetre, potassium, liquorice and ipecacuanha and were a 'sweating' powder. Dover was a surgeon on the ship which rescued Alexander Selkirk, the original of Robinson Crusoe.

[265] *23 May 1811.* Lord Sidmouth's Bill. A repressive measure, claimed to remove incompetent preachers, but which would have had serious consequences for Dissenters, as it would not have allowed any minister to 'settle' over a congregation unless six householders testified to the magistrates that they knew him well, nor any student to go to college unless six ministers who had known him well testified to his suitability. See *Hull Rockingham*, 25 May 1811 re Hull public meeting of protest.

[266] *11 July 1811.* According to the *Hull Advertiser*, 3 August 1811, Charles Newbald and Miss Armstrong, both of Hull, were married on 2 [sic] August 1811 at Holy Trinity church by the Revd Thomas Dikes.

[267] *16 July 1810.* Fish Street baptismal register records that Joseph, son of Joseph and Elizabeth Lambert, was born 15 [sic] July 1811 and baptised 7 October 1811.

[268] *1 August 1811.* See 11 July 1811.

[269] *11 August 1811.* Rev Edward Williams was the first tutor at the Rotherham Academy (see 5 January 1806).

[270] *12 August 1811.* Thomas Paine (1737-1809), Radical author of *The Rights of Man*.

[271] *1 September 1811.* George Fielding (1773-1841), leading Hull surgeon and public figure. See Bickford 42.

[272] *21 September 1811.* Edward Riddell: see 1 January 1781.

[273] *19 January 1812.* Boldero, Lushington & Co, London bankers, stopped payment and Penton, Scott & Co's Leeds and Thirsk banks, involved with them, also stopped payment. (*Hull Advertiser*, 11 January 1812)

[274] *8 April 1812.* B Wright. See note 3 July 1783.

[275] *27 May 1812.* Rev John Beverley: The *Hull Advertiser*, 30 May 1812, gives his age as 79, and states that he had died after an illness of 13 years having been minister in Bowlalley Lane for 21 years.

[276] *28 September 1812.* B Wright. See note 3 July 1783.

[277] *28 September 1812.* William Briggs was a merchant who had shares in whaling ships.

[278] *5 October 1812.* John Staniforth and Sir George William Denys were elected.

[279] *24 March 1813.* GL's funeral sermon on Williams, *Elijah's Translation Foretold*, was published and is available in Dr Williams's Library.

[280] *24 March 1813.* The Rev James Cooper of West Bromwich had been assisting at Fish Street and had been offered a permanent appointment.

[281] *2 May 1813.* Rev George Browne (as he signed himself and as he was recorded in the Church Book, though GL sometimes writes 'Brown') served as GL's assistant 1812-16. His later career was distinguished. See Darwent 39.

[282] *25 December 1813.* Joseph's twin sons, George and John Robinson Lambert, born 30 November 1813, were baptised 25 December 1813.

Vol 12 1814-1816

1814

Thursday, 13 January
This being the day appointed for the day of general thanksgiving for recent victories over the French.[283]

Friday, 8 April
Being Good Friday, the season appointed for the opening of the chapel at Elloughton, I got there about 10 am and preached in the forenoon with much freedom and enlargement to a very attentive audience from Psalm 132.5. In the afternoon Mr Burt from 1 Kings 8.27. But as the place was crowded I stood on the outside of the walls and could not distinctly hear. Returned in the evening and got home soon after 8.

Lord's Day, 15 May
On Monday evening last, a daughter of Captain Anderson, 12 years old, sitting before the fire about 7 in the morning, a spark flew from the fire, caught her cloths, and burnt her in such a manner that she died about 4 o'clock in the afternoon. And on Friday evening Mr William Fearne, who from a boy had frequented my house, died after being in a decline several years. I had visited and prayed with him in the forenoon of the day. He died with great serenity and with only a sigh. He had been in business. Visited Devonshire, Clifton and Cantley [?] with hopes of recovering health, but died not quite 29 years of age. ... I heard that a boy belonging to one of the congregation had fallen from the mast and was killed on the spot.

Wednesday, 15 June
Today our annual Auxiliary Missionary Society commenced. There was a prayer meeting held in Salthouse Lane Chapel from 7-8. The more public services began at Fish Street at half after 10. ... A public meeting was held ½ after 5 in the schoolroom in Salthouse Lane. The Mayor in the chair. A variety of motions were proposed and carried. Several impressive speeches delivered. The place (tho' a rainy evening) crowded so that many were excluded and the business (tho' not finished) did not close till ½ after 9. The place was intensely hot. On the whole, though a busy, it has been a pleasant day.

Tuesday, 19 July
A very wonderful and merciful interposition of Providence I have to record. In going to bed this evening I had the candle in my hand and the night shirt hanging over my arm. The chamber window was open to admit air, and by opening the door suddenly the flame caught hold of the shirt and in a moment it was in flames. I threw it on the floor and by stamping upon it extinguished the fire. What was rather particular, I had on a loose cotton dress which, had the flame communicated to that, I might have been burnt to death.

Tuesday, 30 August
After a fortnight's absence upon a visit to Mr Boyes of Anlaby I got safe home to my own tent about 10 o'clock and found all well. . . . The most delightful situation, richest entertainment and hearty welcome though truly grateful is not like home in a much humbler style.

Lord's Day, 11 September
God has promised that his word shall not return to him void, but accomplish the very thing to which he sends it. Of this I had a pleasing evidence yesterday by a letter received from a young person, a farmer's daughter, at or near Louth in Lincolnshire. It is well written, sensible and signed MBT intimating her occasional attending under my ministry, receiving much spiritual profit and requesting some advice and an answer.

Tuesday, 16 September
I have heard today of the death of the Revd Richard Patrick,[284] vicar of Sculcoates. I remember him a lad under the tuition of my good friend, the Revd Joseph Milner. It is said he obtained that living in rather a clandestine manner, was an odd character, some say at seasons deranged, perhaps the best excuse that could be made for his conduct. He had been injured by the falling of a ladder which raised a tumour on the breast bone. He died in his way to London to obtain advice, tho' informed beforehand that he would die on the road, which he did.

Tuesday, 27 September
This afternoon ½ past 2 my son Samuel left us for London after a visit of better than a fortnight. He has been brought thro' deep waters, mercifully restored, and has been much prospered by Providence since. I wish he saw more of the hand of his deliverer and discovered an humble and grateful sense of God's kindness. But I fear it is not with him as I could wish; as to his soul's concerns, I saw some things which distressed me much.

Lord's Day, 27 November
Mrs Mary Levett sickened last Sunday, died on Tuesday morning, and was deposited in the family vault yesterday afternoon. What a series of changes has composed her life. Born of respectable parents, married to a tradesman in good business, lived in affluence, left on her husband's death in poverty, struggled through serious hardships with four daughters. A few weeks prior to her death remembered by a relative in his will by a legacy of £100 and in a few days hurried into eternity.

Lord's Day, 4 December
The chapel is to have no service in it for the two following Sabbaths as the joiners are to begin tomorrow to erect two galleries for the

Sunday school children. Whether I shall live to return to service therein God only knows.

14 Fish St Day Schools, 1871, now incorpoated into the Hands on History Museum. Photo 1980s

Tuesday, 13 December
I have been called to almost new, and to me, trying work today. My son Joseph needing larger supplies for his family, his wife's father, Mr Robinson, wished to procure him a situation in the Custom House and others have urged the application. To this end I had before written to William Wilberforce Esq. Today I applied to Colonel Burgess, Super Inspector of the Customs. He advised me to write directly to J Staniforth Esq, Member for Hull, which I have done and to procure a memorial signed by some respectable persons, which a friend has kindly and readily procured for me, and is now in a train[285] to forward to London. I have now done all that I can. The lot is cast into the lap, but the whole disposal is of the Lord. However, I can truly say it is more blessed to give than to receive.

Saturday, 31 December
Upon the Ebenezer I have to erect this day I have to inscribe my life and the lives of my family preserved. Daily supply and multiplied blessings. Peace restored to Europe[286] and the Church preserved in peace. A pleasing harmony between my kind assistants in the ministry and myself, and some intimation that our united labours have not been altogether in vain. 16 have been united to the church, 8 have been removed out of it by death, and 2 have been excluded for disorderly conduct.

1815

Lord's Day, 26 February
Being called to preach to the Greenland sailors before they went to sea I spoke from Psalm 107.23. The place was crowded and I had

much more pleasure in speaking than I expected after a very restless and disturbed night in which I heard every clock strike except 4 this morning.

Wednesday, 3 May

This is a season of great commotion in the trading world, and I fear will bring some reflections upon religion. Three persons, respectable as men of business and renowned as leading persons in different Christian societies, have failed. One a preacher and leader amongst the Wesleyan Methodists, another in the Connection separated from them, and the third amongst the Baptists. Not can it be known where it will end for, like the links of a chain, if one break many that depended on it fall with it.

Tuesday, 18 July

The Eastern York Association was this day held at Cottingham. I went in the morning and returned about three to be present at the Hull Juvenile Auxiliary Missionary Society. Engage[d] the whole day till the hour of meeting with company. With difficulty got to the school room in Salthouse Lane where the meeting was held. Called to the chair. Much confused … thro' pain and weakness I was obliged abruptly to leave the chair while [the Revd Mr Bradley of Manchester] was engaged and with some difficulty got home. My friends wish me and think me to be what I am not. I can neither run with the footmen nor contend with those who are on horses. My strength faileth.

Friday, 21 July

Many friends called on me or applied for tickets for the Lord's Supper till about 6 in the evening. Half after, that ordinance was administered at Hope Street Chapel. It was my lot to preach.

Lord's Day, 31 December

Through this year my wife and family have been spared to me, friends have been very kind, every want has been supplied. My third son has commenced a new concern for himself and has the prospect of supporting his family comfortably.

1816

Lord's Day, 7 January

The chapel committee met last Wednesday to whom I addressed a letter proposing to resign the pastoral office; to which they returned a most affectionate reply requesting my continuing to hold not only the office but the emoluments connected with it.

Lord's Day, 10 March

My complaints increase. Spasms frequent. Cough very deep and hard and legs swelled till it is with difficulty I get up and down stairs.

All these things indicate the approaching change. But I bless God. I feel resigned and rather desirous to depart not so much that I may be freed from pain but that I may be with Christ and enjoy in him a fulness which will ever satisfy but never cloy. The Revd A Kidd preached in the forenoon from Isaiah 33.17 and administered the Lord's supper in the evening and Mr Browne preached in the afternoon from John 10.11. [This is the last entry. He died one week later, 17 March 1816.]

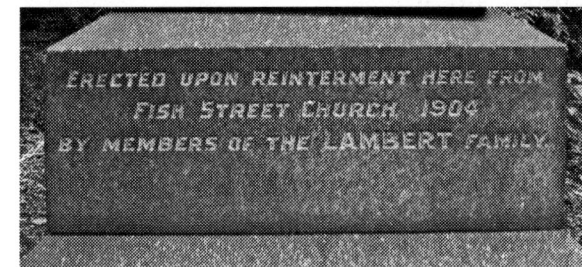

16 Details of Lambert memorial

15 Lambert memorial, Hull General Cemetery, Spring Bank

Notes to Vol 12

[283] *13 January 1814.* During November and December 1813 there had been a number of significant victories against Napoleon.

[284] *16 September 1814.* Rev Richard Patrick (1794-1814) vicar of St Mary's, Sculcoates, was a regular contributor to the *Classical Journal*.

[285] *13 December 1814.* In a train: in course of preparation.

[286] *31 December 1814.* After a series of defeats Napoleon had abdicated and been exiled to Elba.

Appendix A

Some remarks on the experience of me Geo Lambert

I was born on January 31, 1741½[287] at Chelsea in the parish of St George's, Hanover Square. My parents were members of the Church of England. They, particular my Mother, took every opportunity to impress my mind with a sense of the Majesty and Omnipresence of God. In a state of childhood I was not fond of those amusements which are common to that age; but spent much of my time in reading and amusing myself in the garden. My constitution was very weak and I was frequently troubled with fevers and other disorders.

When I was about nine years old I had the smallpox and was so ill that I heard the apothecary pronounce my case beyond hope of recovery. This alarmed me very much. A dread of death and Eternity seized my mind; and I concluded that nothing but Hell could be my portion. But these, and other convictions, were soon passed over and forgotten.

I was much in the same condition at another time in a storm of thunder. Fear drew me to my knees, and my Mother has often observed to me how fervently I prayed. But these were no more than the alarms of natural conscience.

Till about the seventeenth year of my life, I was a stranger to all proper knowledge of God and myself. For after I was removed from under the eye of my Mother, I had neglected prayer, often made the day of the Lord a day of visiting and had pursued some courses which have since given me much concern. And tho' preserved from gross and scandalous sins which some run into, yet my heart was exceedingly wicked. Being brought very low by a nervous fever, I was ordered by the physician into the country. I gained strength very fast and was able to return to London in a few weeks. On the Lord's day following, I called upon an intimate friend when to my great surprise I was informed that he was removed suddenly, and buried that day was a week. This revived [?] my sleeping conscience. I stood amazed at the patience and kindness of God, in sparing me. A sense of my ingratitude for his late deliverance and a solemn dread [?] of Death. Judgement and Eternity pressed with such weight upon my mind so that night and day I could get no rest. I was even afraid to close my eyes, lest I should wake in everlasting burning. The sins of my life, and the opportunities I had neglected, were continually in my view, and I had no one person that I could open my mind to. Such thoughts as these were always upon my mind: 'I have been warned but my friend was removed by a sudden stroke. He had not attained to my age and yet he is removed. Should my case be like his, should death take me away in my present state, I am undone for ever.' I now resolved upon a change of conduct, duties were followed with the rigid severity of a Pharisee. After some time spent in this course I began to fancy that now I was in the favour of God. No pains were spared to establish [?] a righteousness of my own (for all this time I had no knowledge of pardon and salvation thro' Christ). I prayed three times a day. Read *The whole duty of man*,[288] *The Practice of Piety*,[289] and several other books of the same sort.

But after some time spent in this way (and I may add that I found some delight and considerable zeal and fervency in these duties), after some time I was led to reflect more closely on my former course, and to reason thus: 'that tho' I did my duty at present, yet this was no satisfaction for the former neglect of it. If former sins were not pardoned, I was yet as far from the favour of God as ever.' I attended the sacrament at the church, hoping this might do something towards my relief. But there being few communicants I had not time to read over one of the prayers (in the week's preparation) in the course; and this blasted all my hopes and made me more uneasy than I was before. I found many defects in my present course of service. A sense of old sins revived, the thoughts of death still alarmed me. I had a continual dread that all was not right between my soul and God. And tho' I read the Scriptures daily, I had no knowledge of the design and efficacy of the death of Christ. About this time Mr Harvey's Dialogues[290] were published in numbers. I took them in and in reading them my mind was much enlightened, not only so, but my conscience was relieved by John 1.7 which I met with in the course of reading them. These words were opened and applied to my mind, in a very particular manner. Every word was important. My mind was enlightened, so as to have quite a new view of things. I saw that there was pardon thro' the blood of Jesus, that it cleansed from sin – from *all sin*. Sometimes I was ready to hold off the comfort, and conclude it was not for me. My sins were peculiarly great, and in many respects peculiarly aggravated. But then this thought would return: 'If the blood of Christ was sufficient to cleanse from *all sin*, my sins were not too great to be pardoned.' I ventured upon it and found peace, rest and some degree of freedom with God, which I had never found before. I now applied to my Bible with more diligence than ever; tho' I was obliged to do it by stealth, by reason of discouragement that I met with from the family in which I then was. Here I found that gracious declaration of the Redeemer, *he that cometh to me I will in no wise cast out*. This gave further comfort. About the same time I heard a sermon from Isaiah 45.25. (*I even I am he that blotteth out* etc.) I had pleasure in hearing; and found some enlargement of soul afterwards in meditating *on it,* and pleading it before the Lord. This was the first clear gospel sermon that I had heard since I was under any concern. I had been trained up in the strongest prejudices against *such* ministers, whether Churchmen or Dissenters.

From this time I attended upon means with another view. I sat under such ministers as could shew the way of life to a poor ignorant sinner. Such as Messrs Jones, Romaine, Madan and Harris.[291] The *first* and the *last* of these were made very useful to me. In attending at the Leek Chapel I got acquainted with a pious elderly lady who lived near my parents and who frequently invited me to her house. Her conversation was often very instructive and refreshing but frequently speaking of her feelings of a depraved and corrupt heart, I secretly suspected her to be a hypocrite but have since found that she had advanced further in the school of experience than I had. She said after that she was fully persuaded in her mind that I should sometime be a Gospel minister and presented me with a copy of Bishop Reynold's[292] works, desiring that I would read it attentively. This gave umbrage to my relations, but I wanted food for my soul. As they had always discovered the greatest affection to me, it gave me great pain to appear to evidence the least degree of ingratitude towards them, or cause them a moment's uneasiness. But I did not dare to turn my back upon *that*, which was now all my support.

For some time I was carried on in a very comfortable manner, was much refreshed and encouraged under the word. My friends began to be more reconciled to my way of going on. I thought that all was well, my mountain seemed to stand firm. But I now began to find the workings of a depraved nature. Satan assaulted me with temptations, and by the means of a vile young woman (a servant in the family) had well nigh prevailed. My consent was gone. But by an unexpected turn of Providence the snare was broken and my soul delivered. Darkness ensued. I was a terror to myself. My fear was that I was but a hypocrite. Or if I had any grace, that I should surely be ruined before I reached the end of my journey. In this condition my mind was relieved by Isaiah 41.10. (*Fear not thou for I am with* etc.) I now began to see the care of God over me, his kindness to me, his goodness in sparing me while in a state of nature and in calling me out of it. In bringing me to know anything of the blessed Jesus and to see the boundless treasures of grace, merit, righteousness and strength that there were in him. I saw *that* in him which was able to supply all my wants. The 35 and 53 Chapters of Isaiah, as also Hosea 14, were made very refreshing to me about this time.

After some time I was removed into Yorkshire, where for more than a year I had no opportunity to hear a Gospel sermon. But I never knew such a season as this was. The Scriptures were so opened to my understanding. Meditation was so sweet, and I had such great opportunities for it.

Prayer was also very pleasant to me and I found much enlargement in it. But after some time I was brought into great darkness and have since been led to see that I had abused the favours of the Lord, and was placing too much confidence upon these frames and enlargements. It was in mercy the Lord hid his face from me for a season that I might be led to see that, as all good comes from him, so all the glory is due to him. Whilst I was in this solitary situation I gave myself much to reading, and when I had opportunity spoke to such in the family about divine matters as would give me the hearing. I wished to devote the remainder of my time to the service of God in the sanctuary and to have it in my power to minister to Souls. My mind was particularly inclined to the Dissenters and from the Scriptures I was led to approve of the method of those called Independents.

The gentleman under whose care I was fixed by my parents was a Deist. We had many disputes. But at last he attempted my life, protesting he would have my blood. But the Lord enabled me to get away from him. I left the house and never saw him after. But as my Father afterwards told me, that when he saw him on his death bed, he declared that it was his fixed purpose to have killed me, that it was my being so religious that led him to it – and that he had often been sorry that he could not effect his purpose.

I was now in a strange country, far from home, but the Lord raised me up friends. One of them was a member of the church at Heckmondwike to whom I related the thoughts I had formed about the ministry. He prevailed on me to accompany him to Mr Scott,[293] the tutor of the Academy. From him I met with great encouragement to come under his care with a view to preparatory studies. However, I went up to London, and proposed it to my father and mother. They consented. Accordingly I was admitted a student by the Society in London. Dr Conder[294] proposed my being under his direction at Homerton, but I then gave the preference to the Yorkshire Academy, which I have often repented of since. But there might be ends to answer which I can have but very imperfect views of in this imperfect state.

I was with Mr Scott about five years. In which time I recollect nothing very material except the death of my dear mother who was removed suddenly. My being admitted a member of the Church under the care of Mr Scott, and preaching the last year at *Cleckheaton*. My mother died January 27 1767.

Notes to Appendix A

[287] 174½: Until the reform of the calendar in 1765, the new year began officially on Lady Day, 25 March, and '½' indicates *the year* then designated as 1741 but now recognised as 1742.
[288] *The whole duty of man, necessary for all families*, by Richard Allestree, first published anonymously 1657, and extremely influential in the 18th century, reaching its 28th edition in 1790, warned of the perils incurred by neglecting our spiritual nature.
[289] Lewis Bayly, *The practice of piety: directing a Christian how to walk* (1611)
[290] James Hervey, *Theron and Aspasso: a series of dialogues and letters upon the most important and interesting subjects* (1735) See ODNB.
[291] David Jones (1735-1810), Welsh revivalist; William Romaine (1714-95); Martin Madan (1726-90); Howell Harris (1714-73). All had connections with Selina, Countess of Huntingdon, and have entries in ODNB.

Appendix A

[292] Edward Reynolds (1599-1676), Bishop of Norwich, whose works include *A Sermon Touching the Peace and Edification of the Church* (1638)

[293] Rev James Scott, Principal of Heckmondwike Dissenting Academy, died 1783.

[294] John Conder (1714-81) was tutor at Homerton Academy, and its predecessor at Mile End, from 1754 to his death.

Appendix B

The Last Public Execution in Hull:

George Lambert's account, reproduced in the *Criterion*:

Mr J J Sheahan, in his History of Hull, furnishes only brief particulars of the last public execution that took place in this town. We think the following notice, drawn from an unpublished journal kept by the Rev George Lambert, will be an interesting addition to our local history. The account read as follows:-

John Rogerson, being condemned on Saturday, 1st Aug, 1778, for the crime of high treason, in counterfeiting the coin of this kingdom, called half-crowns, on Wednesday, the 5th instant, I waited on him in dungeon, conversed with him for some time, found him very ignorant of the way of Salvation, and flattering himself with the hopes of a pardon, or, at least, a mitigation, of the sentence. I put the New Testament into his hand, and recommended him to read it attentively. After praying with him I left him, as before this, he had signified his desire that Mr Milner and Mr Harris should attend him.

I did not see him again till the Wednesday following; he now evinced much concern about his past life and present situation; before we parted he expressed a great desire to have me repeat my visits more frequently.

On Friday morning I went again; he expressed much concern on account of the hardness and stupidity of his heart. At the same time he remarked that he had found some liberty in prayer, but yet his heart was not as he wished to feel it. 'If,' said he, 'my situation or outward circumstances could effect a change here is everything one would think to do it.'

I told him he must go to God and pray earnestly, and 'that the blood of Jesus Christ cleanseth from all sin.' At first he seemed to stagger at the report, and said, 'How can such a wretch as I, who hath lived in the manner I have done, find mercy for a few days' reading and prayer.' He was answered that *where sin abounded grace did much more abound*; that he who came to Christ would by no means be cast out, and that God could justify such who, tho' ungodly in themselves, believed in Jesus.

On repeating my visit of Saturday evening I found him at prayer. He now said he hoped he had found mercy, and experienced his heart softened; and further that he was not so much concerned for sin on account of its effects as that it was against so good a God.

I read to him Isaiah XLIII, 23, 24, and said 'Now, this is just your case.' He answered, 'Indeed it is.' 'Well,' said I, 'what do you expect will follow upon the words I have now read.' He made a short pause,

Appendix B

and then replied, 'Was it not for the mercy of God in Christ I should be cast into the lake that burneth with fire and brimstone?'

I then read the 25th verse, 'I, even I, am He that blotteth out thy transgressions for My own sake, and will not remember thy sins.' 'Oh,' said he, 'what a merciful God is He.' I then pointed him to the 26th verse as the work he should attend to that night.

Monday morning I found him exulting with Christ; his looks were remarkably composed, and his language very strong; and, amongst other expressions, the following were uttered with such a holy pathos as I still feel the effects of and shall never forget:- 'Christ is my beloved; He is with me at present, and I am sure He will be with me to the end. I am in Christ and he is in me.'

It may be necessary here to remark that the jury having made application to the sheriff to protract the execution as long as was in his power, I was desired by one of them to acquaint him that he was to have one day more. I said to him, 'Your time is very short, could you not wish to live a little longer.' He answered no, he wanted to be gone; and had no doubt but God would be merciful to him. 'But,' said I, 'my friend it is reported that one who wore a crown in England, on her death-bed, was heard to say, "a world of wealth for a moment of time".' 'I believe God will have mercy on my soul,' he replied, 'and I would rather die than live.'

I then informed him that he was to live till Wednesday. 'Well,' said he, 'I hope to spend the time God gives in prayer and reading his word.'

On Tuesday afternoon I was shut up with him two hours. He gave a long and particular account of a very wicked life, and concluded by observing – 'If any one would give me that tub full of gold,' pointing to one that stood in the room, 'with a promise of life and liberty upon condition that I was to live in my old course, I would sooner die than live.' He now earnestly pressed me, as he had done several times before to attend him the next day to the place of execution and expressed great composure in the view of its near approach.

Wednesday morning I met him with Mr Milner and Mr Harris at the gaol.

The keeper's wife informed us that two persons had sat up with him all night, and that he had spent the whole of it in reading and prayer; and when he was weary himself he desired them to read to him. When I went up to him with the other minister he said he had chosen Christ and believed he was going to him.

We left him for a short time, whilst his irons were taken off, and he cleaned himself. When Mr Harris went up to him he was upon his knees, and prayed with such fervency and propriety as struck him much.

The awful moment was now arrived when he was to leave his gloomy mansion.

He walked down the stairs with as much composure as if he was going to liberty, and stepped into the sledge on which lay his coffin, as if it had been a coach to take him on a visit to a friend. He was shewn the words of the Apostle, 1 Cor XV, 55, 57, which he read over several times, appropriating them to himself thus, 'Thanks be to God which giveth me the victory.' He then fixed his eyes upon the heavens, and prayed for a short time in such a devout and fervent manner as I could wish to be in myself when I meet death.

As we all went with him on the sledge we had a full opportunity both to talk to him and hear every word he said.

When we came to the fatal tree he evinced the most unshaken firmness.

After singing part of the lamentation of a sinner, prayer was made. Mr Milner then asked him some questions concerning his faith in Christ, which he answered. The malefactor then spoke to the people, and told them that it was an affecting scene which was now before them, a young man but twenty-five years of age to be launched into eternity. 'This is the halter that will put an end to my life, and above is the Saviour who will receive my soul to glory.' He also warned them against idleness, lying and bad company. But in speaking to the people he was neither so connected nor full as might have been wished; but if we consider him as brought out of a dark, loathsome, solitary dungeon on a clear day into the free air, and a numerous concourse of people, it was not to be wondered at.

When he came down again he prayed in a most humble and scriptural manner. It was amazing how different it was when he spoke to men as when he pleaded with his God. He then ascended once more. Mr Milner prayed, and whilst the halter was being fixed, Rogerson again addressed the people, and said:- 'Young people, take warning, I am going to appear before God, but though my sins are as this scarlet ribbon, through the blood of Christ, God will make them as white as this,' alluding to the bunches of ribbons which they had fixed on his breast. We now took our leave of him. He stood praying for some time, frequently signifying his desire to be gone by putting one foot down from the place on which he stood. At last it was drawn away, and he was sent from our world, accompanied either with a general groan or with a cry for mercy from the numerous spectators.

Appendix C

Place Name Spellings

GL was not always consistent in his spelling of place names. In the edited text all these have been standardised to the accepted modern version. GL's main variations are given below:

Modern spelling	GL's version
Blackheath (London)	Black Heath
Bowlalley Lane	Bowl Alley Lane
Bridlington Quay	Bridlington Key
Caistor	Castor
Cleckheaton	Cleck Heaton
Driffield	Drifield
Drypool	Dry Pool
Gransmoor	Gransmere
Hampstead	Hamsted
Harrogate	Harogate
Heckmondwike	Hickmondwike
Hessle	Hessel
Holton cum Beckering	Houlton
Hornsea	Hornsey
Leeds	Leed
Market Harborough	Market Harbr
Market Weighton	Weighton
North Ferriby	North Ferraby
Norwood (London)	North Wood
Paull	Paul
Ripon	Rippon
Sculcoates	Sculcoats, Scullcotes
Scunthorpe	Scullthorpe
Skipsea	Skipsey
Spital	Spittle
Wapping	Waping
Wincolmlee	Wincolm Lea
	Winkham Lea

Appendix D

George Lambert's Publications

In addition to the sermon preached on the death of Mrs Hannah Gill entitled *The Living Believer's view of his course; and the Dying Believer's confidence in his Lord* (see 19 September 1784), Dr Williams's Library has listed the following works:

The Library has two funeral sermons for him, preached by John Birt and Edward Parsons, and two sermons preached by him, one at Fish Street Chapel on 19 October 1803 on the day appointed for the general fast, entitled *Danger announced, and deliverance sought from God*; the other on 23 March 1813 at Masboro' [Mosborough], near Rotherham, entitled *Elijah's translation foretold*, being a funeral sermon for the Rev Edward Williams. The British Museum catalogue shews some further items. There is a sermon, published in Hull, entitled *Britain's king rejoicing in Jehovah's salvation*, preached on 23 April 1789 on His Majesty's recovery; another, published in Hull, entitled *The confession and support of the godly in times of national danger*, preached on 25 February [1795], being the day appointed for a general fast; and one preached in Hull on 28 October 1810 - published there in 1811 - entitled *True wisdom displayed by family instruction*; and four sermons preached at the second general meeting of the London Missionary Society (1796).

Index

A

Abney, Lady Mary, wife of Sir Thomas, 73, 76, 77
Air Street, 43, 101
Albion Street, 148
Alderson, Dr John, 137, 144, 148, 150, 153, 166, 171, 179, 181, 191, 194, 198, 205
Anlaby, 23, 68, 70, 166, 183, 188, 197, 198, 205, 212
Anlaby Road, 130
Ansley, Brother, 40, 42, 49, 61, 64, 65, 75, 79, 80
Ansley, Hannah (see Lambert, Hannah, née Ansley), 17
Ansley, William, brother-in-law of GL, 24, 31, 33, 42, 47, 61, 65

B

Banks, Mr, 23, 29, 41
Barker, Rev John, 49, 53, 62
Barnard, Rev Samuel, 135, 144, 152
Beatson, Rev John, 76, 78, 120, 124, 141
Bennett, Dr, 64, 77, 117, 125
Beverley, 23, 24, 49, 51, 55, 81, 100, 110, 119, 123, 135
Beverley, Rev John, 175, 204, 209
Binnington, Jane, wife of John, 24
Binnington, John, 42, 45
Blanket Row chapel, 13, 14, 42, 43, 44, 100
Blaydes, 159, 167
Blockhouse Mill, 63, 192
Bottomley, George, 98, 99, 101
Bottomley, Rev Samuel, 98, 99, 101, 129, 179, 188
Bottomley, Richard, 98, 99, 101
Bowden, James Shrapnell, 42, 130, 152, 156, 172, 179, 201, 202, 207
Bowden, Rev Edward, 152, 156, 172
Bowden, William, 129, 130, 137
Bowlalley Lane, 101, 168, 204, 209, 225
Boyes, John, 38, 44, 68, 166, 183, 188, 198, 212

Bradford, Joseph, 192
Bridges, Daniel, 113, 116
Briggs, Christopher, 91, 92, 101
Briggs, Miss, 68, 77
Briggs, William, 206, 209
Bromby, Rev John Healey, 16, 141, 144, 181
Brown, Rev David, 75, 78
Browne, Rev George, 208, 209, 210, 215
Burford, Aubrey, Earl of, 116
Burial ground (Holy Trinity), 74, 78
Burn, Gilbert, 109, 116
Burnett, Rev John, 13, 38, 42, 44, 51, 164, 188
Bush Dike, 86, 100
Butchery, 121, 130

C

Carlill, John, 27, 41, 42, 46, 84
Carlill, John junior, 42, 47, 53, 68, 82, 84, 98, 142
Carlill, Thomas, 42
Carr Lane, 143
Carroll Place, 77
Carter, Rev Thomas, 140, 144
Casson and Penrose, 174, 192
Casson and Stickney, 192
Castle Street, 77, 78
Charity Hall, 26, 27, 42, 148, 152
Charlotte Street, 77
Citadel, 46, 59, 61, 68, 161
Clarke, Dr Charles, 42, 139
Clarke, Rev Thomas, 16, 138, 144, 166
Clough Road, 130
Collison, Rev George, 165, 168, 183, 193, 205
Cooper family, 63, 91, 100, 188, 208, 210
Cooper, Rev James, 208, 210

Cooper, Samuel, 91, 100, 188
Cottingham, 12, 24, 25, 26, 27, 28, 29, 30, 35, 43, 48, 49, 55, 58, 59, 61, 64, 67, 77, 85, 86, 91, 106, 121, 124, 125, 126, 129, 130, 132, 135, 139, 178, 183, 184, 188, 189, 190, 197, 202, 214
Coulson, Edward F, 156
Countess of Huntingdon's Connexion, 44, 144, 220
Crakerode, (otherwise Crakeroad or Crackroad), Mr, 142, 144, 147

D

Dagger Lane new chapel (Ebenezer Chapel), 13, 14, 36, 37, 42, 43, 44, 110, 140, 144, 155, 156, 164, 184, 203
Dansom Lane, 63
Darwent, C E, 7, 11, 15, 16, 17, 43, 44, 78, 85, 130, 144, 154, 156, 192, 210
Denys, Sir George William, 209
Dewhirst, Rev Edward, 43
Dikes (also Dykes), Rev Thomas, 130, 166, 204, 206, 209
Dissenting Academy, North Owram, 153
Dosser, James, 100
Dosser, Peter, 92
Dosser, William, 100
Drypool, 59, 68, 130, 137, 144, 145, 186, 192, 225

E

Ebenezer Chapel (see Dagger Lane new chapel), 42, 44, 140, 144
Egginton, Gardiner, 85, 89, 92, 95, 100
Egginton, Joseph, 100
English, Thomas, 167
Etherington, Sir Henry Bart, 56, 62

F

Fish Street church, 5, 7, 10, 11, 12, 13, 14, 16, 19, 42, 43, 44, 48, 62, 63, 78, 84, 100, 101, 120, 130, 154, 169, 192, 209, 210, 211, 226
French's Gardens, 72

G

Garrison, 46, 59, 61, 68, 161
George Street, 14, 62, 154
George Street chapel, 168
George Yard chapel, 14, 154, 156
Gibson, John, 75, 76, 78
Gifford, Andrew, 146, 156
Gilbert, Mrs, 16
Gilder, John, 28, 37, 39, 40, 41, 42, 46, 86, 91, 92, 96, 106, 122, 207
Gill, Mrs Hannah, 77, 226
Gill, Rev George, 28, 43, 45, 48, 56
Green, Anna, mother of GL (see Lambert, Mrs Anna, née Green, mother of GL), 42
Green, Rev Robert, 155, 156, 208
Groves, the, 124, 130, 145

H

Harcourt (formerly Venables-Vernon), Edward, Archbishop of York, 192
Harris, Howell, 218, 220
Harris, Mr, (Minister of Ebenezer Chapel), 28, 36, 37, 38, 42, 138, 222, 223
Hartley, David, 28, 43, 66, 77
Heckmondwike Academy, 13, 16, 43, 101, 140, 167, 220, 221, 225
Hessle, 68, 100, 225
Hewley, Lady, Sarah, wife of Sir John, 55, 56, 62, 63
Hewley, Sir John, 62
High Street, 42, 62, 63, 78, 130, 144, 156, 167
Hobhouse, Charles, 42
Holy Trinity church, 16, 42, 43, 74, 78, 130, 139, 144, 167, 209
Hope Street chapel, 144, 153, 156, 214
Hornsea, 62, 97, 141, 172, 176, 192, 225
Hotham, 43, 113
Hull Fair, 71, 77
Hull General Infirmary, 54, 55, 56, 62, 69, 74, 99, 116, 138
Hull Grammar School, 42, 78, 167
Hull Missionary Society, 78
Hull Subscription Library, 11, 15, 43, 62, 78

Index

Hull-Anlaby-Kirkella turnpike, 41, 116
Hull-Beverley turnpike, 55, 62, 111, 116
Humber Dock, 8, 192

J

Jewish synagogue, 43
Jones, David, 218, 220
Jones, Josiah, 43, 162

K

Ker, Hugh, 123, 130, 131
Kidd, Rev Anthony, 124, 125, 128, 178, 182, 189, 215
Kidd, Rev Thornhill, 138, 175, 182
King, Rev John, 16, 26, 47

L

Lambert, Elizabeth, daughter of GL, 23, 41, 126, 127, 143, 146, 152, 167, 174, 176, 182, 185, 199
Lambert, George and John Robinson, twin sons of Joseph Lambert, 209, 210
Lambert, George, son of GL, 37, 44, 51, 52, 56, 81, 94, 132, 138, 143, 150, 173, 174, 176, 182, 185, 199, 206
Lambert, Hannah, daughter of GL, 26, 36, 76, 81, 86, 104, 107, 152, 176, 185
Lambert, Hannah, daughter of William and Betsey Lambert, 151, 156
Lambert, Hannah, née Ansley, wife of GL, 17, 22, 23, 24, 27, 28, 30, 31, 32, 33, 35, 36, 38, 46, 48, 52, 53, 58, 59, 65, 68, 69, 70, 85, 86, 96, 98, 104, 106, 109, 110, 111, 112, 114, 117, 132, 135, 136, 138, 143, 154, 163, 171, 173, 176, 186, 187, 188, 191, 194, 195, 198, 199, 214
Lambert, John, born 1 Nov 1782, son of GL, 53, 62, 65, 107, 132, 143, 148, 159, 161, 164, 181, 182, 185
Lambert, John, born 9 Dec 1772, son of GL, 62
Lambert, Joseph, son of GL, 63, 81, 104, 121, 132, 174, 184, 185, 189, 197, 209
Lambert, Joseph, son of Joseph and Elizabeth Lambert, 197, 209
Lambert, Maria, daughter of GL, 112, 116, 120, 122
Lambert, Mrs Anna, née Green, mother of GL, 42, 60, 184, 206, 217, 220
Lambert, Phebe, daughter of GL, 23, 33, 34, 36, 41, 53, 81, 86, 104, 126, 132, 138, 176, 177, 178
Lambert, Samuel Ansley, son of GL, 22, 23, 27, 35, 36, 37, 38, 41, 56, 109, 114, 121, 127, 128, 129, 136, 149, 154, 155, 190, 198, 199, 200, 212
Lambert, Sarah, daughter of William and Betsey Lambert, 163, 168
Lambert, William, father of GL, 24, 41, 42, 49, 54, 67, 105, 106, 120
Lambert, William, son of GL, 23, 41, 50, 57, 103, 104, 105, 108, 111, 114, 116, 118, 120, 123, 124, 125, 127, 134, 136, 137, 141, 143, 144, 150, 151, 174, 177, 178, 184, 191, 209
Leggatt, Rev Richard, 43, 68, 69, 77, 111, 121
Levett, Norrison, 94, 100, 104, 129, 151
Levett, William, 94, 100, 103, 104, 107, 113, 114, 118
Lime Street, 63, 100
London Missionary Society, 11, 15, 131, 133, 144, 156, 165, 168, 206, 226
Lowgate, 16, 42, 61, 62
Lyon, James, 149, 166, 167, 168, 176

M

Madan, Rev Martin, 100, 218, 220
Manor Alley, 156
Manor Street, 78
Market Place, 42, 66, 77, 78, 95, 96, 100, 109, 130, 144, 166, 185
Market Weighton, 11, 175, 192, 225
Markham, Archbishop William, 82
Marsden, Rev Samuel, 167, 168
Mason Street, 77
Milner, Dr Isaac, 166, 167
Milner, Rev Joseph, 16, 42, 139, 167, 212
Mytongate, 18, 42, 44, 62, 91, 118, 205
Mytongates (Mytongate without), 18

N

New Gaol, 66, 77
Newbald, Charles, 192, 197, 209
Newland, 58, 62, 116

Newland Clough, 121, 130
Newland Orphan Homes, 78
Newland Tofts, 45, 57, 61, 120
North Bridge, 65, 100, 116
North End, 100, 112, 116
North Ferriby, 62, 100, 151, 225

O

Old Dagger Lane chapel, 156

P

Paradise Row, 72, 77
Parliament Street, 43
Patrick, Rev Richard, 212, 216
Payne, Rev George, 170, 171, 173, 174, 177, 183, 185, 186, 187, 188, 189, 190, 191, 192, 200, 201, 202, 203, 205
Pead, Benjamin, 71, 77
Penrose, Hannah, daughter of John and Sarah Penrose, 136, 144
Penrose, John and Sarah, 136, 144
Penrose, Sarah, daughter of John and Sarah Penrose, 144
Popplewell, Rev Joseph, 23, 26, 42, 62, 118
Port of Hull Society, 78, 85
Portas, James, 95, 101, 102, 105, 111
Porter, A W, 114, 116
Posterngate, 41, 43
Priestley, Dr Joseph, 95
Prospect Street, 62
Providence chapel (see Hope Street chapel), 152

Q

Queen Street, 130

R

Reaves/Reeves, Timothy, 131, 143
Rennards, Joseph, 90, 100
Rhodes, Josiah, 94, 101, 112, 117, 120
Riddell, Edward, 42, 84, 94, 98, 114, 117, 121, 136, 198, 201, 209
Riddell, Thomas, son of Edward Riddell, 43, 158, 178, 187, 193
Ringrose family, 30, 43, 44, 67, 77
Ringrose, Samuel and William, 30, 43, 67
Rodwell, Rev Josiah, 144, 151, 156
Ross, Hugh, 25, 42, 87, 92
Ross, John, son of Hugh Ross, 42
Rust, William, 42, 74, 78, 85, 129, 131, 143, 172, 183, 198, 200, 203

S

Sailors' Families Society, 78, 85
Salthouse Lane Baptist chapel, 78, 147, 152, 156, 206, 211, 214
Scale Lane, 101
Scarborough, 62, 101
Sculcoates, 43, 95, 100, 101, 106, 110, 120, 178, 191, 212, 216, 225
Skipsea, 151, 164, 172, 175, 205, 225
Smith, [Abel], 144
Sommerville, Rev John, 31, 117, 119, 130, 151, 174
South Cave, 101, 143
South Street, 156
Spooner, Barbara (see Wilberforce, Mrs William), 83, 100
Spyvee family, 57, 63, 71, 91, 100, 108, 137, 194
St John the Evangelist's church, 44, 63, 100, 130
St Mary's church, Lowgate, 16, 42, 47, 49, 53, 62
St Mary's church, Sculcoates, 95, 101
Stanhope, Walter, 62, 77
Staniforth, John, 156, 209
Stickney, Robert, 63
Stillingfleet, Rev James, 29, 43, 69, 113
Sutton-on-Hull, 57, 71, 77, 144

Index

Swanland, 27, 28, 43, 45, 48, 49, 69, 70, 77, 101, 114, 119, 133, 143, 151, 164, 175, 181, 183, 189, 197, 198
Sykes Street, 77
Sykes, Joseph, 42, 75, 78

T

Tapp, Rev William, 132, 141, 143, 178, 184, 199
Thompson, Rev George, 192
Thompson's Bank, 138
Thornton Abbey, 44
Thornton, Godfrey and William, 145
Thornton, Henry, son of John Thornton, 42
Thornton, John, 26, 42, 62, 77, 108
Thornton, Marianne, née Sykes, wife of Henry Thornton, 42, 78
Thornton, Samuel, 51, 62, 64, 77, 116, 156
Thornton, Sarah, sister of John Thornton, 42
Todd, John, 32
Tong, Daniel, 39, 82
Towers, Mary and Sarah, 43
Towers, Mr, miller, 43, 50, 65, 68, 80, 81
Triebner, Rev Christopher Frederick *or* Triebner, Rev Christoph Friedrich, 142, 145, 169
Trinity House, 62, 98, 175, 176, 192
Trippett, 167
Turner, Ralph, 143, 145

V

Vanderkemp, Dr Joannes Theodosius, 146, 152, 156
Venn, Rev Henry, 83, 100
Venn, Rev John, 100
Voase family, 43, 77

W

Walker, Samuel, 99, 101
Welton, 56, 57, 73, 94, 100, 141
West Parade, 130
Whitefriargate, 42, 144
Wilberforce House, 10, 144
Wilberforce, Mrs William, 83, 100
Wilberforce, Robert, 42
Wilberforce, William, 42, 62, 77, 100, 101, 144, 213
Williams, Dr, physician, 46, 61, 137, 138
Williams, Rev David, 133, 143
Williams, Rev Dr Edward, 167, 197, 198, 204, 207, 209, 210, 226
Williams, William, 61
Wright Street, 62
Wright, Benjamin, 42, 57, 63, 75, 91, 108, 113, 118, 203, 206, 209
Wright, Jeremiah, 42
Wright, Samuel, 14, 47, 62, 71, 75, 122, 123